A WILDER WALES

Travellers' Tales 1610-1831

"BRITANNIA directing the attention of HISTORY to the distant view, emblematical of WALES. The ruined castle and bardic circle, in the background, enveloped in clouds, allude to ancient times; and the intermediate space represents the present state of the country."

This is the frontispiece of the Cambrian Register for the year 1795 (printed London 1796). It was founded 'to lay the literary treasures of the Ancient Britons before the world'. Beneath the mountainous hills and bardic circle, lie the ruined castle, some woods, a small church, a hamlet and a solitary figure guiding a plough, pulled by two horses.

A WILDER WALES

Travellers' Tales 1610-1831

David Lloyd Owen

Parthian, Cardigan SA43 1ED
www.parthianbooks.com
First published in 2017
© David Lloyd Owen
ISBN 978 1910901960
Edited by Barbara Whitfield
Typeset by Elaine Sharples
Printed by Opolgraf, Poland
Published with the financial support of the Welsh Books Council
British Library Cataloguing in Publication Data
A cataloguing record for this book is available from the British Library.

A DEDICATION

Er cof annwyl am
Patricia Owen
1925-2012

"Ust, saif y nos o'th gylch y gangell glaear
Ac arflladen nef yn croesi â i bendith y ddaear."

[gan Saunders Lewis, Y Pin / The Pine]

CONTENTS

ACKNOWLEDGEMENTS

This book emerged from lunches, dinners and sundry conversations with Richard Lewis Davies and Gillian Griffiths at Parthian. Michael Gibbon QC, through his rather more recherche endeavours, has also been a spur. Barbara 'Qui Timet Deum Faciet Bona' Whitfield has been a blessing with the editing, teasing my vulgar errors and sundry howlers from the good copy. Bethan and Trystan have shown me life with 'yr hen iaith' regained, along with their wit and love. Above all, Polly made all of this possible and has lovingly and cheerfully endured all the consequences of life with a middle aged writer.

INTRODUCTION

Before the second half of the Eighteenth Century visitors to Wales were few, Wales being thought of as a poor rural backwater of Britain albeit it one with its own rich identity. This view of Wales changed with a shift in aesthetic judgement. As mountains, once objects of fear, became viewed as places of awesome beauty, North Wales was hailed as the 'British Alps' and South Wales became a sought after destination for seekers of sublime views. This willingness to travel into Wales coincided with the Napoleonic Wars of 1799-1815 which forced many of those seeking to go on a Grand Tour of Europe's classical sights and sites to root out enlightenment and new experiences closer to home just as later, visitors crossed the border enticed by the innovations of the Industrial Revolution.

Under the Wales and Berwick Act 1746, England was formally defined as including Wales. That did not change until 1967. Before this time, Wales barely existed in any legal or political sense. With the passing of the Tudors, Welsh heraldic insignia and references to Wales ceased to feature in national flags or royal shields. The 'Acts of Union' of 1536 and 1543 stated that "this said Country or Dominion of *Wales* shall be, stand and continue for ever from henceforth incorporated, united and annexed to and with this Realm of *England*."

A Council of Wales and the Marches carried on until it was abolished in the Glorious Revolution of 1689 and the Courts of Great Sessions in Wales was set up in 1543 to preside over more serious legal cases until 1830. English

Law succeeded Welsh Law, with all trials being held exclusively in English and almost all judges being English.

Despite this incorporation of Wales into England and the insistence that English, and English alone, was to be used in all official roles and functions, one aspect of Wales hardly changed; outside the plantations of South Pembrokeshire and the Gower, Wales remained overwhelmingly Welsh speaking and mainly monoglot.

Language was perhaps a greater barrier than the symbols and separate constitutions of Scotland and Ireland despite their greater physical distance from London. Scottish Gaelic had always been confined to the Highlands and Western Islands (many of the surviving early Welsh poems were composed in what is now the Central Scottish Lowlands) and Irish Gaelic was steadily being pushed westwards by waves of repression and plantation. The Welsh language, on the other hand, formed a border more immediately tangible than Offa's Dyke or any county boundary. Needing an interpreter to transverse what was meant to be a western part of England gave the Welsh counties an exoticism that remained almost undiminished throughout this time.

* * *

The study of travel and tourism has been a flourishing academic discipline for some decades and the experience of visitors to Wales over the years has provided much material for the devotee. For example, the Journal 'Studies in Travel Writing' had a special issue (18/2) in 2014 entitled 'Travel Writing and Wales', while during 2016, an exhibition 'EuroVisions: Wales through the Eyes of European visitors, 1750-2015' was the result of a collaborative project between

Swansea, Aberystwyth and Bangor Universities, examining 360 travel accounts and a plethora of images. Meanwhile, a website 'sublime Wales' (sublimewales.wordpress.com) is currently under development covering early (18th and 19th century) tourists' comments about Wales, as well as looking at 'Curious Travellers: Thomas Pennant and the Welsh and Scottish Tour 1760-1815', a project being managed by Aberystwyth University's Centre for Advanced Welsh and Celtic Studies. Some illustrative examples of these studies have been included in the bibliography to give an idea of the depth and breadth of these endeavours.

This book makes no attempt to contribute towards any academic discourse. I am a behavioural ecologist by training who has subsequently strayed into the field of water policy. My perspective is that of the engaged returnee; childhood memories of Ceredigion forty or fifty years ago are of a more exotic, distinct place compared to say, the Home Counties of the day. All places change with time, especially through our individual perspectives. That is one thing that earlier travel accounts help to highlight.

Rather than taking an academic approach, my aim is to present a selection of travellers' accounts published between 1610 to 1831 with the hope that it will encourage readers not only to peruse the original accounts in greater depth but to appreciate the generosity of spirit and open-mindedness reflected in many of these passages. There has been a tendency to assume that English writers in particular, have visited Wales in order only to look down upon it. Happily, this is not evident in these accounts.

Satires and polemics have also been omitted. For example, William Richards' 'Wallography, or the Britton describ'd: Being a pleasant relation of a journey into Wales, wherein are set down several remarkable passages that occur'd in the way thither. And also many choice observables, and notable commemorations, concerning the state and condition, the nature and humor, actions, manners, customs, &c. of that countrey and people' (London: Printed for Edward Caudell, bookseller in Bath, 1682) which is a satire of social pretensions in England and Wales rather than a travel book.

There are two reasons for adopting an 1831 cut-off date for visitors' accounts. Firstly, because of the sheer wealth of material being published from the start of the Nineteenth Century and secondly, to draw a line between two quite distinct social and political eras. In the period between 1740-1800, 11 riots were noted in Wales, with two deaths. In that between 1801-1820, there were nine riots, with three deaths in Merthyr Tydfyl; two hanged and one shot. These were so unremarkable as to not catch the attention of early travellers. After this relative calm, came the storm of the Scotch Cattle movement (enforcing strikes in coal mines and ironworks, chiefly between 1822 and the 1840s), the Merthyr Rising (1831), Chartism (from 1836), the Rebecca Riots (1839-43, against toll gates), and land enclosure (the 1845 Enclosure Act encouraged the enclosure of once common lands in Wales).

Before 1831, we also find a Wales in which the Welsh language and culture were largely unchallenged, as, by and large, were the local Gentry, since voters did what they were expected to do. The 'Treachery of the Blue Books' in 1847 unleashed state and social hostility against the Welsh language, and South Wales starting with the schools, steadily became Anglicised. In rural Wales, democracy was as unwelcome to the landed interests as enclosure was to their subjects. Finally, the diverse forms of nonconformity and religious dissent brought their own conformities when it came to music and public life.

Did something change after this? Did a desire for progress impel travellers to disdain local culture and custom? These are questions for academics. As an 'aboriginal Briton' I have been generally refreshed by the degree of nuance in many of those accounts predating 1831. By going back and looking beyond times when linguistic difference has been despised, we can reconnect with a time when educated or intrepid people appreciated the value of variety and the elemental importance of sustaining the language and cultures that a place may hold.

Early accounts are often of a pragmatic nature; appraising fortifications and fertilisers, pondering wrecked castles, commenting on agricultural improvements and the prospect for gainful employment through industry. A more flamboyant language flourished, one that employed the overblown imagery deemed necessary when describing an aesthetically perfect curve of the River Wye, for instance, usually spiced with soaring rhetoric. Mountains were meant to be majestic, while picturesque landscapes could be classified according to their components. Writers vied with each other to unearth intriguing customs and local mannerisms, while seeking to draw broader conclusions about human nature from their sundry observations.

These accounts are about perceptions as much as they are about realities. When we look at how Wales is seen by the English and others subsequently, attitudes have been distorted by a *negative* view of Welsh culture that persisted until relatively recently. Conversely, the accounts offered here often emphasise the need to preserve a 'British' tongue and chroniclers regard the practicalities of traversing a land inhabited by foreign speakers in the manner recommended when visiting continental Europe.

* * *

'English Language Travel Books Dealing with Wales', an invaluable compilation by Diana Luft, notes 153 accounts written by 1831; three from Medieval and Tudor times, seven in the Seventeenth Century, five in the first and fifty-one in second half of the Eighteenth Century, and eighty-seven from 1800 to 1831. In this work, I have used thirty-eight accounts by thirty-six authors dating between 1610 and 1831, with a total of approximately 2.2 million words. Thirty-three were written with publication in mind while five (Dineley, Fiennes, Lyttleton, Johnson and Skinner) are manuscripts that were posthumously published. Two are by women (Fiennes and Morgan), five are identified as Welshmen (Pennant, Davies (two), Jones and an anonymous correspondent) and two (Skrine and Malkin) had married into Welsh families. Brief biographies have been included for thirty-one of the authors. Two other named authors remain a mystery, while three were either pseudonymous or anonymous accounts.

The recycling rate in these accounts is prodigious. This is not usually a case of plagiarism, rather one of various tales that each visitor is aware of from previous narratives, and, therefore, may be expected to be included. Stories about Holywell in North Wales and flowers on graves in the South are prime examples. Some of these have been included here to show how they recurred and evolved.

Editing has been kept to a minimum. For ease of reading,

the archaic 'f' is replaced by the contemporary 's', while gaps between words and quotation marks, colons and semicolons have been closed. Otherwise, spelling and punctuation have been retained. Where possible, first editions were used and exceptions are noted. Many of the writers at times displayed a numbing verbosity and a propensity to insert quotations at the least excuse. I have aimed to mitigate the former and excise the latter.

I have not sought a complete coverage of towns and traverses, concentrating only on accounts that best reflect the authors and their approaches. Many of the books are dominated by history and biography which lie outside the scope of this publication, as do natural history (Pennant was a leading naturalist in his day) and geology. The exceptions here are mining and industry, due to their development and transformative role during, and immediately after, this period, and farming, given the nature of its direct impact on people's livelihoods.

Perhaps 'A Wilder Wales' is a case of the past being another country – in public life and politics it was English rather than Welsh, yet culturally more identifiably Welsh than English. There is little room for sentimentality when looking back at the past as it is depicted here, yet it is difficult not to admire how a distinct culture endured when outside churches and chapels it enjoyed no formal recognition. The final chapter presents a contemporary riposte to generalisations and clichéd observations, a reminder of the diversity which existed within a place that could beguile and bemuse the visitor at the same time.

1

EARLY VISITATIONS: 1610 – 1698

Such was the low profile of Wales after its conquest in 1282 that the 1188 visit to Wales by Gerallt Cymro (Gerald of Wales) written in 1191 as Itinerarium Cambriae ('Journey through Wales') was seen as the primary source of information about the country until William Camden published his Britannia in 1584. Indeed, just as others were to base their accounts on Camden's observations, he used the Journey as his starting point. John Leland's 'labryouse journey' included at least one visit to Wales between 1536 and 1539, but was not published until Thomas Hearne's edition of 1710-12. Leland does not appear to have been used as a source by later writers about Wales.

During the seventeenth century, visits to most of Wales for the sake of curiosity were unusual to say the least. Those that were published often included long historical and genealogical accounts. The six travel accounts included here have been retained in some detail. While they offer new encounters they also show Camden's influence. Outside Monmouth, Flint and Carmarthen they depict an overwhelmingly rural Wales, punctuated by towns and castles in varying degrees of size and ruin. George Owen's description of Pembrokeshire was written in 1603, but remained unpublished until it was serialised in the Cambrian Registers for 1796 and 1799.

When the Stuarts succeeded the Tudors, it appears that interest in Wales eased somewhat and with it Welsh antiquarianism. Matters improved with the polymath Edward Lhuyd (1660-1709) who travelled extensively through Wales, first in 1688 and then from 1697, and who pioneered the comparative study of Celtic languages. Two of these accounts (Dinley and Fiennes) were not published until the Victorian era.

In 1586 William Camden published Britannia in Latin. Britannia was the first attempt to fully describe the whole of the British Isles, and by 1607 the sixth edition had expanded from 556 pages of octavo text to 860 pages of folio. In 1610 the final edition was translated into English by Philemon Holland. Camden wrote his work at a time when Welsh antiquarianism was flourishing. Sir John Prise's Historiae Britannicae Defensio (1573) pioneered the study of British history and David Powell expanded this book in his Historie of Cambria, published in 1584. Sir Edward Stradling and Rice Merrick specialised in the topography of Glamorganshire as did George Owen in Pembrokeshire. Outside such circles, accounts about Wales were few. Until the nineteenth century, Camden's Britannia remained the primary point of information and comparison for travellers to Wales.

In Britannia, the counties of Wales are divided according to the tribes described by the Romans. Radnor, Brecknock, Monmouth, and Glamorgan, along with Hereford are grouped as the Silures, Carmarthen, Pembroke, and Cardigan under the Demetae, and Montgomery, Meirioneth, Caernarfon, Anglesey, Denbigh, and Flint as the Ordovicae.

....
"Nature hath loftily areared it up farre and nere"
....

William Camden visited Wales to revise and expand his 'Britannia' in the summer of 1590, enabling him to develop a feel for the Welsh landscape as well as its history. He was being strictly correct in describing Wales as part of the Kingdom of England in a pre-union Britain.

RADNORSHIRE

The East-side hath to beautifie it, besides other castles of the Lords Marchers, now all buried well neere in their owne ruines, Castle Paine, built and so named of Paine a Norman, and Castle Colwen, which, if I be not deceived, was sometime called the Castle of Mawd in Colwent. ... But of especiall name is Radnor the principall towne of the whole Shire, in British *Maiseveth*, faire built, as the maner of that country is, with thatched houses. In times past it was firmely fensed with a wall and castle, but after that Owen Glendowerdy what notable rebell had burnt it, it beganne by little and little to decrease and grow to decay, tasting of the same fortune that the mother thereof did before, I meane Old Radnor, called in British *Maiseveth hean,* and for the high situation *Pencrag*, which in the reigne of King John Rhese Ap Guffin had set on fire. ... Scarce three miles Eastward from hence you see Prestaine, in British *Lhan Andre*, that is, *Saint Andrews Church*, which of a very little village within the memorie of our grandfathers is by the meanes of Richard Martin Bishop of Saint Davids growne now to be so great a mercate towne and faire withall, that at this day it dammereth and dimmeth the light in some sort of Radnor. From whence also scarce foure miles off, stands Knighton, a towne able to match with Prestaine, Called in British, as I have heard say, *Trebuclo* in steed of *Trefcyluadh,* of a famous ditch lying under it which Offa King of the Mercians with admirable worke and labour caused to be cast from Dee-Mouth unto Wy mouth by this towne, for the space of foureskore and ten miles, to separate the Britans from his Englishmen. Wherupon in British it is called *Claudh Offa*, that is, *Offaes ditch*. Concerning which, John of Salisbury in his *Polycraticon* writeth thus: *Harald ordained a law that what Welshman soever should be found with a weapon on this side the limite which he had set them, that is to say Offaes Dike, he should have his right hand cut off by the Kings officers.*

When yee are past this place, all the ground that lieth toward the West and South limits, being for the most part baren, leane, and hungry, is of the inhabitants called *Melienith*, for that mountaines be of a yellowish colour. Yet remaine there many footings as it were of castles to be seene heere and there, but especially Kevenles and Timbod, which standing upon a sharpe pointed hill, Lhwellin Prince of Wales overthrew in the yeere 1260. This *Melienith* reacheth as farre as to the river Wy, which cutteth overthwart the West corner of this shire, and, being hindered in his streame with stones lying in his way, upon a sudden for want of ground to glide on hath a mighty and violent downfall, hath a mighty and violent downfall, where upon the place is tearmed *Raihader Gowy*, that is, *The fall or Fludgats of Wy*. And I cannot tell whether thereupon that British word *Raihader* the Englishmen forged this name first for the whole shire, and afterwards for the chiefe towne. ... Hard by there is in some sort a vast and wide wildernesse, hideous after a sort to behold by reason of the turning and crooked by-waies and craggy mountaines, into which as the safest place of refuge Vortigern, that pestilent wretch and bane of his native country, odious both to God and man, (whose memorie the Britans may wish damned) withdrew himselfe, when after he had called the Saxons into this Iland in horrible incest married his owne daughter.

[…]

BRECHNOCKSHIRE

Farre greater this is than Radnorshire, but thicker set with high hils, yet are the valleies fruitfull every where.

[…]

On the North side, as [Gerallt Cymro] said, it is more open and plaine, namely where the river Wy severeth it from Radnorshire, by which stand two townes well knowen for their antiquity, Buelth and Hay. Buelth is pleasantly situate with woods about it, fortified also with a Castle, but of a later building, by the Breoses and Mortimers, whenas Rhese ap Guffin had rased the ancient Castle. … And as for Hay, which in British is called *Trekethle*, that is, *The towne in a grove of Hasel trees*, in the very utmost skirt of this shire next unto Herefordshire, it standeth hard by the river Wye, well known, as it seemeth, to the Romans, whose coines is is often digged up there, and it sheweth also by the ruins that in old time it was walled. But being now as it were decaied it complaineth of that most lewd rebell Owen Glendoweredwy for his furious outrages, who in wasting and spoiling all those countries most villanously did depopulate it and set it on fire.

As this river Wy washeth the North side of this shire, so doth Uske a notable river likewise runne through the middest thereof, which Uske, springing out of the Blacke-Mountain, passeth along with a shallow streame beside Brechnock the shire towne, standing in the very hart in maner of the country, which the Britans call *Aber-Hodney* because the two rivers Hodney and Uske doe meet in that place. That this town was inhabited in the Romans time appeareth by the coines of Romane Emperours now and then digged up here.

[…]

Leveney a little river, after it is run into this Poole, keepeth his owne hew and colour still by himselfe, as disdayning to be mingled therewith (which the very colour sheweth), is thought to carry out his owne water, entertained a while there by the way, and no more than he brought in with him. It hath beene a currant speech of long continuance among the neighbours there about, that where now the Meere is there was in times past a City, which being swallowed up in an earth quake, resigned up the place unto the waters. And beside other reasons, they allege this for one, that all the high waies of this shire come directly hither on every side. Which if it be true, what other City should a man thinke stood by the river Leveney than Loventium, which Ptolomee placeth in this tract? And in no place hitherto could I finde it (albeit I searched diligently for it) either by the name, or situation, or ruines remaining.

[…]

MONMOUTHSHIRE

In the utmost angle, called Ewias, to the Northwest, not farre from the river Munow, among the Hatterell hils which, because they rise up in height like a chaire, they call *Munith Cader*, there stood Lanthony, a little ancient Abbay which Walter Lacy founded.

[...]

In other other corner North-east-ward, Munow and Wy at their confluence doe compasse almost round about the chiefe towne of the shire and give it the name. For in the British tongue it is called *Mongwy* and in ours Monmouth. On the Northside, where it is not defended with the rivers, it was fortified with a wall and ditch. In the midest of the towne hard by the mercate place standeth a castle.

[...]

From hence Wy with many windings and turnings runneth downe Southward, yeelding verie great plenty of delicate Salmons from September to April. And is at this day the bound betweene Glocestershire and Monmouthshire, in times past betweene the Welsh and Englishmen, according to this verse of Nechams making:

By Wales on this side runeth Wy,
And of the other England he doth eye.

Who, when he is come almost unto his mouth, runneth by Chepstow, that is, if one interprete it after the Saxons tongue, a *Mercat*. The Britans call it *Castle-went*. A famous towne this and of good resort, situate upon the side of an hill, rising from the verie river, fortified round about with a wall of a large circuite, which includes within it both fields and orchyards. It hath a very spatious castle situate over the river, and just against it stood a Priory, the better part whereof beeing pulled downe, the rest is converted into a Parish Church. As for the bridge that standeth over Wy, it is of timber and verie high built, because the river at every tide riseth to a great height. ... This towne is not verie ancient to speake of. For may there be that constantly affirme, and not without good reason, that not many ages agoe it had his beginning from Venta, a verie ancient citie that in the daies of Antonine the emperour flourished about foure miles hence Westward and was named *Venta Silurum* (as one would say, *the Principall citie of the Silures*). which name neither hostile fury nor length of time hath as yet discontinued: for it is called even as this day *Caer went*, that is, *The City Wet*. But as for the citie it selfe, either time or hostility hath so caried it away that now, were it not only for the ruinate wals, the checker worke pavements, and peeces of Roman money, it would not appeere there was such a city. It tooke up in compasse above a mile. On the South side a great part of the wal standeth, and there remaine little better than the rubbish of three bulwarks. And yet of how great account it was in ancient times, wee may gather if it were but by this, that before the name of Monmouth once heard of, all this whole country was of it called *Guent, Went-set*, and *Wents-land*.

[...]

Beneath these places upon the Severn Sea, nere unto Wy-mouth, standeth Portskeweth, which Marianus nameth Portscith ... And adjoining to it is Sudbrok the church wherof called Trinity Chappell standeth so neere the sea that the vicinity of so tyrannous a neighbour hath spoiled it of halfe the Church-yarde, as it hath done also of an olde fortification lieng thereby, which was compassed with a triple ditch and three rampiers as high as an ordinary house, cast in forme of a bowe, the string whereof is the sea-cliffe. That this was a Romane worke the Britaine brickes and Roman coynes there found are most certaine arguments... Then Throgoy, a little river neere unto Caldecot, entreth into the Severn Sea, where saw the wall of a castle that belonged to the high Constables of England, and was holden by the service of Constableship of England. Hard by are seene Wondy and Penhow, the seats in times past of the noble family of Saint Maur, now corruptly named Seimor.

[...]

Beneath this lieth spred for many miles togither a mersh, they call it the Moore, which when I lately revised this worke, suffered a lamentable losse. For when the Severn sea at a spring tide in the change of the Moore, what beeing driven backe for three daies together with a Southwest winde, and what with a verie strong pirrie from the sea troubling it, swelled and raged so high that with surging billowes it came rolling and in-rushing amaine upon this tract lying so low, as also upon the like states in Somersetshire over against it, that it overflowed all, subverted houses and drowned a number of beasts, and some people withall. Where this mersh coast bearing out by little and little runneth forth into the sea, in the verie point thereof standeth Goldclyffe aloft.

[...]

Neere to this place there remaine the reliques of a Priorie, that acknowledge those of Chandos for their founders and patron. Passing thence by the merish country, wee came to the mouth of the river Isca, which the Britans name *Usk* and *Wiisk,* and some writers terme it Osca. This river as it runneth through the midest, as I said before, of this County, floweth hard by three townes of especiall antiquity. The first, in the limite of the shire North-west, Antonine the Emperour calleth Gorbanium, at the very meeting of Uske and Geveny, whereof it had the name, and even at this day, keeping the ancient name, as it were, safe and sound, is tearmed Aber-Gevenny, and short Abergenny, which signifieth the confluents of Gevenny or Gorbanny. Fortified it is with wals and a Castle.

[...]

The second little Citie, which Antonine named Burrium and setteth downe twelve miles from Gobannium, standeth where the river Birthin and Uske mete in one streame. The Britans at this day, by transposing of the letters, call it *Brunebegy* for *Burenbegie,* and *Caer Uske.* Giraldus tearmeth it *Castrum Oscae,* that is, *The Castle of Uske,* and we Englishmen Uske. At this day it can shew nothing but the ruins of a large and strong Castle, situate most pleasantly betweene the river Uske and Oilwy, a riveret, which beneath it runneth from the East by Ragland, a faire house of the Earle of Worcesters, built castle-like.

The third Citie, which Antonine nameth Isca and *Legio Secunda,* is on the other side of Uske twelve Italian miles just distant from Burrium, as he hath put it downe. The Britans call it *Caer Leon* and *Caer Leon ar Uske,* that is, *The citie of the Legion upon Uske,* of the second Legion Augusta, which is also called *Britannica Secunda.*

[...]

GLAMORGANSHIRE

The North part by reason of the mountaines is rough and unpleasant, which as they bend downe southward by little and little become more mild and of better soile, and at the foote of them there stretcheth forth a plaine open to the South-Sunne … For this part of the County is most pleasant and fruitfull, beautified also on every side with a number of townes.

[…]

The river Rhemnie, falling from the mountaines, is the limite on the Eastside, whereby this Country is divided from Monmouthshire, and *rhemni* in the British tongue signifieth to *Divide*. Not farre from it were the river holdeth on his course through places hardly passable, among the hills, in a marish ground are to be seene the tottering wals of Caer-philli Castle, which hath beene of so huge a bignesse, and such a wonderfull peece of worke beside, that all men wel nere say it was a garison-fort of the Romans. Neither will I denie it, although I cannot as yet perceive by what name they called it. And yet it may seeme to have beene re-edified anew, considering it hath a chappell built after the Christians maner (as I was enformed by John Sanford, a man singular well learned and of exact judgment), who diligently tooke view of it.

[…]

A little beneath hath Ptolomee placed the mouth of Ratostabius or Ratostibius, using a maimed word in steed of *Traith-Taff,* that is, *The sandy Trith of the river Taff.* For the said river Taff, sliding downe from the hilles, runneth toward the sea by Landaff, that is, *the Church by*

Taff, a small Citie and of small reputation, situate somewhat low, yet a Bishops See, having within the Dioecesse 154 parishes, and adourned with a Cathedral Church consecrated to Saint Telean Bishop of the same. Which Church German and Lupus, … From hence goeth Taff to Caerdiff, called of the Britans *Caer-did*, a proper fine towne (as townes goe in this country) and a very commodious haven, which the foresaid Fitz-Haimon fortified with a wall and Castle, that it might bee both a seat for warre and a Court of Justice.

[…]

Scarce three miles from the mouth of Taff, in the very bending of the shore, there lie aflote as it were two small but pleasant Ilands, separated one from another and from the maine land with narrow in-lettes of the sea. The hithermore is called Sullie of the towne right over against it, which tooke the name name, as it is thought, of Robert Sully (for it fell to his part in the division), if you would not rather have him to take his name of it. The farthermore is named Barry of Baruch, an holy man buried there, who as hee gave name to the place, so the place gave the surname afterwards to the Lords thereof. … Beyond these Islands, the shire runneth directly westward and giveth entrance and passage to one river, upon which more within land standeth Cowbridge (the Britans of the Stone-bridge call it *Pont-van*), a mercate towne, and the second of those three which Fitz-Haimon the Conqueror kept for himselfe. … Neath, a towne very well knowne, retaining still the old name, in manner, whole and sound, and here at Lantwit, that is, *The Church of Iltut*, that joyneth close thereto, are seene the foundations of many houses, for it had divers streetes in old time. A little from hence in the very bout well nere of the shore standeth Saint Donats Castle, a faire habitation of the ancient and notable familie of the Stradlings, neere unto which were lately digged up antique peeces of Roman money, but those especially of the thirty Tyrants, yea and some of Aemilianus and Marius, which are seldome found. The river Ogmor, somewhat higher, maketh him selfe way into the sea, falling downe from the mountaines by Coitie.

[...]

From hence coasting along the shore, you come within the site of Kinefeage, the castle in old time of Fitz-Haimon him selfe; also of Margan, hard by the sea side, sometime an Abbay founded by William Earle of Glocester, but now the habitation of the worshipfull family of the Maunsells, knights. Neere unto this Margan, in the very top of an hill called *Mynyd Margan* there is erected of exceeding hard grit a monument or grave-stone, foure foote long and one foote broad, which an Inscription,which whosoever shall happen to read, the ignorant common people dwelling about give it out upon a credulous error that hee shall be sure to die within a little while after. Let the reader therefore looke to him selfe, if any dare read it, for let him assure himselfe that he shall for certaine die after it.

[...]

After you are past Margan, the shore shooteth forth into the North-easy by Aber-Avon, a small mercate town upon the river Avons mouth (whereof it tooke the name) to the river Nid or Neath, infamous for a quick-sand, upon which stands an ancient towne of the same name ... Beneath this river Neath, whatsoever lieth betweene it and the river Loghor, which boundeth this shire in the West, we call Gower, the Britans and Ninnius *Guhir* ... This is now divided into the East part and the West. In the East part Swinesey is of great account, a towne so called by the Englishmen of Sea-Swine, but the Britans *Aber-Taw* of the river Taw running by it, which the foresaied Henry Earle of Warwick fortified. But there is a towne farre more ancient than this by the river Loghor, which Antonine the Emperor called Leucarum, and we by the whole name, Loghor. ... Beneath this lieth West-Gower, and by reason of two armes of the sea winding in, on other side one, it becommeth a Biland, more memorable for the fruitfulnesse than the townes in it, and in times past of great name in regard of Kined, canonized a Saint, who lived heere a solitarie life, of whom if you desire to know more, read our countryman Capgrave, who hath set out his miracle with great commendation.

CAERMARDENSHIRE

CAERMARDEN-SHIRE is plenteous enough in corne, stored abundantly with cattaile, and in some places yeeldeth it cole for fewell. On...the South with the Ocean, ...with so great a bay or creeke getteth within the land that this country seemeth as it were for very feare to have shrunke backe and withdrawne it selfe more inwardly.

Upon this Bay, Kidwelly first offreth it selfe to our sight ... Kidwelly with a wall and Castle to it, which now for very age is growen to decay and standeth, as it were, forlet and forlorne. For the inhabitants, having passed over the little river *Vendraeth Vehan*, built a new Kidwelly, entised thither by the commodity of the haven; which notwithstanding, being at this day choked with shelves and barres, is at this present of no great use. ... A few miles beneath Kidwelly, the river Tovie, which Ptolomee calleth Tobius, falleth into the Sea after he hath passed through this region from North-east to South, first by Lanandiffry, so called, as men thinke, of rivers meeting together, which Hoel the sonne of Rhese overthrew for malice that he bare unto the English; then by Dinevor, a princely castle standing aloft upon the top of an hill and belonging unto the Princes of South-wales whiles they flourished; and last of all by Caer-Marden, which the Britans themselves call *Caer-Firdhin* ... This is the chiefe Citie of the country, for medowes and woods pleasant, and in regard of antiquity to be respected ... Straight after the Normans entring into Wales, this Citie was reduced (but I wote not by whose conduct) under their subjection, and for a long time sore afflicted with many calamities and distresses, being oftentimes assaulted, once or twice set on fire, first by Gruffin ap Rise, then by Rise the said Gruffins brother. At which time, Henrie Turbervill an Englishmen succoured the castle and heawed downe the bridge. But afterwards by the meanes of Gilbert de Clare, who fortified both the walles thereof and the castles adjoining, it was freed from these miseries; and being once eased of all grievances, and in security enduring afterwards more easily from time to time the tempests of warre and all assaults.

[...]

Neere unto this Citie on the Eastside lieth *Cantred Bichan*, that is *The lesse Hundred* (for the Britans terme a portion of land that containeth 100 villages a *Cantred*), in which, beside the ruins of Careg Castle, situate upon a rocke rising on every side steepe and upright, there are many under-mines or caves of very great widenesse within the ground, now covered all over with greensord and turfe, wherein it is thought the multitude unable to beare armes hid themselves during the heate of warre.

[...]

But on the North-east side there stretcheth it selfe a great way out *Cantred Maur*, that is, *The great hundred*, a most safe refuge for the Britans in times past, as being thicke set with woods, combersome to travaile in by reason the waies are intricate by the windings in and out of the hils. Southward stand Talcharn and Lhan-Stephan Castles upon rockes of the Sea, which are most notable witnesses of martiall valour and proesse as well in the English as in the Welsh. Beneath Talcharn, Taff sheddeth it selfe into the Sea, by the side whereof was in times past that famous *Twy Gwn ar taf*, that is *The white house upon the river Taf*, because it was built of white hazels for a summer house, where in the yeere of our redemption 914 Hoel, surnamed *Dha*, that is is, *Good*, Prince of Wales, in a frequent assembly of his States (for there met there, besides others, of the Cleargie one hundred and fortie), abrogated the ancient ordinances and established new lawes for his subjects, as the Prooeme to the very lawes themselves doe witnesse. In which place afterward a little Abbay named White Land was built. Not farre from whence is Killmayn Lhoyd, where of late daies

24

certaine country people hapned upon an earthen vessell, in which was hourded a mighty deale of Romaine coine of embased silver ... Now it remaineth that I should relate how upon the river Tivy that separateth this County from Cardiganshire, there standeth New-castle (for so they call it at this day) ... before time it was named Elmelin. Which name, ...the Englishmen gave unto it of elme-trees.

[...]

PENBROKSHIRE

First and formost upon the shore descending Southward, Tenby, a proper fine towne well governed by a Major, and strongly walled toward the land, looketh down into the sea from a drie cliffe, very famous because it is a commodious road for ships, and for abundance also of fish there taken, whereupon in the British tongue it is called *Tenby-y-Piscoid*, and hath for Magistrates a Maior and a Bailiffe.

[...]

From hence runneth the shore along not many miles continuate, but at length the land shrinketh backe on both sides giving place unto the sea, which, encroching upon it a great way, maketh the haven which the Englishmen call Milford haven, than which there is not another in all Europe more noble or safer, such variety it hath of nouked bayes, and so many coves and creekes for harbour of ships, wherewith the bankes are on every side indented... For, to make use of the mariners words and their distinct termes, there are reckoned within in

16 Creekes, 5 Baies, and 13 Rodes, knowen every one by their severall names. Neither is this haven famous for the secure fastnesse thereof more than for the arrivall therein of King Henrie the Seventh ... Upon the innermore and East creeke of this haven, in the most pleasant country of all Wales, standeth Penbroke the Shire-towne, one direct street upon a long narrow point, all rock, and a forked arme of Milford haven ebbing and flowing close to the Towne walles on both sides. It hath a Castle, but now ruinate, and two Parish-churches within the walles, and is incorporate of a Maior, Balives and Burgesses.

[...]

Upon another creeke also of this haven, Carew Castle sheweth it selfe, which gave both name and originall to the notable family de Carew.

[...]

Into this have there discharged themselves, with their out-lets joined almost in one, two rivers, which the Britans tearme *Gledawh*, that is, if you interpret it, Swords, whereupon themselves use to tearme it *Aber du gledhaw*, that is, *The outlet of two swords*.

[...]

That tract was inhabited by Flemings out of the Lowcountries, who by the permission of King Henrie the First were planted heere when the Ocean, by making breaches in the bankes, had overwhelmed a great part of the said Low-countries. These are distinctly knowen still from the Welsh, both by their speech and manners, and so neere joined they are in society of the same language with Englishmen, who come nighest of any nation to the low Dutch tongue, that this their little country is tearmed by the Britans Little England beyond Wales.

[…]

By the more westward of these two rivers is Harford West, called by the Englishmen in times past Haverford, and by the Britans *Hulphord*, a faire towne and of great resort, situat upon an hil side, having scarce one even street, but is steepe one way or another, which, being a County by it self, hath for magistrates a Major, a Sheriff, and two Baliffs. The report goeth that the Earles of Clare fortified it with rampier and wall on the North side, and wee read that Richard Earle of Clare made Richard Fitz-Tancred Castellan of this Castle.

Beyond Ros, there shooteth out with a mighty front farre into the Western Ocean a great Promontorie, which Ptolomee called Ocltopitarum, the Britans *Pebidiauc* and *Candred Devi*, we Saint Davids land. A stony, barraine, and unfruitfull ground … Devi, a most religious Bishop, translated the Archiepiscopall see from Isca Legionum into the most remote and farthest angle heereof, even to Menew or Menevia, which afterwards the Britains of his name called *Tuy Devy*, that is *Devi his house*, the Saxons *Davy S. Mynster*, the Englishmen at this day Saint Davids, and was for a long time an Archbishops See. … What this Saint Davids was and what maner of thing in times past, a man can hardly tell, considering it hath beene so often by pirates raised. But now it is a very small and poore Citie, and hath nothing at all to make shew of but a faire Church dedicated to Saint Andrew and David, which, having beene many times overthrowen, Petre the Bishop, in the reigne of King John, and his successours erected in that forme which now sheweth, in the vale (as they tearme it) of Ros under the towne, and hard by it standeth the Bishops pallace, and faire houses of the Chaunter (who is next unto the Bishop, for there is no Dean heere), of the Chauncellor, Treasurer, and foure Archdeacons, who be of the number of the XXII Canons, all enclosed round within a strong and seemely wall, whereupon they call it the Close.

[…]

A noble kinde of falcons have their Airies here and breed in the rocks, which King Henry the Second, as the same Giraldus writeth, was wont to prefer before al others. For of that kinde are those, if the inhabitants thereby doe not deceive mee, which the skilful faulconers call Peregrines … But from this promontorie, as the land draweth backward, the sea with great violence and assault of waters inrusheth upon a little region called Keimes, which is reputed a Barony. In it standeth, first, Fishgard, so called in English of the taking of fish, in British *Aber-gwain*, that is, *The mouth of the river Gwain*, situate upon a steepe cliff, where there is a very commodious harbour and road for ships. Then Newport at the foote of an high mountaine by the river Neverns side, in British *Tref-draeth*, i. e. *The towne upon the sands* … Who founded likewise Saint Dogmaels Abbay according to the order of Tours, by the river Tivy low in a vale environed with hils, unto which the Borrough adjoyning (as many other townes unto Monasteries) is beholden for the original thereof.

[…]

More inward, upon the river Tivy aforesaid is Kilgarran, which sheweth the reliques of a castle built by Girald, but being at this day reduced unto one only street, it is famous for nothing else but the most plentifull fishing of Salmon. For there have you that notable Salmon Leap, where the river from on high falleth downright, and the Salmons from out of the Ocean, coveting to come up further into the river, when they meet with this obstacle in the way, bend backe their taile to the mouth, otherwhiles also to make a greater leap up hold fast their taile in the mouth, and as they unloose them selves from such a circle, they give a jirke, as if a twig bended into a rondle were sodainly let go, and so with the admiration of the beholders mount and whip themselves aloft from beneath.

[…]

CARDIGANSHIRE

The river Tivy, which Ptolomee calleth Tuerobius, but corruptly in steed of *Dwy-Tivius*, that is, *The river Tivy*, issueth out of the poole Lin-Tivy, beneath the hils whereof I spake before: first combred, as it were, with stones in the way, and rumbling with a great noise without any chanel, and so passeth through a very stony tract (nere unto which at Rosse the mountainers keepe the greatest faire for cattaile in all those parts), untill it come to Strat-fleur, a monastery long since of the Cluniack monks, compassed about with hils. From thence, being received within a chanel, it runneth downe by Tregaron and Lhan-Devi-brevi, built and so named in memoriall of David Bishop of Menevia, where he in a frequent Synode refuted the Pelagian heresie springing up againe in Britaine, both by the holy scriptures and also by a miracle, while the earth whereon hee stood as he preached arose up under his feete, by report, to a hillock. Thus farre and somewhat farther also Tivy holdeth on his course Soutward to Lan-Beder a little mercate towne. From hence Tivie, turning his streame Westward, carith a broader chanell, and maketh that Salmons Leape whereof I spake ere while.

[...]

Scarce two miles from hence standeth upon a steepe banke Cardigan, which the Britans name *Aber-tivy*, that is, *Tivy-mouth*, the shire towne, strongly fortified.

[...]

From Tibv mouth the shore gently giveth back, and openeth for itself the passage of many riverets, among which in the upper part of this shire ... being called in common speach Ystwith: at the head whereof are veines of lead, and at the mouth the towne Aber-y-stwith, the most populous and plentuous place of the whole shire ... At the same mouth also the river Ridol dischargeth it self into the Irish sea. This river, descending out of Plinlimon, an exceeding steepe and high hill that encloseth the North part of this shire, and powreth out of his lap those most noble rivers Severn and Wy, whereof I have already often spoken. And not much above Y-stwith mouth the river Dev, that serveth in steed of a limite betweene this and Merionithshire, is lodged also within the sea.

MONTGOMERYSHIRE

Five miles hence, the Hil Plinlimon, whereof I spake, raiseth it selfe up to a wonderfull height, and on that part where it boundeth one side of this shire, it powreth forth Sabrina, the greatest river in Britaine next to Thamis, which the Britains tearme *Haffren*, and Englishmen Severn.

[…]

This river immediatly from his spring head maketh such a number of windings in and out in his course that a man would thinke many times he returns againe to his fountaine, yet for all that hee runneth forward, or rather slowly wandereth through this Shire …, it being overshadowed with woods, after much strugling hee getteth out Northward by Lanidlos, Trenewith or Newtowne, and Caer-fuse, which, as they say, is both ancient and enjoieth also ancient priviledges, and not farre from his East banke leaveth behind him the Castle and towne of Montgomery upon the rising of a rocke, having a pleasant plaine under it.

[…]

Hard by this, Corndon Hill mounteth up to a very great height, in the top whereof are placed certaine stones in a round circle like a coronet, whence it taketh that name, in memoriall as it should seeme of some victorie. A little higher, Severn glideth downe by *Trellin*, that is, *The towne by a poole*, whereupon it is called Welch Poole in English. It hath a Castle joining unto it on the South-side, called Castle Coch of a kind of reddish stone wherewith it is built, which within the compasse of one wall containeth two Castles, the one belonged to the Lord of Powis, the other to the Baron Dudley.

MERIONETHSHIRE

The inhabitants, who for most part wholy betake themselves to breeding and seeding of cattaile, and live upon white meates, as butter, cheese &c. (however Strabo mocked our Britans in times past as unskilfull in making cheese) are for stature, cleere complexion, goodly feature and lineaments of body, inferiour to no nation in Britaine, but they have an ill name among their neighbours for being so forward in the wanton love of women, and that proceeding from their idlenesse.

[…]

Where the river Avon runneth downe more Westward there is Dolegethle a little mercat town, so called of the vale wherein it is built. Hard by the sea in the little territory named Ardudwy, the castle Arlech, in times past named Caer Colun, standeth advanced upon a very steepe rock and looketh downe into the sea from aloft, which being built, as the inhabitants report, by King Edward the First, tooke name of the situation. For *Arlech* in the British tongue signifieth as much as *upon a Stony rocke*… A little higher, in the verie confines of the shires, two notable armes of the sea enbosom thermselves within the land, *Traith Maur* and *Traith Bachan*, that is, *the Greater wash, and the Lesse*. And not farre from hence neere unto a little village called Fastineog, there is a street or Port-way paved with stone, that passeth through these combersome and, in manner, unpassable mountaines. Which, considering that the Britans name it *Sarn Helen*, that is, *Helens street*, it is not to bee thought but that Helena mother to Constantine the Great, who

32

did many such like famous workes throughout the Roman Empire, laied the same with stone.

[…]

In the East side of this shire the river Dee springeth out of two fountaines, whence some thinke it tooke the name, for they call it *Dwy*, which word importeth also among them *the number of two* (although others would needes have it so termed of some Divinity, others of the blacke colour), and forthwith passeth entier and whole through Lhinteged, in Engish Pimble-Meare and Plenlin-meare, a lake spreding far in length and breath, and so runneth out of it with as a great a streame as it entred in. For neither shal a man see in Dee the fishes called *guiniad*, which are peculiar to the Meare, nor yet Salmons in the Meare, which neverthelesse are commonly taken in the river.

[…]

On the browe or edge hereof standeth Bala, a little towne endowed with many immunities, but peopled with few inhabitants, and as rudely and unhandsomely built, neverthelesse it is the chiefe mercate towne for these mountainers.

CAERNARVONSHIRE

Nature hath loftily areared it up farre and nere with mountaines standing thick one by another, as if she would here have compacted the joints of this Island within the bowells of the earth, and made this part thereof a most sure place of refuge for the Britans in time of adversitie. For there are so many roughes and rocks, so many vales full of woods, with pooles heere and there crossing over them, lying in the way betweene, that no armie, nay not so much as those that are lightly appointed, can finde passage. A man may truely, if hee please, terme these mountaines the British Alpes: for, besides that they are the greatest of the whole Island, they are no lesse steepe also with cragged and rent rockes on every side than the Alpes of Italie, yea and all of them compasse one mountaine round about, which over-topping the rest so towreth up with his head aloft in the aire as hee may seeme not to threaten the skie, but to thrust his head up into heaven. And yet harbour they the Snow, for all the yeere long they bee hory with snow, or rather with an hardened crust of many snowes felted together. Whence it is that all these hilles are in British by one name termed *Craig Eriry*, in English Snow-don, which in both languages sound as much as *Snowye Mountaines* ... Neverthelesse, so ranke are they with grasse that it is a very comon speech among the Welsh, that the mountaines Eriry will yeeld sufficient pasture for all the cattaile in Wales, if they were put upon them together. Concerning the two Meare on the toppe of these, in the one of which floteth a wandering Island, and in the other is found great store of fishes, but having all of them but one eye apeece ... certaine it is that there bee in the very top of these mountains pooles indeed and standing waters.

[...]

But come wee downe now from the mountaines into the champian plaines, which because wee finde no where else but by the sea side, it may suffice to coast onely along the shore. The Promontory ... that the inhabitants name it at this day *Lhein*, ... runneth forth with a narrow and even by-land, having larger and more open fields than the rest of the Country, and the same yeelding barley most plentuously. Two little townes it sheweth, and no more, that are memorable. Farther within upon the creeke is *Pullhely*, that is, *that salt Meare or Poole*. More outward, by the Irish sea (that beateth upon the other side of the Biland) is Nevin, a village having a mercate kept in it.

[...]

From Nevin the shore, pointed and endented with one or two elbowes lying out into the sea, tendeth Northward, and then, turning afront North-east, by a narrow sea or Firth (they call it *Menai*), it severeth the Isle of Anglesey from the firme land. ... It tooke the name of a river running by the side of it, which yet at this day is called Seiont, and issueth out of the poole Lin-Peris. In which there is a kinde of fish peculiar to that water ... King Edward the First[,] [w]ho out of the ruines of this towne at the same time raised the Citie Caer-narvon somewhat higher upon the rivers mouth, so as that on the West and North-sides it is watered therewith. Which, as it was called *Caer-narvon* because it standeth right over against the Island Mona (for so much doth the word import), so it hath communicated that name unto the whole Country, for heereupon the English men call it Caer-narvonshire. This is encompassed with a verie small circuite of walles about it and in manner round, but the same exceeding strong, and to set it the better out, sheweth a passing faire Castle which taketh up the whole West side of it. The private buildings (for the manner of that Country) are sightly enough, and the inhabitants for their courtesie much commended ... About seven miles hence by the same narrow sea standeth Bangor or Banchor low seated, enclosed on the south side with a mountaine of great height, on the North with a little hill. ... The Church was consecrated unto Daniel sometime Bishop thereof, but that which now standeth is of no especiall faire building. For Owen Glendoverdwy ... set it on fire ... and defaced the ancient Church, which albeit Henry Deney Bishop of the same repaired about the time of King Henry the Seventh, yet it scarcely recovered the former dignity. Now the towne is small, but in times past so large that for the greatnesse thereof it was called *Banchor Vaur*, that is, *Great Banchor*, and Hugh Earle of Chester fortified it with a Castle, whereof I could finde no footings at all, though I sought them with all diligent inquiry. But that castle was situate upon the verie entry of the said narrow sea.

[...]

From thence the shore, raising itself with a bending ascent, runneth on by *Pennaen-maur*, that is *the great stony head*, a very exceeding high and steep rock, which, hanging over the sea when it is floud, affourdeth a very narrow path way for passengers, having on the one side huge stones over their heads, as if they were ready to fall upon them, on the other side the raging Ocean lying of a wonderfull steepe depth under it. But after a man hath passed over this, together with *Pen-maen bychan*, that is, *the lesser stony head*, he shall come to an open broad plaine that reacheth as farre as to the river Conwey, which limiteth this shore on the East side. ... For a very smal and poore village standing among the rubbish thereof is called *Caer hean*, that is, *the ancient City*. Out of the spoile and ruines whereof King Edward the First built a new towne at the very mouth of the river, which thereupon they call *Aber-Conwey*, that is, *the Mouth of Con-wey*, which place Hugh of Chester had before time fortified. But this New Conovium or Aber-Conwey, being strongly situated and fensed both with wals and also with a very proper castle by the rivers side, deserveth the name rather of a pety City than of a towne, but that it is not replenished with inhabitants.

Opposite unto this towne, and yet on this side of the river, which is passed by ferry and not by bridge, reacheth out a huge Promontory with a bending elbow (as if nature purposed to make there a road and harbour for ships), which is also counted part of this shire and is named Gogarth, wherein stood Diganwy, an ancient City just over the river Conwey, where it issueth into to the sea, which was burnt many yeeres ago with lightning.

MONA INSULA SIVE ANGLESEY

This Isle, called of the Romans *Mona*, of the Britans *Mon* and *Tir-Mon*, that is *the land of Mon*, and *Ynis Dowil*, that is, *A shadowy or darke Iland*, of the ancient Anglo-Saxons *Moneg*, and at last, after that the Englishmen became Lords of it, *Engles-ea* and *Anglesey*, as one would say, *The Englishmens Iland*, being severed from the continent of Britaine with the small narrow streight of Menai, and on all parts besides beatten upon with that surging and troublous Irish sea … In cattaile also it is passing rich, and sendeth out great multitudes. It yeeldeth also grind-stones, and in some place an earth standing upon Alum, out of which some not long since beganne to make Alum and Coperose. But when they saw it not answerable to their expectation at first, without any further hope they gave over their enterprise.

[...]

The next town in name to Beau-Marish is Newburg, called in British *Rossur*, standing ten miles off Westward, which having bin a long time greatly annoyed with heaps of sand driven in by the sea, complaineth that it hath lost much of the former state that it had. Aber-fraw is not far from hence, which is now but an obscure and meane towne, yet in times past it excelled all the rest farre in worth and dignity, as having beene the Royall seat of the Kings of Guineth or North-wales. And in the utmost Promontorie Westward, which wee call Holy-head, there standeth a little poore towne, in British Caer-Guby, so named of Kibie, a right holy man and a disciple of S. Hilarie of Poitiers, who therein devoted himselfe to the service of God, and from whence there is an usuall passage over into Ireland. All the rest of this Iland is well bespred with villages, which because they have in them nothing materially memorable, I will crosse over into the Continent and view Denbighshire.

DENBIGHSHIRE

The West part, but that it is somewhat more plentifull and pleasant toward the sea side, is but heere and there inhabited, and mounteth up more with bare and hungry hils, but yet the painfull diligence and witty industrie of the husbandmen hath begunne a good while since to overcome this leannesse of the soile where the hils setle anything flattish, as in other parts of Wales likewise. For after they have with a broad kind of spade pared away the upper coat, as it were, or sord of the earth into certaine turfes, they pile them up artificially on heapes, put fire to them, and burne them to ashes, which being throwen upon the ground so pared and flayed, causeth the hungry barainnesse thereof so to fructifie that the fields bring forth a kind of Rhie or Amel corne in such abundance as it is incredible. Neither is this a new devise thus to burne grouind, but very ancient, as we may see in Virgil and Horace. Among these hilles there is a place commonly called *Cerigy Drudion*, that is, *The stones of the Druidae*, and certaine little columnes or pillers are seen at Yvoellas, with inscriptions in them of strange characters, which some imagine to have beene erected by the Druides.

[…]

By the vale side whre these mountaines begnne now to wax thinner, upon the hanging of a rocke standeth Denbigh, called of our Britans by a more ancient name *Cled Fryn-yn Ross*, that is *A rough hill in Ross*, for so they call that part of the Shire … with a wall about, not large in circuit, but strong, and on the Southside with a proper castle, strengthned with high towres. … And then, either because the inhabitants like not the steep situation therof (for the cariage up and down was very incommodious), or by reason that it wanted water, the removed downe from thence by little and little, so as that this ancient towne hath now few or none dwelling in it. But a new one farre bigger than it sprung up at the very foote of the hill, which is so well peopled and inhabited that by reason that the Church is not able to received the multitude, they beganne to build a new one in the place where the old towne stood.

[...]

Now are we come into the very hart of the shire, where Nature, having removed the hilles out of the way on both sides to shew what she could doe in a rough country, hath spred beneath them a most beautifull pleasant vale reaching 17 miles in length from South to North and five miles or thereabout in bredth, which lieth open onely toward the sea and the cleering North Wind: otherwise environed it is on every side with high hills, and those from the Eastside, as it were, embatled. For such is the wonderfull workmanship of nature that the tops of these mountaines resemble in fashion the battlements of walles. Among which the highest is Moilenlly, on the top whereof I saw a warlicke fense with trench and rampier, also a little fountaine of cleere water. This vale for wholsomenesse, fruitfulnesse and pleasantnesse excelleth. The colour and complexion of the inhabitants is healthy, their heads are sound and of a firme constitution, teir eie sight continuing and never dimme, and their age long lasting and very cheerefull. The vale it selfe, with his greene medowes, yellow corne-fields, villages, and faire houses thicke, and many beautifull Churches, giveth wonderfull great contentment to such as behold it from above. The river Cluid, encreased with beckes and brookes resorting unto it from the hilles on each side, doth from the very spring-head part it in twaine running through the midst

of it, whence in ancient time it was named *Strat Cluid*.
… On the East banke of Cluid, in the South part of the
vale, standeth Ruthin, in Latin writers *Ruthunia*, in
British *Ruthun*, the greatest market towne in all the vale,
full of inhabitants and well replenished with buildings,
famous also not long since by reason of a large and very
faire Castle able to receive and entertaine a great
houshold.

[…]

When you ascend out of the vale Eastward, you come
to Yale, a little hilly country, and in comparison of the
regions beheath and round about it passing high, so that
no river from elswhere commeth into it, and it sendeth
forth some from it. By reason of this high situation it is
bleake, as exposed to the winds on all sides. Whether it
tooke that name of the riveret Alen, which rising first in
it, undermineth the ground and once or twice hideth
himselfe, I know not. The mountaines are full of neat,
sheepe, and goats, the vallies in some places plenteous
enough of corne, especially Eastward,on this side of
Alen. But the more Westerly part is not so fruitfull, and
in some places is a very heath and altogither barraine.
Neither hath it any thing memorable, save onely a little
Abbay, now wholy decaied, but standing most richly
and pleasantly in a vale, which among the woody hils
cutteth it selfe overthwart in maner of a crosse,
whereupon it was called in Latin *Vallis Crucis*, that is,
the vale of the Crosse, and in British *Lhane-Gwest*.

From hence more Eastward, the territory called in
Welsh *Mailor Cymraig*, that is, *West Mailor*, in English
Bromfield, reacheth as far as to the river Dee. A smal
territory, but verie rich and pleasant, plentiful withal of

41

lead, especially nere unto Moinglath, a little towne which tooke the name of mines. Heere is Wrexham to be seene, in the Saxons tongue *Writtles-ham*, much spoken of for a passing faire towre steeple that the Church hath, and the Musical Organs that be therein.

[...]

Beneath Bromfield Southward lieth Chirke, in Welsh *Gwain*, being also very hilly, but wel knowne in elder ages for two Castles, Chirk, which gave it the name, built by Roger Mortimer, and *Castle Dinas Bran*, situate in the hanging of a mighty high hill pointed in the top, where of note there remaineth nothing but the very ruines.

FLINTSHIRE

Beneath this Varis, or *Bodvari*, in the vale glideth Cluid, and streightwaies Elwya, a little riveret, conjoineth it selfe with it, where there is a Bishops see. This place the Britains call according to the river Llan-Elwy, the Englishmen of Asaph the Patron thereof Saint Asaph, and the Historiographers *Asaphensis*. Neither is the towne for any beauty it hath, nor for the Church for building or braverie memorable, yet some thing would bee said of it in regard of antiquity.

[...]

Above this, Rughlan, taking the name of the ruddy and red banke of Cluid on which it stands, maketh a good shew with a Castle, but now almost consumed by very age. ... Beneath this we saw the little town of Haly-well, as one would say Holy-well, where there is that fountaine frequented by Pilgrimes for the memoriall of the Christian Virgin Winefride, ravished there perforce and beheaded by a tyrante, as also for the mosse there growing of a most sweet and pleasant smell. Out of which well there gusheth forth a brooke among stones, which represent bloudy spottes upon them, and carrieth so violent a streame that presently it is able to drive a mill. Over the very well there standeth a Chappell built of stone right curiously wrought, whereunto adjoineth a little Church, in a window whereof is portraied and set out the history of the said Winifride, how her head was cut off and set on againe by Saint Benno.

[…]

This part of the Country, because it smileth so pleasantly upon the beholders with a beautifull shew, and was long since subject unto Englishmen, the Welsh named *Teg-Engle*, that is, *Faire England*. But whereas one hath termed it *Tegenta*, and thought that the Igeni there planted themselves, take heede I advise you that you bee not overhasty to beleeve him.

[…]

Through the South part of this shire, lying beneath these places above named wandereth Alen, a little river, neere unto which in a hill hard by Kilken, a small village, there is a well, the water whereof at certaine set times riseth and falleth after the manner of the sea-tides. Upon this Alen standeth Hope Castle, in Welsh *Caer-gurle*, in which King Edward the First retired himselfe when the Welshmen had upon the sodaine set upon his soldiers, being out of array, and where good milstones are wrought out of the rocke; also Mold, in Welsh *cuid Cruc*, a castle belonging in ancient time to the Barons of

Monthault, both which places shew many tokens of Antiquity.

William Camden,
Britain, or, a Chorographicall Description of the most
flourishing Kingdomes, England, Scotland, and Ireland,
1607 (Translated by Philémon Holland, 1610)

William Camden (1551-1623) lived most of his life in London, apart from spending five years at Oxford. He was a master at Westminster School, and subsequently became its headmaster. Camden made good use of long vacations, spending twenty five summers traversing England, and in 1590, Wales. His chapters on Wales benefited from his learning Welsh. He was also Clarenceux King of Arms at the Royal College of Heralds and his 'Remaines Concerning Britain' (a series of historical essays and the first collection of English proverbs) was published in 1605, along with his 'Annales' (a history of Queen Elizabeth's reign) which was published posthumously in 1625. An enlarged edition was edited by Edmund Gibson in 1695, including detailed accounts of the archaeology of Wales by Edward Lhwyd and further expanded in 1722. Finally, in 1789, Richard Gough's edition encompassed three folio volumes with four in 1806.

....
"With a wide wild heath under me"
....

John Taylor spent 28 days riding and walking through Wales, sometimes on all fours. He did not approve of the use of churches as places of recreation on Sundays.

On Fryday the 30. of July, I rode (and footed it) ten miles to Flint (which is the shire town of Flintshire), and surely war hath made it miserable; the sometimes famous castle there, in which Richard the Second of that name, king of England, was surprised by Henry of Bullinbrook, is now almost buried in its own ruins, and the town is so spoiled, that it may truely be said of it, that they never had any market (in the memory of man). They have no sadler, taylor, weaver, brewer, baker, botcher, or button maker; they have not so much as a signe of an alehouse, so that I was doubtfull of a lodging, but (by good hap) I hapned into the house of one Mr. Edward Griffith, where I had good meat and lodging for me and my dumb Dun beast, for very reasonable consideration, and this (me thinks) is a pitifull discription of a shire town.

Saturday, the last of July, I left Flint, and went three miles to Holy-well, of which place I must speak somewhat materially. About the length of a furlong, down a very steep hill, is a well (full of wonder and admiration); it comes from a spring not far from Rudland castle; it is and hath been many hundred yeares knowne by the name of Holy-well, but it is more commonly and of most antiquity called Saint Winifrids well, in memory of the pious and chaste virgin Winifrid, who was there beheaded for refusing to yield her chastity to the furious lust of a pagan prince: in that very place where her bloud was shed, this spring sprang up; from it doth issue so forcible a stream, that within a hundred yards of it, it drives certain mils, and some do say that nine corn mils and fulling mils are driven with the stream of that spring. It hath a fair chappell erected over it, called Saint Winifrids chappell, which is now much defaced by the injury of these late wars. The well is compassed about with a fine wall of free-stone; the wall hath eight angles or corners, and at every angle is a fair stone piller, whereon the west end of the chappell is supported. In two severall places of the wall there are neat stone staires to go into the water that comes from the well, for it is to be noted that the well it selfe doth continually work and bubble with extream violence, like a boiling cauldron or furnace, and within the wall, or into the well very few do enter. The water is christalline, sweet and medicinable; it is frequented daily by many people of rich and poore, of all diseases, amongst which great store of folkes are cured, divers are eased, but none made the worse. The hill descending is plentifully furnished (on both sides of the way) with beggers of all ages, sexes, conditions, sorts and sizes; many of them are impotent, but all are impudent, and richly embrodered all over with such hexameter poudred ernins (or vermin) as are called lice in England.

Monday, the second of August, when the day begun, I mounted my dun, having hired a little boy (to direct me in the way) that could speak no English, and for lack of an interpreter, we travelled speachless eight miles, to Rudland, where is an old ruined winde and war-shaken castle; from that town, after my horse and the boy, and my selfe had dined with hay, oats, and barrow causs, we hors't and footed it twelve miles further, to a fine strong walled towne, named Aberconwy; there I lodged at the house of one Mr. Spencer (an English man) ; he is a post-master there, and there my entertainement was good, and my reckoning reasonable. There is a good defensive castle which I would have seen, but because there was a garrison, I was loath to give occasion of offence, or be much inquisitive.

The next day, when the clock strok two and foure,
I mounted Dun, Dun mounted Penmen Mawre;
And if I do not take my aime amisse,
That lofty mountain seems the skies to kisse:
But there are other hils accounted higher,
Whose lofty tops I had no mind t' aspire:
As Snowdon, and the tall Plinnillimon,
Which I no stomack had to tread upon.
Merioneth mountains, and shire Cardigan
To travell over, will tire horse and man:
I, to Bewmaris came that day and din'd,
Where I the good lord Buckley thought to find:
But he to speak with me had no intent,
Dry I came into's house, dry out I went.
I left Bewmaris, and to Bangor trae'd it,
Ther's a brave church, but time and war defae'd it:
For love and mony I was welcome thither,
Tis merry meeting when they come together.

Thus having travelled from Aberconwy to Beumorris
and to Bangor, Tuesday 3. August, which in all they are
pleased to call 14 miles, but most of the Welsh miles are
large London measure, not any one of them but hath a
hand bredth or small cantle at each end, by which
means, what they want in broadness, they have it in
length; besides the ascending and descending almost
impassable mountains, and the break-neck stony ways,
doth make such travellers as my selfe judge that they
were no misers in measuring their miles; besides, the
land is courser then it is in most parts about London,
which makes them to afford the larger measure: for
course broad-cloth is not at the rate of velvet or satten.

Wednesday the 4. of August, I rode 8 miles from Bangor to Carnarvon, where I thought to have seen a town and a castle, or a castle and a town; but I saw both to be one, and one to be both; for indeed a man can hardly divide them in judgement or apprehension; and I have seen many gallant fabricks and fortifications, but for compactness and compleatness of Caernarvon I never yet saw a parallel. And it is by art and nature so sited and seated, that it stands impregnable; and if it be well mand, victualled and ammunitioned, it is invincible, except fraud or famine do assault, or conspire against it.

I was 5. hours in Caernarvon, and when I thought that I had taken my leave for ever of it, then was I meerly deceived; for when I was a mile on my way, a trooper came galloping after me, and enforced me back to be examined by Colonell Thomas Mason (the governour there), who, after a few words, when hee heard my name and knew my occasions, he used me so respectively and bountifully, that (at his charge) I stayd all night, and by the means of him, and one Mr. Lloyd (a justice of peace there), I was furnished with a guide, and something else to beare charges for one weeks travaile; for which curtesies, if I were not thankfull, I were worth the hanging for being ingratefull.

The 5. of August I went 12 miles to a place called Climenie, where the noble Sire John Owen did, with liberall welcome, entertain me.

The 6. day I rode to a town called Harleck, which stands on a high barren mountaine, very uneasie for the ascending into, by reason of the steep and uneeven stony way; this town had neither hay, grass, oats, or any relief for a horse: there stands a strong castle, but the town is all spoild, and almost inhabitable by the late lamentable troubles.

So I left that towne (for fear of starving my horse) and came to a place called Bermoth (12. miles that day, as narrow as 20.) That place was so plentifully furnished with want of provision, that it was able to famish 100. men and horses: I procured a brace of boyes to goe two miles to cut grasse for my dun, for which I gave them two groats; for my selfe and guide, I purchased a hen boyld with bacon, as yellow as the cowslip, or gold noble. My course lodging there was at the homely house of one John Thomson, a Lancashire English man.

Saturday the 7. of August, I horst, footed (and crawling upon all 4.) 10. slender miles to Aberdovy, which was the last lodging that I had in Merionethshire, where was the best entertainment for men, but almost as bad as the worst for horses in all Merionethshire.

August 9. I gat into Cardiganshire, to a miserable market town called Aberistwith, where before the late troubles there stood a strong castle, which being blown up, fell down, and many fair houses (with a defensible thick wall about the town) are transformed into confused heaps of unnecessary rubbidge: within foure miles of this town are the silver mines, which were honourable and profitable, as long as my good friend Thomas Bushell, Esquire, had the managing of them, who was most industrious in the work, and withall by his noble demeanour and affable deportment deservedly gain'd the generall love and affection of all the countrey of all degrees of people: but since he hath left that important imployment, the mines are neglected.

From Aberistwith, I went to the house of Sir Richard Price, knight and baronet, where my entertainment was freely welcome, with some expression of further curtesies at my departure, for which I humbly thank the noble knight, not forgetting my gratefull remembrance to Mr. Thomas Evans there: that whole dayes journey being 9. miles.

Tuesday the 10. of August, having hired a guide, for I that knew neither the intricate wayes, nor could speake any of the language, was necessitated to have guides from place to place, and it being harvest time, I was forced to pay exceeding deare for guiding; so that some dayes I payd 2s., sometimes 3, besides bearing their charges of meat and drinke and lodging; for it is to bee understood that those kind of labouring people had rather reap hard all the day for six pence, then to go ten or twelve miles easily on foot for two shillings. That day, after sixteen miles travell, I came to the house of an ancient worthy and hospitable gentleman, named sure Walter Lloyd; he was noble in bountifull house-keeping, and in his generositie caused his horse to be saddled, and the next day hee rode three miles to Conway, and shewed me the way to Caermarden, which they do call 18 small miles, but I had rather ride 30 of such miles as are in many parts of England; the way continually hilly, or mountainous and stony, insomuch that I was forced to alight and walke 30 times, and when the sun was near setting, I having foure long miles to go, and knew no part of the way, was resolved to take my lodging in a reeke of oats in the field ; to which purpose, as I rode out of the stony way towards my field chamber, my horse and I found a softer bed, for we were both in a bog or quagmire, and at that time I had much ado to draw myselfe out of the dirt, or my poore weary Dun out of the mire.

I being in this hard strait, having night (of Gods sending) owl-light to guide me, no tongue to aske a question, the way unknown, or uneven, I held it my best course to grope in the hard stony way againe, which having found (after a quarter of an houres melancholy paces), a horsman of Wales, that could speak English, overtook me and brought me to Caermarden, where I found good and free entertainment at the house of one Mistris Oakley.

Caermarden, the shire town Caermardenshire, is a good large town, with a defencible strong castle, and a reasonable haven for small barks and boats, which formerly was for the use of good ships, but now it is much impedimented with shelvs, sands, and other annoyances; it is said that Merlyn the prophet was born there; it is one of the plentifullest townes that ever I set my foot in, for very fair egs are cheaper then small pears; for, as near as I can remember, I will set down at what rate victuals was there.

Butter, as good as the world affords, two pence halfepenny, or three pence the pound.

A salmon, two foot and a halfe long, twelve pence.
Biefe, three half pence the pound.
Oysters, a penny the hundred.
Egs, twelve for a penny.
Peares, six for a penny.

And all manner of fish and flesh at such low prices, that a little money will buy much, for there is nothing scarce, dear, or hard to come by, but tobacco pipes.

My humble thanks to the governour there, to William Guinn of Talliaris, Esquire; to Sure Henry Vaughan; and to all the rest, with the good woman mine hostess.

Concerning Pembrookshire, the people do speak English in it almost generally, and therefore they call it little England beyond Wales, it being the furthest south and west county in the whole principality. The shire town, Pembrook, hath been in better estate, for as it is now, some houses down, some standing, and many without inhabitants; the castle there hath been strong, large, stately, and impregnable, able to hold out any enemy, except hunger, it being founded upon a lofty rock, gives a brave prospect a far off. Tenby towne and castle being somewhat near, or eight miles from it, seems to be more usefull and considerable. My thanks to Mistris Powell at the Hart there.

Tenby hath a good castle and a haven, but in respect of Milford Haven, all the havens under the heavens are inconsiderable, for it is of such length, bredth, and depth, that 1000 ships may ride safely in it in all weathers, and by reason of the hills that do inclose it, and the windings and turnings of the haven, from one poynt of land to another, it is conjectured that 1500 ships may ride there, and not scarce one of them can see another. The haven hath in it 16 creekes, 5 bayes, and 13 rodes, of large capacity, and all these are known by severall names.

The goodly church of St. Davids hath beene forced lately to put off the dull and heavy coat of peacefull lead, which was metamorphosed into warlike bullets. In that church lies interred Edmund earle of Richmond, father to King Henry the seventh, for whose sake his grandson (K. Henry the eight) did spare it from defacing, when hee spared not much that belonged to the church.

Thus having gone and riden many miles, with two many turning and winding mountains, stony turning waies, forward, backward, sidewaies, circular and semicircular, upon the 17. of August I rode to the house of the right honourable Richard Vaughan, earle of Karbery, at a place called Golden Grove; and surely that house, with the faire fields, woods, walks, and pleasant scituation, may not onely be rightly called the Golden Grove, but it may without fiction be justly stiled the Cambrian Paradise, and Elizium of Wales; but that which grac'd it totally, was the nobleness, and affable presence and deportment of the earle, with his faire and vertuous new married countess, the beautiful lady Alice, or Alicia, daughter to the right honourable the late earle of Bridgwater, deceased: I humbly thank them both, for they were pleased to honour me so much, that I supp'd with them, at which time a gentleman came in, who being sate, did relate a strange discourse of a violent rain which fell on the mountains in part of Radnorshire and into Glamorganshire; the story was, as near as I can remember, as followeth.

That on Saturday the 17. of July last, 1652, there fell a sudden showre of rain in the counties aforesaid, as if an ocean had flowed from the clouds to overwhelm and drown the mountains: it poured down with such violent impetuositie, that it tumbled down divers houses of stone that stood in the way of it; it drowned many cattell and sheep, bore all before it as it ran, therefore a poore man with his son and daughter forsook their house, and the father and son climed up into a tree for their safety; in the mean time the merciless waters took hold of the poore maid, and almost furiously bare her away down between two mountains, rolling and hurling her against many great stones, till at last it threw her near the side of the stream, and her hair and hair-lace being loose, it catched hold of a stump of an old thorn bush, by which means she was stayed, being almost dead; but as she lay in this misery, she saw a sad and lamentable sight, for the water had fiercely unrooted the tree, and bore it down the stream, with her father and brother, who were both unfortunately drowned: the maid, as I was certified, is like to live and recover.

My humble thanks to the good yong hopefull lord Vaughan, and to all the rest of the noble olive branches of that most worthy tree of honour, their father, not omitting or yet forgetting my gratitude to Mr. Steward there, with all the rest of the gentlemen and servants attendant, with my love to Mr. Thomas Ryve, unknown, and so Golden Grove farewell.

The 18. of August, I hired a guide who brought me to Swansey (sixteen well stretch'd Welch mountainous miles), where I was cordially welcome to an ancient worthy gentleman, Walter Thomas, esquire, for whose love and lebirality I am much obliged to him and the good gentlewoman his wife; he staid me till the next day after diner, and then sent his man with me a mile to his sons house, named William Thomas, esquire: there, as soon as I had rewarded my guide he slip'd from me, leaving me to the mercy of the house, where I found neither mercy nor manners, for the good gentleman and his wife were both rode from home; and though there were people old enough, and big enough, yet there was not one kind enough or good enough to do me the least kind of courtesie or friendship; they did not so much as bid me come into the house, or offer me a cup of drink; they all scornfully wondred at me, like so many buzzards and woodcocks about an owle: there was a shotten, thin scul'd, shallow brain'd, simpleton fellow, that answered me, that he was a stranger there, but I believed him not, by reason of his familiarity with the rest of the folks; there was also a single soal'd gentlewoman, of the last edition, who would vouchsafe me not one poor glance of her eye beams, to whom I said as followeth : —

Fair gentlewoman, I was sent hither by the father of the gentleman of this house, to whom I have a letter from a gentleman of his familiar acquaintance; I am sure that the owner of this place is famed and reported to be a man endowed with all affability and courtesie to strangers, as is every way accomodating to a gentleman of worth and quality; and that if I were but a meer stranger to him, yet his generosity would not suffer me to be harbourless, but by reason of his fathers sending his servant with, and a friends letter, I sayd that if Mr. Thomas had been at home I should be better entertained.

To which Mrs. Fumpkins, looking scornfully ascue over her shoulders, answered me with, It may be so. Then, most uncourteous mistress, quoth I, I doubt I must bee necessitated to take up my lodging in the field: to which the said ungentle gentlewoman (with her posteriors, or butt end, towards me) gave me a finall answer, that I might if I would.

Whereupon I was enraged, and mounted my dun; and in a friendly maner I tooke my leave, saying, that I would wander further and try my fortune, and that if my stay at that house, that night, would save either Mr. Shallow-pate or Mrs. Jullock from hanging, that I would rather lie, and venture all hazards that are incident to hors, man, or traveller, then to be beholding to such unmanerly mungrils.

Thus desperately I shaked them off, that would not take me on; and riding I knew not whither, with a wide wild heath under me, and a wider firmament above me, I roade at adventure, betwixt light and darkness, about a mile, when luckily a gentleman overtook mee, and after a little talk of my distresse and travail, he bad me be of good chear, for he would bring me to a lodging and entertainment; in which promise he was better than his word, for he brought me to a pretty market town called Neath, where he spent his money upon me; for which kindness I thank him. But one doctour (as they call him) Rioc Jones (or doctor Merriman) came and supt with mee, and very kindly payd all the reckoning. That dayes journey being but six miles sterling.

The 19. of August I hired a guide for 3s. (16 miles) to a place called Penline, where sometime stood a strong castle, which is now ruined; adjoining to it, or in the place of it, is a fair house, belonging to Anthony Tuberville, esquire, where, although the gentleman was from home, the good gentlewoman his wife did with hospitable and noble kindnesse bid me welcome.

Fryday, the 20. of August, I rode a mile to an ancient

town, named Coobridge, from whence I scrambled two miles further to Llanstrithyott, where the noble gentleman Sure John Awbrey, with his vertuous lady, kept me three dayes; in the mean space I rode two miles to the house of the ancient and honorable knight Sir Thomas Lewis, at Penmark, to whom and his good lady I humbly dedicate my gratitude. The same day, after dinner, I returned back to Llanstrithyott, which was to me a second Golden Grove, or Welch paradice, for building, scituation, wholsome ayre, pleasure, and plenty : for my free entertainment there, with the noble expression of the gentlemans bounty at my departure, I heartily do wish to him and his, with all the rest of my honorable and noble, worshipfull and friendly benefactors, true peace and happinesse, internall, externall, and eternall.

Monday, the 23. of August, I rode eight miles to the good town of Cardiffe, where I was welcome to Mr. Aaron Price, the town clark there, with whom I dined, at his cost and my perrill: after dinner he directed me two miles further, to a place called Llanrumney, where a right true bred generous gentleman, Thomas Morgan, esquire, gave me such loving and liberall entertainment, for which I cannot be so thankfull as the merit of it requires.

Tuesday, being both Saint Bartholomews day, my birthday, the 24. of the month, and the very next day before Wednesday, I arose betimes, and travelled to a town called Newport, and from thence to Carbean, and lastly to Uske, in all 15 well measur'd Welsh Monmouthshire miles: at Uske I lodg'd at an inn, the house of one Master Powell.

The 25. of August I rode but 12 miles; by an unlook'd

for accident, I found Bartholomew Fair at Monmouth, a hundred miles from Smithfield; there I stayed two nights upon the large reckoning of nothing to pay, for which I humbly thank my hospitable host and hostess, Master Reignald Rowse and his good wife.

Monmouth, the shire town of Monmouthshire, was the last Welsh ground that I left behind me. August 27. I came to Glocester, where, though I was born there, very few did know me... Of all the places in England and Wales, that I have travelled to, this village of Barnsley [in Gloucestershire] doth most strictly observe the Lords day, or Sunday.

[...]

There is no such zeale in many places and parishes in Wales; for they have neither service, prayer, sermon, minister, or preacher, nor any church door opened at all, so that people do exercise and edifie in the church yard, at the lawfull and laudable games of trap, catt, stool-ball, racket, etc., on Sundayes.

[...]

Those that are desirous to know more of Wales, let them either travell for it as I have done, or read Mr. Camdens *Britania,* or Mr. Speeds laborious *History,* and the geographicall maps and descriptions will give them more ample or contenting satisfaction.

John Taylor,
A Short Relation Of A Long Journey Made Round or
Ovall By Encompassing the Principalitie of Wales
Through Wales, 1653

John Taylor 'the water-poet', was born in Gloucester in 1578, moved to London as a bound apprentice to a waterman, and was afterwards for many years a servant in the Tower. In 1612, he started writing 'doggerel poems'. A six hundred mile 'painfull circuit' of Wales and and the Marches carried out between 13th July and 7th September 1652 was written up and published in March 1653. He died in Phoenix Alley later that year. Many of his journeys were funded by issuing "bills" inviting subscribers to pay his travel costs in return for an account of the journey on his return. James O. Halliwell republished this account in 1859 in an edition of 26 copies. Taylor entered Wales in the second quarter of his journey, offering a brief insight into the country as it recovered from the English Civil War.

"The Vulgar here are most miserable and low"

Thomas Dineley accompanied the eighth Duke of Beaufort to write an "account of the Progress, and magnificent reception and hearty welcome which awaited his Grace at the various places through which he passed."

"MARGHAM is a very noble Seat...it appears by some noble ruines about it to have been form'd out of an ancient Religious House; the modern additions are very stately, of which the Stables are of free-stone, with fair standings capable of . . . horses, the roof being ceiled, and adorned with cornishes and fretwork of goodly artifice. ... The ancient *Gate-house* before the Court of the house remains unaltered because of an old *Prophesie* among the Bards thus concerning it and this family; viz. That as soon as this Porch or Gate-house shall be pulled down this family shall decline and go to decay; *ideo quaere.*

Haverford West Is called in Welsh Hulforth ... DYVET, or WEST WALES, where better English is spoke than

Welsh, though anciently were here a Colony of Flemings...and they are a sort of people of *Industry*, exceeding their neighbours, improving of their lands lime, and Tennants renting greater parcells than usuall in the other parts of Wales, viz. from £10 to £60 a-yeer.

[LHANDDHEWIBREVI] This is a fair Church in Cardiganshire named *Llandewy brevy*, the Etimology whereof in English is *Church David* bellowing from a very large Ox, one of them which drew the stones for the building thereof, which had so large an head that the Pith of one of its Horns would equall in bigness a middle-siz'd man's thigh, thence its addition *bellowing* is said to be derived.

This Pith I saw; it is kept in a Chest in the high Chancel to shew strangers. This hath been view'd also by several Persons of quality and Judges going this Circuit, as Sir Francis Manley, &c., as the Inhabitants here relate. As for the Church, it has no other manner of Antiquity but itself, and an od kind of a long marble stone erect att the entrance into the great west door, marked A, which they would fain perswade you has carried some Inscription, but I can discern no footsteps thereof. It appears to me as if it has been pick't with a pickax to create a fallacy, rather than ever to have born any character.

[CARDIGAN] The Vulgar here are most miserable and low, as the rich are happy and high, both to an extream. The Poorer sort for bread eat Oaten cakes and drink small beer made of Oaten Malt; some drink onely water for necessity. Those of Estates have their Tables well spread; French Wines (Clarets especially) plenty and good, at the rate of five pounds per hogshead, as I was inform'd. They have choice Wine also of their own growth off the mountains, which the Welsh Gentlewomen make of Resberryes and which abound in these parts. But as Usquebauh in Ireland, so the celebrated liquor here is *Punch*, which they make to a Miracle.

BALA, exhibited on the other side, is where the River Dee issueth out of Lhintegid or Pimble-meare, in the County of Merioneth, neer this Town; and the foot of the Bridge there, […] were the Foot of this County is drawn up, giving his Grace severall Volleyes in his passage. The great Lake there, called Lhyn Tegyd.

Thomas Dineley,
An Account of the Progress of His Grace Henry the First
Duke of Beaufort Through Wales, 1684
Edited from the Original MS in the possession of His
Grace the Eighth Duke of Beaufort by Charles Baker,
Strangeways & Walden, London 1864

The Duke (Henry Somerset, 1629-1700) was appointed President of the Council for the Marches of Wales, which comprised of the "great officers of state, and other noblemen, bishops, and gentry possessing local influence and importance." Its ostensible purpose was to keep the peace by acting as a higher court for all applicable disputes and cases of particularly lawless behaviour. In reality, it was concerned with gathering support for the Tory Party amongst the gentry and commoners, and for allowing James, Duke of York to succeed to the throne. By making his stays brief, he redoubled the loyalty of his hosts, as their expenses were that much smaller. Dineley used the formalities as an excuse to visit local buildings and record their inscriptions.

The great majority of the MS is a description of local militia, market days, church inscriptions, genealogy, history and loyal receptions with bells ringing, hat doffing, wine proffering and soldiery paraded.

....
"The Air is sharp and piercing"
....

James Brome was taken aback to discover echoes of the Old Faith at St Winifred's well, where people mumbled over their beads in a manner this low churchman could not countenance.

[*From the first journey*]

Having spent some time in *Hereford*, and being now upon the Borders of *Wales*, we resolved to make a visit to some parts of that Country: To this purpose we Travelled into *Monmouthshire*, in some places very Fruitful, and in others as Barren, through Nature supplies those Defects, by giving the Inhabitants great plenty of Iron, which provides to them a very advantageous Commodity.

We found the ways near *Monmouth* very hard and rugged, and that Town to be environ'd with Hills on all sides, the Ruins of its Wall and Castle argue its great Antiquity, it hath a fair Church and Market-place, with a Hall for the Assizes and Sessions; 'tis govern'd by a Mayor, Recorder, and Aldermen, and the Inhabitants do generally speak both the *Welsh* and *English* Tongue: They told us there of great Immunities and Privileges granted to them by the House of *Lancaster*; but for nothing is it so much Renown'd, as itt that it was the Native place, of *Henry* V. that dreadful Scourge of the *French*, and glorious Pillar of the *English* Nation.

[…]

After we were past this Town, we found the Ways still more troublesom and uneasie, and were entertained with no other Objects, but what the stony Rocks, and dangerous Cliffs, the towring Mountains, and craggy Precipices, did afford us, being covered with Flocks of Sheep, or Herds of Goats, or Multitudes of Oxen, which they call Runts. The *Rusticks* will tell you, that upon the Black Mountain, or near it, are some Hills which are so high, and whose Tops are so sharp, that two Persons may stand upon two different Point thereof, and discourse with one another, and understand one onother with great Facility, although they must be forced to traverse a long Circuit of Ground before they can meet to embrace each other; But though I will not answer for the Truth of this Story, sure I am, that there are many of those Mountains of so unconceivable a Height, and so steep an Ascent, that they seem to be, as It were, Nature's Stair-Cases, by which we may climb up to some higher Regions, and have an Entercourse and Correspondence with the Inhabitants of the Moon, or converse more frequently and familiarly with the *Aereal Daemons.*

Having, with much difficulty, scrambled over some of these Mountaias, we arrived at a Town in the furthermost part of this County, which is called *Chepstow,* which signifies in the *Saxon* Language, a Market, or place of Trade; this Town hath formerly been Fortified with Walls, though more naturally with Rocks, with which it is environ'd on all sides. It is still remarkable for its Castle built, as some affirm, by *Julius Caesar,* after he had conquer'd *Britain,* which is strong, and generally well guarded with a convenient Garrison: 'Tis seated upon the *Wye,* with a strong wooden Bridge over it near its fall into the *Severn.* The Water flows here 11 or 12 Ells high at every Tide, as likewise at *Bristol,* and extraordinary proportion in comparison of most places besides on the *English* Shore.

[...]

Near to this Town is a Dike, called in *Welsh, Clauda Offa,* i.e. *Offa's.* Dike, made by *Offa* the puissant King of the *Mercians,* which beginning at the Influx of the *Wye* into the *Severn,* extendeth 84 or 90 Miles in length, even as far as *Chester,* where the *Dee* is mingled with the Sea.

[...]

Whilst we were in these parts, we made the best Enquiries after South-*Wales,* which we had not then an opportunity to travel over, and from some of the Natives, who were very Communicative, and ready to make what discoveries they could of the Rarities of their own Country, we made a shift to Collect this short Account.

Brecknockshire is one of the most Mountainous of all *Wales,* but between its Mountains there are many fruitful Vallies; it has four Market Towns, amongst which *Brecknock* is the chief; Three Miles from which is a Hill, called *Mounth-Denny.*

[...]

Two Miles East from the same place is a Mere called *Lynsavathan,* which (as the People dwelling there say) was once a City, but was swallowed by an Earthquake, and this Water, or Lake, succeeded in the place: They Report likewise, that after a long Frost, when the Ice of this Lake breaks, it makes a fearful Noise like Thunder, possibly, because the Lake is encompass'd with high steep Hills, which pen in the Sound, and multiply it, or else the Ground may be hollow underneath, or near the Lake.

Through this Lake runs a River called *Levenny*, without mixtures of its Waters, as may be perceived both by the Colour of the Water, and also by the quantity of it, because it is no greater afterward than when it entred the Lake.

Cadier Arthur, or *Arthur's* Chair, is a Hill so called on the Southside of this County, from the Tops resembling the form of a Chair, proportionate to the Dimensions of that great and mighty Person, upon the Top whereof riseth a Spring as deep as a Well, four-square, having no Streams issuing from it, and yet there are plenty of Trouts to be found therein.

Radnorshire, in the East and South parts thereof is more fruitful than the rest, but is uneven and rough with Mountains, yet it is well stored with Woods, watered with running Rivers, and in some places with standing Pools; the Air is cold and sharp, because the Snow continues long unmelted under the shady Hills, and hanging Rocks, whereof there are many.

[...]

Glamorganshire hath a temperate Air, and is generally the most pleasant part of all South-*Wales*. It is replenished with divers convenient Towns, amongst which *Cardiff*, which stands near the Sea, where *Robert* the Eldest Son of *William* the Conrqueror, died after a long Imprisonment, is reputed the most Eminent, a Mile above which stands also on the River *Taff Landaff*, one of the four Episcopal Sees of *Wales*; 'Tis one of the most ancient Sees either in *England* or *Wales*, claiming a direct Succession from the Arch Bishops of *Caerleon* upon the River *Uske* in *Monmouthshire*, where formerly was placed an ancient School of Learning for the *Britains*, by the Roman Powers ... It is adorn'd with a Cathedral consecrated to St. *Teliawe,* who was Bishop here, which Church *Germanus* and *Lupus,* French Bishops, then Erected when they had suppressed the *Pelagian* Heresie, preferring *Dubritius,* a very devout Person, to this Bishoprick, unto whom *Meurick* a *British* Lord, gave all the Lands which lie betwixt the two Rivers *Taff* and *Elri.*

[…]

Clement Alexandrinus saith, That in *Britain* is a Cave under the bottom of a Hill, and on the top of it a gaping Chink, where when the Wind is gathered into that Hole, and toss'd to and fro in the Womb of it, there is heard, as it were, a Musical sound like that of Cymbals: It is not unlikely that he might point at the Cave at *Aberbarry* in this Shire, the Story agreeing very near with the Quality of this Cave: It is mention'd by my Lord *Bacon,* in his History of Winds, to this effect, That in a certain Rocky Cliff, in which there are Holes, if a Man lay his Ears to them, he shall hear divers Noises, and rumbling of Winds; now these Noises *Cambden* saith, are as well as be heard at the lowest Ebb, as the highest Flood.

Caermarthenshire, though a most Hilly Country yet hath a wholsom Air, and though the Soil be not very fruitful in Corn, 'tis well stored with Cattle, and, in some places, yields good Pit Coal for Fuel, and the best Lead. On the South side the Ocean hath, with so great violence, encroach'd upon the Land, that the Country seems to have shrunk back in a fright, and withdrawn it self more inwardly for Security.

Caermarthen, the chief place of it, being a pretty distance from the Sea, is situated between pleasant Meadows and Woods: The Residence kept here by the

Princes of *South-Wales,* made it anciently very Eminent, and it became a Prey to the *Normans* in the Reign of *William* the Conqueror.

Near *Carreg* Castle are many Caves of great wideness within the Ground, now covered all over green-Sword and Turf, wherein 'tis probable, the Multitude, unable to bear Arms, when the *Normans* made their first Incursions into these parts, hid themselves during the heat of the War; where also is a Well that, like the Sea, Ebbs and Flows twice in 24 hours.

That *Cardiganshire* being a Hilly Maritime Country, was not formerly planted, or garnished with Cities, may be gathered from that Speech of their Prince *Caratacus,* who being taken Prisoner by the *Romans,* and carried to *Rome;* when he had throughly viewed the Magnificence of that City, *What mean you,* saith he, *when you have such stately Buildings of your own, to covet such poor and, mean Cottages as ours are?*

Its chief Town is *Cardigan,* pleasantly seated upon the *Tivy* near its fall into the Sea, which River parts this County from *Pembrokeshire;* and over it here is a Stone-Bridge, supported by several Arches.

Pembrokeshire hath a good temperate Air, considering it lies so near to *Ireland;* the Inhabitants are now many of then *Dutch* Men, and formerly, as it appears from *Giraldus Cambrensis,* they were like the *Romans* of old, very skilful in Soothsaying, by looking narrowly into the Entrails of Beasts, and by their Manners and Language are so near a-kin to the *English,* that upon this Account this Country is call'd Little *England* beyond *Wales.*

[...]

About *Kilgarran* are abundance of *Salmons* taken, and

there is a place called the *Salmons- Leap*, as there is also in other Rivers, probably for this Reason, the *Salmon* coveteth to get into fresh Water Rivers to Spawn, and when he comes to places where the Water falls down right, almost Perpendicular, as some such like places there be, he useth this Policy; he bends himself backwards, and takes his Tail in his Mouth, and with all his force unloosing his Circle, on a sudden with a smart Let-go he mounts up before the fall of the Stream; and therefore these downright-falls, or little Cataracts, are call'd the *Salmons Leap*.

In this County is *St. David's*, now only a Bishop's, though formerly an Archbishop's See.

[...]

'Tis reported by some Historians, That while *David*, Bishop of this See, who was a very sharp Stickler against the Pelagian Heresie, was one day very zealously disputing against those erroneous Tenents, the Earth, whereon he then stood arguing, rose up by a Miracle to a certain height under his Feet, and a white dove descending, as is supposed, from Heaven, sat all the while he preached upon his right shoulder.

[From the Third Journey]

When we left this City [Chester] we took the Opportunity of the Sands, and passed with a Guide over the Washes into *Flintshire* in *North-Wales*, where *Flint* Castle saluted us upon our first Arrival. This Castle was begun by King *Henry* the Second, and finished by *Edward* the First, where King *Richard* the Second was deposed, and King *Edward* the Second met his great Favourite *Gaveston* at his Return out of *Ireland*.

The Air is healthy, without any Fogs or Vapours, and the People generally very aged and hearty; the Snow lyes long upon the Hills; the Country affords great Plenty of Cattle, but they are small: Mill-stones are also digged up in these Parts as well as in *Anglesey:* Towards the River *Dee* the Fields bear in some Parts Barley, in others Wheat, but generally throughout Rye, with very great Encrease, and especially the first Year of their breaking up their Land, and afterwards Two or Three Crops together of Oats.

Upon the River *Cluyd* is situated St. *Asaph,* (anciently *Elwy)* a Town of greater Antiquity than Beauty, and more Honourable for a Bishop's See, placed here about 560 by *Kentigerne,* a *Scot,* Bishop of *Glascow,* than for anything else contained therein, by whom the Cathedral was Built on the *Elwy.* whence the Town is called *Land-Elwy* by the *Welsh,* and the Bishop *Elwensis* in the Ancient *Latin:* After that he returned into *Scotland* he deputed *Asaph,* a Religious and Devout Man to succeed him in the Bishoprick, from whom the Place received its Denomination.

But most remarkable is this County for a little Village called *Holy-Well,* so Famous for the strange Cures which have been wrought (as is supposed) by the Virtue and Intercession of St. *Winifrid,* who is the grand Patroness thereof: The Water hereof is extream Cold, and hath so great a Stream that flows from it that it is presently able to drive a Mill; the Stones which are at the bottom being' of a Sanguine Colour, are believed to have received that Rubicund Tincture from the Drops of Blood which trickled down this Holy Virgin's Body, when she was here Beheaded by the Bloody Tyrant that would have Ravished her; and the Moss which grows upon the

Sides, and bears a very Fragrant Smell, is averred to have been the Product of her Hair; tho' I find by some we brought away with us that in Process of Time it loseth all its sweetness. Over the Well stands a Chapel, Dedicated to her, Built of Stone after a Curious Manner, to which formerly was much Resorting by Pilgrims, who came hither out of a Blind Devotion; and the generality of the Commonalty hereabouts, who are too much addicted to Popish Superstition, are so extreamly Credulous to believe the Legend of this Martyrd Virgin, and the great Miracle that was wrought by St. *Benno*, who restored her to Life again, as they say, by clapping on her Head immediately after it was cut off upon her Shoulders, that we happening to smile at this Fabulous Relation, which we had from an Old Romish Zealot, who gave his Attendance, it seeming indeed as ridiculous to us as the Story of *Gartgantua*, or the Wandring *Jew*, he presently observed us, and replied, That he supposed we e'er long would not believe the very Scriptures to be true; as if the Holy and Undoubted Oracles of God had now no more Certain and Infallible Grounds of Veracity to enforce an Assent to the Credibility thereof, than such Idle and Extravagant Fables as these, which have only been the Chymical Extracts of some Enthusiastick hot-brained Monks, dress'd up finely with some outward Shews of Probability to Cheat the Vulgar into a Belief hereof.

At this Place we met divers Persons of as different Qualities as Designs; some came hither for the good of their Bodies, and others, as they hoped for, the Benefit of their Souls; some we saw kneeling about the Well, mumbling, over their Beads with such profound

Murmurs as the Conjurers did of Old, who used to invocate Old *Hecate's* Assistance, and kissing the Stones on which they kneeled with as great Reverence as if the Sacred Feet of St. *Winifrid*, or the Pope's Toe, had been there present before; others were crossing themselves from Head to Foot with the Holy Water in which they bathed, supposing it as effectual to drive away all Evil Spirits from their Bodies:, as the *Spaniard* did in *Flanders*, who seeing a Demoniack exorcised that looked earnestly upon him, a thing which he had never seen before, and being told that the Devil, when dispossessed of his former Hold, had a great mind to enter into his Posterities, leaps up immediately and clapp'd his Backside into a Basin of Holy Water, by that Means hoping to keep it free from that Black intruding Inmate: Others were gathering up the bloody Stones, and picking up the sweet Moss from the sides of the Well, which Holy Relicks they resolved to treasure up as carefully as the Nuns in *Britany* did the Bones of Eleven Hundred Martyr'd Virgins. And in fine, others went in purely for their Pleasure and Diversion, to cleanse and purifie themselves from Bodily Pollutions, reserving their Souls for other kind of Lustrations, more suitable and congruous to their Divine Nature.

Amongst these Persons we passed away some Days, in which time, by conversing with the *Welsh*, we gathered up from them again an Account of some Curiosities in these Northern Counties, which we had not then time enough personally to survey, which I shall next decypher with as much brevity as I can.

Montgomeryshire is a mountainous Country, and yet very fruitful, because well irrigated, but nothing more observable than for its excellent Breed of Horses, which are of most excellent Shapes, strong Limbs, and very swift.

The Hill *Plim-limmon* raiseth it self up to a wonderful Height, and on that part where it boundeth on this Shire it poureth forth the *Severne,* the greatest River in *Britain* next the *Thames*; as likewise in the other Parts of it riseth the River *Wye,* and the River R*ideal.*

Upon *Cerdon-Hill* are placed certain Stones in a round Circle like a Coronet, in all Probability to commemorate some notable Victory.

Merionethshire may have a wholesome Air, but is very Barren, and exceeding full of spir'd Hills, and good for little but Cattle: It was not conquered by the *English* till the Reign of *Edward* the first, *A.D.* 1283. And in the Reign of *Henry* the IVth, *Owen Glendower* having drawn this and all *Wales* into a Combination against that Prince, endangered the Loss of the whole, but that he had to do with too Martial a Prince.

Near *Bala* is a great Pool of Water, that drowns at least 200 Acres of Ground, whose Nature is such, as they say, that the High-land Floods cannot make this Pool swell bigger, tho' never so great; but if the Air be troubled with violent Tempests of Wind, it riseth above the Banks; the River Dee runneth into this Pool with a swift Stream, and glides through it without Mixture of Water; for in this Pool is bred the Fish called *Gulmad,* which is never seen in the *Dee*; and in *Dee* Salmons are taken, which are never found in the Pool. Upon the Sea Coasts of this County great Store of Herrings are taken at time of Year, and upon the West side of it the Sea beats so sore and hard, that it is thought it hath carried away part of it.

Anglesey is a considerable Island in the North-West

Part of *Wales*, parted from the Continent by a narrow Arm of the Sea named the *Menay*: The *Welsh* call this Island *Mon*, or *Tie-Mon*, but since *Edward* the First conquered it from *Llewellen*, King or Prince of *North-Wales*, it got the Name of *Anglesey*, that is, the *English* Land. 'Tis in Length about Twenty Miles, though in Breadth scarce Seventeen; and herein are frequently found and digged up in the Low Grounds Bodies of huge Trees with their Roots, and Fir Trees of a wonderful Bigness and Length, which Trees some believe were cut down by the *Romans*; so that it appears this Island was in Times past full of Woods and Timber, but instead thereof it yeildeth now Plenty of Corn, Sheep and Cattle; the Air is reasonably Healthful, save only a little Aguish at some Time, and in some Places, by reason of the Fogs that do arise from the Sea. It yeildeth also great Store of Milstones and Grindstones, and in some Places a Sort of Earth, of which they make Alum and Copperas; but more especially it affords such Plenty of Wheat, that it is deservedly entitled the Mother *of Wales*.

In *Caernarvanshire* the Air is sharp and piercing, and in it are the highest Hills in *Wales*, for which Reason it is justly called the *English Alps*; on some of which the Snow lyes long, and on others all the Year long hard crusted together.

In the Pool called *Lin-paris*, there is, as 'tis reported, a kind of Fish called *Torroch*, having a red Belly, which is nowhere else to be seen but here: 'Tis affirmed likewise, that on some of the high Hills of this Shire are Two Meers, one of which produceth Fish which have but one Eye, and in the other is a movable and floating Island, which as soon as any Person treads on it presently falls into a moving Posture.

Snowdown-Hills, although they have always Snow lying upon them, yet they are exceeding Rank with Grass, insomuch that they are become a Proverb amongst the *Welshmen*, that those Mountains will yield sufficient Pasture for all the Cattle in *Wales:* And 'tis certain that there are Pools and standing Waters upon the top of these Mountains; and they are so coated with a snowy Crust that lyes on them, that if a Man doth but lightly set his Foot upon the top of them he shall perceive the Earth to stir for several Foot from him, which probably might Occasion the Story of the floating Island before mentioned.

Penmaen-Mour, i.e. the great stony Head, is an exceeding high and steep Rock, which hanging over the Sea when it is Flood, affordeth a very narrow Way for Passengers, having on the one side huge Stones over their Heads, as if they were ready to fall upon them, and on the other side the raging Ocean, lying of a wonderful depth under it; but after a Man hath passed over this, together with *Penmean-Lychan*, the less stony Head, he shall come to an open broad Plain, that reacheth as far as the River *Conway*, in which are bred a Sort of Shell-Fish, which being conceived of an Heavenly Dew, as is conjectured, bring forth Pearl.

[...]

In *Denbighshire* the Air is cold, but very wholesome, and the Snow lyes long upon the Hills, which resemble the Battlements of Walls, and upon the top of *Moilenny-Hill*, which is one of the largest in this Shire, is a Spring of clear Water.

In this County is *Wrexham*, a Market Town, distant about Fifteen Miles from *Holy-Well*, and much admired for the Steeple of its Collegiate Church, being a Curious Fabrick, contrived according to the most exact Draught and Model of Architecture, and nowhere to be parallelled in those Parts for Workmanship of which taking a transient View, we passed on again through *Shrewsbury*.

James Brome,
Travels over England, Scotland and Wales, 1694

James Brome (c. 1650-1719) was a clergyman and travel writer. This work was originally published in 1694 as 'Mr Roger's Three Years Travels over England and Wales' and republished under Brome's own name in 1700. This account is taken from the second edition of 1707. He observed in the preface that 'it is very incongruous to pretend to be acquainted with other Countries, and to be Strangers to their Own, which is an Epitome of all other'.

··
"Several strange Apparitions"
··

Wales was a land of supernatural qualities to Nathaniel Crouch, perhaps due to an abundance of mead.

Remarkable Observations upon the most memorable Persons and Places in Wales. And an Account of several considerable Transactions and Passages that have happen'd for many hundred Years past. Together with the natural and artificial Rarities and Wonders in the several Counties of that Principality.

Yet *South Wales*, called by the Inhabitants *Dehenbarth*, or the right side, as being nearer the Sun, was the largest, most fruitful and rich, but more subject to the Invasions and Depredations of the *English* and *Flemings*, and therefore *North Wales* being secured by its Hills and Mountains was preferred before it, and retaineth more of the Purity of the *Welsh* Tongue. However this makes the Soil lean and hungry, but that is supplied by the large Quantity thereof, which occasioned this pleasant Passage: An *English* Gentleman in Discourse with a worshipful Knight of *Wales* boasting that he had in *England* so much Ground worth 40s an Acre, the *Welsh* Gentleman replied, *You have ten Yards of Velvet, and I have two hundred Yards of Prize, I shall not exchange with you.*

There are likewise in *Wales* very pleasant Meadows water'd by fine Rivers; and as the sweetest Flesh is said to be near the Bones, so the moft delicious Valleys are interposed betwixt these Mountains. The Natives are generally healthy, strong, swift, and witty, which is imputed to the clear and wholesome Air of the Mountains, the cleanly and moderate Diet of the People, and the Hardship to which they are inur'd from their Childhood.

[...]

The Principality of *Wales* produceth Mines, and among others, Royal Mines of Silver in *Cardiganshire* in the Mountains of *Cosmelock, Tallabant, Gadarren, Bromgoid, Geginnon* and *Cummerrum*. The *Romans* began to mine here, as appears by their Coins found in the trenches wherein they worked about twenty four fathom deep, and found Plenty of Lead, till the Waters drowned their Works. The *Danet* and *Saxons* work'd a hundred Fathom deep, and gain'd much Lead, till the Waters drowned their Works. Sir Tho. *Smith* discover'd

Silver in *Cosmelock* in the latter end of Queen *Elizabeth's* Reign. Which Design was prosecuted after his Death by Sir *Hugh Middleton*, coining the Silver, to his great Charge, at the Tower of *London*, as his Predecessor had done. Next Sir *Francis Godolphin* of *Cormwal*, and *Tho. Bushel* Esq; undertook it, having Power from King *Charles* I. to coin it at Aberruski in that County: Sir *Francis* dying, and *Cosmelock* being deserted, Mr. *Bushel* adventur'd on the other five Mountains, and at last these Mines yielded an hundred Pound a Week, and half so much more in Lead. The Silver was coin'd into Pence, Groats, Shillings and Half Crowns, and had the Ostrich Feathers, being the Arms of the Prince of *Wales*, stamp'd in them for distinction. They had an ingenious Invention to supply the Miners with fresh Air, which was done by two Men blowing Wind with a Pair of bellows on the Outside of the Entrance into a Pipe of lead, which was daily lengthen'd as the Mine grew larger, whereby the Candle in the Mine was daily kept burning, and the Diggers were constantly supplied with a Sufficiency of Breath. But the Civil Wars in 1642. discomposed all the Work. … As for manufactures, the *British* valuing themselves upon their Gentile Birth and Extraction, are better pleased in employing their Valour than Labour and therefore have but few Commodities, as Cottons and Frieze, of which King Henry V. when Prince of *Wales* having a Suit, and being check'd by a bold Courtier for wearing the same many weeks together, 'I wish', *said he*, 'that the Cloth of my Country would last forever.' Then they have Cheese very tender and palatable, the Pedigree whereof was by one arily derived:

Adam's nawn Cusson was by her Birth
Ap Curds, ap Milk, ap Cow, ap Grass, ap Earth.

They have likewise Metheglin, first invented by *Matthew Glin,* their own Countrymen. It is compounded of Milk and Honey, and very wholesome. ... It is like Mead, but much stronger. Queen *Elizabeth,* who by the *Tuders* was of *Welsh* Descent much loved this her native Liquor.

The Buildings of *Wales* are generally like those of the old *Britons,* neither large nor beautiful, the *Italian* Humour of Building not having affected (not to say Infected) the *British* Nation.

[...]

ANGLESEY, called by the *Britains Tir Mon,* or the land of *Mon,* in *Latin Mona,* and by the *English Anglesey* or the *English* Island, being separate from the Continent, and surrounded on all sides by the *Irish* Sea, save on the South, where it is joined by a small and narrow Streight of the River *Menai,* and almost square, containing twenty Miles from *Beaumaris* to *Holy-Head* East and West, and from *Llanbaderick* North to the point of *Menai* South, seventeen, in the whole Circuit about seventy Miles. The Air is generally healthy and the Soil seemingly barren, but really fruitful, affording Corn and Cattle sufficient both for the Natives and their Neighbours, therefore the *Welsh* Proverb, *Mon Mam Cymbry, Anglesey* is the Mother of *Wales,* because when other Countries fail, this plentifully feeds their markets, and is said to afford Corn enough to supply all *Wales.* This County produceth likewise the best Mill-stones to grind it; also Alom and Copperas: And in divers Places in the low Fields and champaigne Grounds, there are several Trees, digged up, black within like Ebony, and are used by Carvers for inlaying Cupboards; yea, Haslenets are found under Ground with sound Kernels in them. It is hard to resolve how they came hither. Some imagine the *Romans* cut them down as being Coverts for their Enemies. Others think they fell of themselves, and with their own Weight were buried in those marshy Places, and that, the clammy bituminous Substance which is found about them, keeps them from Putrefaction.

[...]

The chief Town, *Beumaris*, formerly called *Bonc-per*, built by this King *Edward* I. (together with a strong Castle) is governed by a Mayor, two Bailiffs, two Serjeants at Mace, and a Town-Clerk.

[...]

BRECKNOCKSHIRE ... is full of Hills, and difficult in travelling. The Mountains of *Talgar* and *Ewias* on the East seem to defend it from the excessive Heat of the Sun, which makes an wholesome and temperate Air, from whence likewise rise many curious Springs that render the Valleys fruitful both in Corn and Grass, and thereby make amends for their own Barrenness. ... [O]ne Mountain in the South is of such an height and occult Quality, that saith Mr. *Speed*, I should blush to relate it, had I not the Alderman and Bayliffs of the Town of *Brecknock* for my Vouchers, who assured me, that from this Hill, called *Mounchdenny*, they have oft-times cast down their Hats, Cloaks and Staves, which yet would never fall to the bottom, but with the Air and Wind still returned back and blown up again, neither will any thing but a stone or hard Metal fall from thence;

and the Clouds are oft seen lower than the top of it. There is likewise *Cadier Arthur*, or *Arthur's* Chair, a Hill so called on the South side of this Country, the top thereof somewhat resembling the form of a Chair, proportionate to the Dimension which the *Welsh* imagine that great and mighty Person to be of. Upon the top thereof riseth a spring as deep as a Well, four square, having no stream issuing from it, and yet there are plenty of Trouts to be found therein. They also told him, that when the *Meer Lynsavathan* two Miles from the *Brecknock*, hath its frozen Ice, first broken, it yieldeth a dreadful noise like thunder. And it is reported, that where this *Meer* now spreadeth its Waters, there formerly stood a fair City, which was swallowed up by an Earthquake, and it seems probable, both because all the highways of this County led thither, and likewise the learned *Cambden* judgeth it might be the City *Leventrium*, which *Ptolomy* placeth in these parts, and Mr *Cambden* could not discover, and therefore likely to be drowned in this Pool, which the River *Levenny* running hard by, farther confirms, the Waters whereof running through this *Meer* without mixing with them, as appears in the Colour and Breadth of the Stream, which is the same through the whole length of the Pool.

[...]

Brecknock still retains some Beauty in its Building, it had formerly three Gates for entrance, and ten Towers for Defence, with a very fine Castle.

[...]

CARDIGANSHIRE ...The Air is open and sharp, for besides the great and high Mountain of *Plinillimon*, it hath a continued Range of lesser Hills. The Valleys are rich in Pasture and Corn, and well watered with Pools and Springs. In the River *Tivy* Beavers were formerly found, a Creature living both by Land and Water, having the two fore Feet like a Dog, wherewith he runs on Land, and the two hinder like a Goose with which he swims, his broad Tail served for a Rudder, but now none are found, the Salmon seeming to succeed, who coming out of the Sea into fresh Waters, and meeting with some downright Water-falls in this River, he bends himself backward, and putting, his Tail in his Mouth, gives a Spring up those Ascents, which are called the Salmon's Leap, many of which are caught in this River.

[...]

John Lewis, Esq; a Justice of Peace at *Glaskerrigg* near *Aberystwith,* in this County, in the Year 1656. by several Letters to Mr. *B.* a late worthy Divine, deceased, gives an Account of several strange Apparitions in *Caermarthen, Pembrokeshire,* and this County about that Time, confirmed by divers Persons of good Quality and Reputation, the substance whereof are as followeth. A Man and his Family being all in Bed, he being awake about Midnight perceived a Light entring the little Room where he lay, and about a Dozen in the shapes of Men, and two or three Women with small Children in their Arms following, they seemed to dance, and the Chamber appeared much wider and lighter than formerly. They seemed to eat Bread and Cheese, all about a kind of a Tick upon the Ground, they offered him some, and would smile upon him, he heard no Voice, but calling upon God to bless him, he heard a Whispering Voice in *Welsh,* bidding him hold his Peace. They continued there about four Hours, all which Time he endeavoured to awake his Wife but could not. Afterward they went into another Room, and having danced a while departed; he then arose, and though the Room was very small, yet he could neither find the door, nor the way to Bed again, until crying out his Wife and Family awaked. He living within two Miles of Justice *Lewis* he sent for him, being a poor honest Husbandman, and of good Report and made him believe he would put him to his Oath about the Truth of this Relation who was very ready to take it.

This Gentleman adds a second account of the strange and usual Appearance of Lights (called in *Welsh, Canhwyllan Cyrth, Corps or dead Mens Candles)* which are so ordinary in these Counties, that scarce any die, either young or old, but this is seen before Death, and often observed, to part from the very Bodies of the Persons all along the way to the Place of Burial, and infallibly Death will ensue. There is that Evidence for these Candles, that few or none of any age but have seen them, and will depose it. A while since (saith this Gentleman) some of my Family saw two Candles, one less than the other passing the Church way under my House, my Wife was then big with Child, and it caused much Apprehension both in us and her, but just a Week after, her self came first to me, as something joyed that the Danger might be over, with the News that an old Man and a Child of the Neighbourhood were carried that way to be.buried.

[…]

Now for the Particulars. At *Lanylar* late at Night, some of the People saw one of these Candles hovering up and down along the River's Bank, which they continued to view till they were weary, and at last left it so and went to Bed. A few Weeks after came a proper young Woman from *Montgomeryshire,* to see her Friends who dwelt on the other side that River *Istwyth,* and thought to ford the River at that very place where the Light was seen, but being dissuaded by some standers by, (who probably had seen the Light) not to venture on the Water, which was high by a sudden Flood, she walkt up and down the River's Bank as the Light had done, waiting for the falling of the Water, which at last she went into, but too soon for her, for she was therein drowned.

[...]

Mrs. *Catherine Wyatt* an eminent Woman in the Town of *Tenby,* being in an Evening in her Bed-Chamber, saw two little Lights just upon her Belly, which she endeavoured to strike off but could not, within a while they vanished of themselves. Not long after she was delivered of two still-born Children.

[...]

In this County also, in the Silver and Leaden Mines nothing is more ordinary than that some Subterranean Spirits called Knockers (where a good Vein is) are often heard and seen in the shape of Men little statured, about half a Yard long. And living Mens Ghosts are commonly seen in these parts, unawares to the Party.

[...]

CARMARTHENSHIRE ... It is not so hilly as others in Wales and therefore affords plenty of Corn, Cattle, Grass, Wood, Pit-coal, Fowl and Fish, especially Salmon which are very large and plentiful. ... Carmarthen, the principal Town, is pleasantly seated near the River Towy, which runs through the midst of the Shire, and falls south into the Sea, where there was formerly a good Haven for Ships, but now so choaked up with the sands, that only small Vessels can come up to the Bridge, which is built of Freestone, and over it, on an hanging Rock, a large Castle, from whose Stone Wall another mingled with Brick incompassed the Town, being in Circuit 1400 Paces.

[...]

CARNARVANSHIRE ... The Air is sharp and piercing, by reason of the high mountains, which may be properly termed the *Britsh Alps* (for steepness and cragginess not much unlike those that divide *France* from *Italy)* all tow'ring into the Air, and some far higher than the rest, called *Snowdon* Hills, or *Snowy* Mountains, being all the Year round crusted over with Snow, though liable to the Sun and Wind. This made them a secure Refuge to the *Britains* against their Enemies, no Army, though never so potent, nor any Traveller, never so lightly cloathed, being able to *find* a Passage among so many rough and hard Rocks, so many Pools, Vales, and Sloughs, as are to be encountred with in the middle of this County. Yet it is sufficiently fruitful, for the Mountains are so rank with Grass, that it is become a Poverb amongst them, *Craig Eriry,* or *Snowdon, will yield sufficient Pasture for all the Cattle of* Wales *put together.* And it is certain there are Ponds and standing Waters upon the Tops of them, though generally cover'd with snow, and if a Man sets his Foot any where upon the Top of them, he shall perceive the Earth to move at a considerable distance from him. *Penmen-maur,* or the great stony head, is an exceeding high and steep Rock or Hill in this County, which hanging over the sea, when it is Flood affordeth a very narrow Way for Passengers, huge stones hanging over Head as if ready to fall upon them, and the tempestuous Ocean lying under of a very great Depth. But after the passing this, and *Penmen-bibam,* the less stony Head, there is a great open Plain, reaching as far as *Aber-Conwey,* in which River are found a sort of shell-fish, conceived as they say by the heavenly Dew, which are thought to bring forth Pearl, formerly much valued.

[…]

The *Welsh* report that the Corps of 20000 saints are interr'd in a small Island called *Berdsey,* lying within a mile of the south Promontory of this County. It is I confess more easy to find Graves there for so many saints, than saints for so many Graves.

[…]

DENBIGHSHIRE … It is generally mountainous, cold and barren, yet not without some fruitful Valleys, by the Industry of the Husbandmen, who may be said to fetch their Bread out of the Fire, by cutting up Turfs, which being burnt in great Heaps, the Ashes spread on these hungry Grounds, cause them to bring forth a kind of Rye in very great plenty. … *Denbigh*…with a strong Wall, a fair Castle, and several high Towers … is reckon'd the most beautiful in all *North Wales;* and this is remarkable, that in 1575 a great Earthquake, which much terrify'd the People … caused the Bell in the Shire-Hall of *Denbigh* to toll twice, with shaking of the Earth, yet no farther Mischief happen'd.

[…]

FLINTSHIRE … It is the least county of Wales, and not so mountainous as other Parts, but lies pleasantly along by the river Dee. The Air is healthful, and the Soil plentiful of corn and cattle. The rivers abound with Fish. There are not as many Woods or Trees in this, as there are in the other Parts of *Wales,* the frequent rebellions of the Inhabitants having occasion'd the *English* to make great Devastations of them, to prevent their being the retreats of these unquiet people. Fruits are not very common; but of milk, butter, cheese and honey there is plenty; of the last of which they make great Quantities of a Drink like Muscadine, call'd Metheglin.

[…]

This County hath not any River of Note within it; but near *Rutland* Castle is a famous spring, called *Holy Well or* St. *Winifred's* Well. … To this Well *Romish* Pilgrims resort to this Day, and others bathe therein, supposing that there is much Virtue in the Water. In the bottom of it are many red Stones, which the superstitious People believe are the Spots of this Lady's Blood, which all the Water in the Spring can never wash away; and that the green Moss which grows on the sides of the Well is her Hair, which though every Stranger almost carries away a part of, yet they say it never wastes: And the Truth is, the Moss smells exceeding sweet, which confirms these weak Believers in their fond Opinion.

[…]

GLAMORGANSHIRE … The North part of this Shire is mountainous, the South plain and very fruitful, being called the Garden of *Wales* abounding with Cattle, pleasant Springs and Fruits. *Tare* is the chief River, upon the Eastern Shore of which, *Cardife*, the fairest Town all *South-Wales* is situated, which *Fitz Hannon* fortified with a Wall and Castle.

[…]

Likewife near *Newton,* on the Bank of the River *Ogmore* near the *Severn,* there is a Well, the Water whereof is so low at the flowing of the Sea, that you can hardly get a Dishful, but at the Ebb and Fall of the Tide it riseth amain, which may be occasioned by the Wind or Air, which not finding a Passage out, stops up the Passages of the Springs, but when the Water is gone, and the Air has Room to vent it self, the Water boils up abundantly. On the same Shore of *Severne,* on the Top of an Hill called *Minyd Morgan,* is erected a Monument, inscribed with strange Characters, and the People thereabout have a Tradition that if any Man read the same he shall die soon after, meaning, I suppose, that it it [sic] impossible to be read.

[...]

MERIONETHSHIRE ... The Form of this County is like a *Welsh* Harp, though it yields but dull Musick to the Inhabitants, being the roughest and most barren Shire of all *Wales,* as *Giraldus,* the *Welsh* Historian acknowledges, the Air giving little Pleasure, unless to those that admire the furious and blustring Winds that roar from the adjacent Hills and Mountains, which are so high, and yet so near together, that it is reported Men may discourse from the tops thereof one to another, and yet hardly meet in a Day's time; so that if the Shepherds should fall out in the Morning, and challenge one another to fight, before they can come together, the Day will be spent, and the Heat of their Fury abated, after they have slept till Morning. ... now the Hills are cover'd with Flocks of Sheep, which are the only Riches of this County, for by reason of the Unnevenness and Rockiness of the Soil, the Plow cannot go, nor the Corn thrive here, though some have causelesly imputed the scarcity of Grain to the Sloth of the People.

[...]

There are only three Market-towns in this Shire. *Bala,* near which is a Pool called *Pimble Meer* or *Lin Tegid* in *Welsh,* covering near an hundred and sixty Acres of Ground, of which it is reported that the Land Floods, though never so great, do never cause it to rise or swell, whilst a Blast of Wind will quickly make it mount above its Bounds and Banks. Into the South Part of it runs the River *Dee* with a swift stream, and glides through the same without any Mixture of its Waters, as the People imagine, because the Salmon usually taken in *Dee* is never found in that Pool; and, on the contrary, the Fish called *Guinead,* bred in that Meer, is never seen in the River *Dee.*

Dolgethe is another Market-town in this Shire, of which I know not whether it be worth relating what is known for a Truth. 1. That the Walls thereof are three Miles high, that is, the Mountains which surround it. 2. That Men come into it over the Water, but go out of it under the Water; because they go in over a fair Bride, but the Water falling from a Rock, is convey'd in a wooden Trough, under which Travellers make shift to pass. 3. The Steeple thereof doth grow therein, since the Bells, if they have more than one, hang in a Yew-tree. 4. There are more Ale-houses than Houses, for Tenements are divided into two or three Tipling Houses, and Barns without Chimneys are used to that purpose.

Harlech is the last Market-town, standing on the Sea-shore, cold and barren enough, but only of Fowl and Fish, having few Houses, and meanly built. Here is a little decay'd Chapel, and out of use, wherein Sir *Richard Thimbleby,* an *English* Knight, lies buried, who, for the Delight he took in fishing and fowling, remov'd his

Dwelling from a far better Soil. Here likewise was erected a strong and beautiful Castle upon an Hill, with a double-Bulwark walled about, commanding the Sea, to impede the Entrance of all Invaders. Near this are two great Inlets into the Sea, which People pass over at low Water, and upon the Shore, as upon all the Sea-coasts in this Country, abundance of Herrings are caught, and are therefore much frequented at the Season of the Year by People of several Nations.

[…]

Mr. *Cambden* takes especial notice of the Beauty and Comeliness of the Inhabitants of this Shire.

[…]

MONMOUTHSHIRE … The Air is temperate, clear, and healthful; the, soil hilly, woody and fruitful of Cattle, Corn, and all other Accommodations of Life. …*Caerleon*. This Town, though now but small, was once a great City, reaching a Mile in length, and comprehending St. *Julian's*, a House of late Sir *William Herbert's*, now a Mile distant from the Town. But as all human Glory hath its Period, so this City, formerly renowned for Beauty, Circuit and Magnificence, is now deplorably decay'd.

Monmouth is a Market-town in this County, and had antiently a very strong Castle, with many lofty Towers, as the Ruins do still demonstrate. The Town is pleasantly situated between the Rivers *Monnow* and *Wye*, and hath an handsome Church with three Isles: And at the East End of the Town is another decay'd one, called the Monks Church. …Several Monasteries were erected and suppressed in this County, the most memorable being at *Caerleon, Chepstow, God-cliff, Monmouth,* and *Llanthony*, which last stood so solitary among the high Hills, that the Sun did shine upon it not above two or three Hours in a Day. As for Manufactures, the best Caps were formerly made at *Monmouth,* where the Cappers Chapel doth still remain. In Queen *Elizabeth's* Reign an Act of Parliament was made, enacting, That all Persons should wear *Monmouth* Caps; but about twenty five Years after, it was repealed.

[...]

Monmouthshire may be called an *English Welsh* County, whereas formerly all *Welsh* Counties sent but one Knight to Parliament, this has the Privilege of two, and is not subject to the Welsh Jurisdiction, but to the Governance of the Itinerant Judges who ride *Oxford* Circuit.

[...]

MONTGOMERYSHIRE ... In this County are many high Hills, and divers Vales, Springs and Rivers, of which the *Severn* is the chief, being the second River in the Kingdom, whose Head rising from the vast high Mountain *Plymlimon,* and being joined with other smaller Streams, runs through the East Part of this Shire.

[...]

Montgomery is the chief Town, and is one of the new Shires taken out of the Marches of *Wales,* and made a County by King *Henry* VIII. so called from *Roger de Montgomery,* a noble *Norman* Earl of *Shrewsbury,* who gaining much Land hereabout from the *Welsh,* first built it to secure his Conquests, as likewise a very fine Castle, standing not far from the Banks of the River *Severn,* upon the rising of a Rock, from whence it hath a very pleasant Prospect into a curious Plain that lieth beneath it.

[...]

In the Year 1661. *Dec.* 20. about Sunsetting, the Inhabitants of *Weston* in *Montgomeryshire* discover'd a great Number of Horsemen about 400 Paces from them, marching two a-breast in military order upon the Common, and were half an Hour before the Rear came up, seeming to be about five hundred in all. The Spectators were amazed, thinking them to be an Army of Roundheads, going to release the Prisoners at *Montgomery* (there being, at that time several Ministers and Gentlemen in Prison) and therefore several of them went to the top of the next Hill, where they had another full view of them, and could distinguish their Horses to be of several Colours, as white, grey, black, *&c.* and that they marched in three Companies, and betwixt every Division they had two Horse-colours flying; but as they drew toward them, they still marched from them, so that they could not come nearer than a hundred Yards. They asked a Man (who was thatching a House all that Day, which they judged the Horsemen went by) whether he faw all those Soldiers which marched by, who said that he saw none; neither was there any Track of the Horses to be seen that Night, nor the next Morning, so that they concluded it to be a wonderful Apparition, and deposed the Truth of these Particulars before the Lord *Herbert*, and several other Justices of the Peace of this County.

[...]

This County is very plentiful of cattle, especially Horses, which for their shape and swiftness are much valued.

[...]

PEMBROKESHIRE ... Part of this County was after inhabited by the *Flemings,* sent thither by King *Henry* I.

who lost their Country by the breaking in of the sea, whereby a great Part of *Flanders* was drowned, and whose Posterity continue there to this Day, and speak so good *English,* that their Division is called, *Little* England Be*yond* Wales. The Commodities of this shire are Corn, Cattle, Sea-fish and Fowl; and in the Days of *Giraldus Cambrensis* they had Wines for sale.

[...]

Pembroke, the Shire-town, which appears more antient than it is, was formerly walled, and had three Gates, with a large Castle, and a Causey leading over to the decay'd Priory of *Monton.* The Town consists principally of one long Street, on a long narrow Point of a Rock, and hath within the Walls thereof two Churches.

St. *David's* is a barren old City, having neither Trees to defend it, nor is it pleasant with Fields or Meadows, but lies exposed to Winds and Storms. It is now the Seat of a Bishop, but was once an Archbishoprick in the *British* Church. ...The Cathedral here hath been often ruined by the *Danes, Norwegians,* and other Pirates, as standing near the Sea in an extream Corner of this County, that which we now see was built by Bishop *Peter,* and by him dedicated to St. *David.* ... The Roof of' this Church is higher than any in *England.*

[...]

RADNORSHIRE ... The Air is sharp and cold, as generally it is through all *Wales,* whereby the Snow lies long uumelted under those vast Mountains, Hills and Rocks that overshadow the Valleys, yet the East and South parts are somewhat fruitful, indifferently stored with Woods, and watered with Rivers and Mears. The Riches of the North and West consist chiefly in the Cattle which they produce.

[…]

Radnor is the chief Town in this County, from whence it receives its Name, called antiently *Magi,* where the *Pacensian* Legion of the *Romans* lay, and thought to be *Magnos* mentioned by the Emperor *Marcus Antoninus,* It had formerly a Wall, with a large and strong Castle.

Presteyn is the best Town in this Shire for handsome Buildings, and good Trading. *Keynton* is also a Market Town, under which is to be seen the Tract of Offa's Ditch, along the Edge of the Mountain. The fourth place remarkable is, *Rhibader Gowy,* from which Word *Rhibader,* the *English,* it is thought, named the County *Radnor.* It is also called *Melineth,* from the yellowish Mountains thereof, which Stretch from *Offa's* Dyke to the River *Wye,* which River cutteth overthwart the West corner of this Shire, where meeting with some Rocks that impede its Passage, for want of Ground to glide on, it hath a violent Downfall, with a continual Noise, and is called, The *Fall of Wye.*

[…]

There are several other Proverbs in *Wales* besides those already mentioned, as 1. *Hur Welsh Blood is up:* and 'tis no Wonder that a very antient Gentleman being deprived of his Country, should digest his Losses with great Difficulty.

2. *As long as a Welsh Pedigree;* and as high too, seeing commonly a *Welsh* Gentleman can climb up to a Princely Extraction.

3. *Give your Horse a Welsh Bait.* That is, stop on the Top of the Mountains, where the poor Palfrey is forced to make shift with Cameleons Commons, the clear Air.

4. *Calen y Sais wrah Gimro.* That is, the Heart of an

Englishman toward a *Welshwoman:* This was invented while *England* and *Wales* were at dreadful feud, and applied to such as are possessed with Prejudice, and only carry an outward Compliance without cordial Affection.

5. *Ni Cheitw Cymhro oni Golle.* That *the Welshman keeps nothing until he hath lost it.* When the *British* recovered their lost Castles from the *English,* they doubled their Diligence and Valour, keeping them more tenaciously than before.

6. *Afo Pen, bid Bont.* That is, he that would be a Head let him be a Bridge. This is of a fictitious Original, for *Benigridan,* a *Welsh* General is said to have carried his Army (one by one, we must imagine) upon his Back, over a River in *Ireland,* where there was neither Bridge nor Ferry, and therefore deservedly was made their Prince.

7. There was an antient Play in *Wales,* wherein the stronger put the weaker into a Sack, from whence came the Proverb, H*e is able to put him up in a Bag.*

[...]

In 1662, *July* 2, were seen above an hundred Porpoises together near *Newport,* which seemed very strange and prodigious to the Inhabitants.

[...]

To conclude, the Principality of *Wales* was modelled into Shires, in the Reign of King *Henry* VIII. In the thirteen Counties whereof aforementioned are reckoned one Chace, thirteen Forests, thirty three Parks, two hundred thirty Rivers, an hundred Bridges, four Cities, fifty five Market Towns, forty one Castles of old Erection, four Bishopricks, and a thousand and sixteen Parish Churches, and elects thirty Parliament Men.

Nathaniel Crouch,
The History of the Principality of Wales, III, 1695

Nathaniel Crouch (c.1632-c.1725) was a bookseller and writer, who in the words of John Dunton 'melted down the best of our English Histories into Twelve-Penny Books'. His contemporary and friend also noted that 'his title pages are a little swelling' and he 'has got a habit of leering under his hat'. These histories were written under the name of Richard Burton or R.B. and published by himself. In total he produced 46 books on British history along with accounts ranging from a 'General History of Earthquakes' to 'The History of Daemons, Spectres, Witches ... and other Supernatural Delusions and malicious Impostures of the Devil'. This extract is taken from the 1730 reissue.

....

"Here, Mutton is noe bigger than Little Lamb"

....

Coal mining thrived in North Wales when Celia Fiennes briefly visited in 1698, but the rutted roads and floods made its transport perilous.

Cross this River by this Bridge Enters Fflintshire and so Crossed over ye marches wch is hazardous to strangers, therefore Mr Wm Allen – wch was ye major of Chester that time and gave me a very Civil treate being an acquaintance of my Brother Sr Edmund Harrison – so order'd his son and another Gentleman to Ride wth me to Direct, to Harding wch was 5 miles. Just by that was a very fine new built house of Brick and in ye Exact forme of ye London Architecture wch was this Mr Majors house and good gardens.

Att Harding, where was my Relation Dr Percivalls wife who was Minister of y^t place: his parish was 8 miles in Extent and 2 lordships in it, and ye ruines of two great Castles in it remaines – its good Rich Land here, much on Enclosures and woods.

In a tarresse walke in my Relations garden I could very plainly see Chester and ye River Dee with all its Washes over the Marsh ground wch look'd very finely: here are sands wch makes it very difficult for strangers to passe wth out a guide. From hence my Relation Carry'd me to Holly Well and pass'd thro' Flint town wch is the shire town 5 mile from harding; its a very Ragged place many villages in England are better, ye houses all thatched and stone walls, but so decay'd that in many places Ready are to tumble down. There was a town hall such a one as it was; it was at a Session tyme w^n I was there wch shew'd it at its Prime. There is a Castle wch still remaines wth its towers built of stone, its down to ye water side: from thence to Holy well is 3 mile mostly by ye water side wch is Reckon'd the sea – here I went just in sight of high Lake where were many shipps Rideing along that harbour.

St Winfreds Well is built over wth stone on Pillars Like a Tryumphall arch or tower on ye gates of a Church, there is a pavem^t of stone wth in – round 3 sides of ye well wch is joyn'd on ye fourth side by a great arch of stone wch Lies over ye water y^t runs of from ye well; its many springs wch bubbles up very fast and Lookes Cleane in a Compass wch is 8 square walled in wth stone. In ye bottom wch you see as Clear as Chrystall are 9 stones Layd in an oval on wch are dropps of Red Coullour some almost quite Covering the top of ye stone, wch is pretended to be ye blood of this holy saint whose head was struck off here and so where her body Laid this spring burst forth and remaines till now a very Rapid Current, wch runs off from this well under a barre by wch there are stone stepps for ye persons to descend wch will

bathe themselves in the well, and so they walke along
ye Streame to the other End and then come out, but there
is nothing to Shelter them but are Exposed to all the
Company that are walking about ye well and to ye Little
houses and part of ye Streete wch runs along by it but y^e
Religeuse are not to mind it, it seemes the saint they do
honour to in this place must beare them out in all things.
They tell of many lameness's and aches and distempers
wch are Cured by it, its a Cold water and Cleare and runs
off very quick so y^t it would be a pleasant refreshm^t in
ye sumer to washe ones self in it, but its shallow not up
to ye Waste so its not Easye to Dive and washe in, but I
thinke I Could not have been persuaded to have gone
in unless I might have had Curtains to have drawn
about some part of it to have shelter'd from ye Streete,
for ye wett garments are no Covering to ye body; but
there I saw abundance of ye devout papists on their
Knees all round a well. Poor people are deluded into an
ignorant blind zeale and to be pity'd by us y^t have the
advantage of knowing better and ought to be better.
There is some stones of a Reddish Coullour in ye well s^d
to be some of St Winifred's blood also, wch ye poore
people take out and bring to ye strangers for Curiosity
and Relicts, and also moss about ye bancks full of great
virtue for Every thing. But its a Certaine gaine to y^e
poore people – every one gives them something for
bringing them moss and ye stones, but lest they should
in length of tyme be quite gather'd up they take Care to
replenish it dayly from some mossy hill and so stick it
along ye sides of ye well – there is good streames runs
from it and by meanes of steepe descent runs down and
turns mills. They come also to drinke of ye water w^ch

they take up in ye first square wch is walled round and where the springs Rise and they say its of wonder full operation. Y^e taste to me was but like good spring water wch wth wine and sugar and Lemons might make a pleasant Draught after walking amongst those shady trees of wch there is a great many and some straight and tall like a grove but not very uniforme. From thence I went back to Harding wch is 8 very Long Miles. At Holly well they speake Welsh; the inhabitants go barefoote and bare leg'd – a nasty sort of people. Their meate is very small here, Mutton is noe bigger than Little Lamb, what of it there is was sweete; their wine good being Neare ye Sea side, and are well provided with ffish – very good Salmon and Eeles and other ffish I had at Harding. This shire is improperly Called Fflintshire there being noe flints in all ye Country. There are great Coale pitts of the Channell Coale thats Cloven huge great pieces: they have great wheeles that are turned wth horses y^t draw up the water and so draine the Mines wch would Else be over flowed so as they Could not dig the Coale; they have also Engines y^t draw up their Coale in sort of baskets Like hand barrows wch they wind up like a Bucket in a well, for their mines are dug down through a sort of well and sometymes its pretty Low before they Come to ye Coales; it makes ye Road unsafe because of ye Coale pitts and also from ye Sloughs and quicksands, all here about being mostly near ye bancks of ye water. In this Country are quarrys of Stone, Copper and Iron Mines and salt hills, its a hilly place, very steep descents and great many very high hills, but I went not so farre as Pen Ma Mower but Cross'd ye river Dee haveing first went two mile by these Coale mines (at least 10) in a place (?) its a thing wch holds neer two bushell that is their Basket they draw up wch is bought for 6 pence. I forded over ye Dee when ye tide was out all upon the sands at Least a mile, wch was as smooth as a Die being a few hours left of ye flood. Y^e sands are here soe Loose y^t the tydes does move them from one place to another at Every flood, y^t the same place one used to ffoard a month or two before is not to be pass'd now, for as it brings the sands in heaps to one place so it leaves others in deep holes wch are Cover'd wth water and Loose sand that would swallow up a horse or Carriages; so I had two Guides to Conduct me over. The Carriages wch are used to it and pass Continually at ye Ebbs of water observes ye drift of sands and so Escape ye danger. It was at least a mile I went on ye sands before I Came to ye middle of ye Channell wch was pretty deep and with such a Current or tyde wch was falling out to sea together wth ye wind, the horses feete could scarce stand against it, but it was but narrow just the deep part of the Channell and so soone over. When the tyde is fully out they frequently fford in many places wch they marke as the sands fall and Can go near 9 or 10 mile over ye sands from Chester to Burton or to Flint town almost; but many persons that have known the ffoards well y^t have Come a year or halfe a year after, if they venture on their former knowledge have been overwhelm'd in the Ditches made by ye sands wch is deep enough to swallow up a Coach or waggon; but they Convey their Coales from Wales and any other things by waggon when the tyde is out to Chester and other parts.

Celia Fiennes,
The Diary of Celia Fiennes, 1698

Celia Fiennes (1662-1741) was the grand-daughter of a William Fiennes, 1st Viscount of Saye and Sele. She made several journeys across England between 1684 and 1713, usually accompanied by one or two servants. She wrote up her travels in 1702, in a manuscript 'soe not likely to fall into the hands of any but my near relations'. This was published in 1888 under the title 'Through England On a Side Saddle'. Her visit to Flintshire took place during a journey in 1698. Otherwise, she looked at Wales from its bordering counties on a number of journeys, observing that Herefordshire and Shropshire were once parts of Wales.

2

SETTING OUT: WHAT
YOU NEED TO KNOW

Travelling across Wales was evidently not something to be undertaken lightly. Visitors needed to be suitably equipped as well as forewarned about the exertions and possible discomforts involved. That said, as the following account shows, travel had become easier by the end of the Eighteenth Century.

"reckoned among the first of the kingdom."

By the end of the Eighteenth Century, travelling across Wales was less of a challenge than it had previously been.

Like a variety of other parts of Great Britain, the mode of travelling through Wales has been much changed of late. Travellers going from Chester to Holyhead for Ireland, were once obliged to take a guide to see them safe over the almost trackless mountains in Flintshire and Denbighshire, which is now performed with ease and safety, in less than a one third of the time it formerly took. Wales, in many respects, as to accommodation for travellers, as well as improvement in the roads, within late years, may be reckoned among the first of the kingdom.

Anon., A Collection of Welch Tours: or, a display of the
beauties of Wales, selected principally from celebrated
histories and popular tours, with occasional
observations and remarks, 1797

....

"It would save him many a languid hour"

....

The 'Cambrian Traveller' needed to consider the best mode of transport and the subjects to be recorded whether in words or pictures.

You determine wisely, not to visit other countries till you have become acquainted with the wonders and beauties of your own. Your intention is equally judicious, to devote a part of the University long vacation to a Tour through Wales. Interesting and instructive it will certainly be, and in after life an opportunity may not so readily occur again. Wales is indeed almost a foreign country within our own; its features, inhabitants, language, manners, and customs, are so very different from those of England, that the Cambrian Traveller is abroad—a stranger, yet at home.

Your plan is to walk and sketch the scenery, — this too is well. The best way undoubtedly of seeing a country is on foot. It is the safest, and most suited to every variety of road; it will often enable you to take a shorter track, and visit scenes (the finest perhaps) not otherwise accessible; it is healthy, and, with a little practice, easy; it is economical: a pedestrian is content with almost any accommodations; he, of all travellers, wants but little […]

And last, though not least, it is perfectly independent. Expedition it cannot boast; but this is to you rather an advantage: three miles an hour would be found fast enough for your pursuit; and twelve or fourteen miles a day (more or less), for two months, would carry you through a considerable tour, allowing for a halt on the march, sometimes of two or three days, in order to explore.

Your principal object is to exercise your pencil. Perhaps every tourist would do well to have a principal object, adding as many secondary ones as he pleases. A journal too, or short notes regularly kept, may be recommended: it would save him many a languid hour, and make his tour more pleasant and profitable, both to himself and others. One object there is, which I need not remind *you* to keep in view—a constant reference of these stupendous scenes to that Being whose *"hands formed the dry land."*

As to some general direction for taking a view, an eminent artist, when I first began to sketch from nature, gave me this—*Choose the most handsome objects, and the best assemblage of parts.* But this, masterly as it is, would no more satisfy you, I apprehend, than it did me, because it cannot be followed without *experience.* You shall therefore have the benefit of mine (such as it is) — a detail of "the most handsome objects," in my excursions, and "the best assemblage of parts;" in other words, my choice of subjects, and of situations for drawing them. In planning your route, you would find it useful to look over the catalogues of our public exhibitions, for such views as might be included in it. It is safe to study scenes chosen by professors, and a stimulus to recollect that they *have been* drawn. I will send you a list. Your first aim, of course, will be the characteristic features of the country, and then to exercise your taste and judgment in selecting them. Artists, of merit in other respects, sometimes fail in this. With considerable facility and fidelity of pencil, and even skill in colouring, they have little notion of catching the grand peculiarities of a country, or of choosing them judiciously. I have met with such indefatigable fellows, drawing all day long all that came in their way; and this may be good practice, and help to fill the hint book, but it surely neither improves the taste of the artist, nor displays his genius. Be it your care then to study, and bring back with you, such scenes of sublimity and beauty as wear Cambrian features, and are not to be found at home; and to which I very sincerely wish my sketches were a better introduction.

R. H. Newell, Letters on the scenery of Wales; including a series of subjects for the pencil,1821

The Reverend Robert Hasell Newell (1778-1852) was the rector of Little Hormead, Herts. and also wrote 'The Poetical Works of Oliver Goldsmith' (1811) in which he sought to ascertain the actual site of Goldsmith's 'The deserted village'. His son, Charles Alexander Newell (1817-1882), the recipient of the above letter, did indeed have a sketchbook, but there is no evidence that he visited Wales.

"To study nature in her works, and man in society"

It was best to have a clearly stated objective before setting out. What you encountered should be seen as confirming your beliefs rather than challenging them.

Behold us, then, more like two pilgrims performing a journey to the tomb of some wonder-working saint, than men travelling for their pleasure and amusement. We are so completely metamorphosed, that I much doubt whether you would recognise us through our disguise; we carry our clothes, &c. in a wallet or knapsack, from which we have not hitherto experienced the slightest inconvenience : as for all ideas of appearance and gentility, they are entirely out of the question – our object is to see, not to be seen; and if I thought I had one acquaintance who would be ashamed of me and my knapsack, seated by the fire side of an honest Welsh peasant, in a country village, I should not only make myself perfectly easy on my own account, but should be induced to pity and despise him for his weakness.

[...]

The chief object of this expedition, and from which I hope to derive the greatest pleasure, is to explore the hidden beauties of nature unmechanized by the ingenuity of man; as well as to make some observations upon the human character under every different attitude it may assume; in short, to study nature in her works, and man in society. The lower orders of people in this part of Great Britain have as yet presented to me only a picture of humiliation and wretchedness. Whether this be the general character, or but a partial appearance of the country, I shall have other opportunities of discovering in the prosecution of my journey: at present I am far from entertaining a favourable opinion of their stock of happiness; undeniably there are numerous examples of apparent cheerfulness and content to be found amongst the poor inhabitants of a mud-built cottage; but are not the social endearments of domestic life (the only source of enjoyment amongst the lower orders of mankind), too often imbittered by repeated difficulties and distresses, and rendered so many aggravating circumstances to the wounded recollection of a parent, surrounded by a numerous and helpless family who look up to him for protection and support, which he is utterly unable to afford them? I believe and hope that such instances of want and degradation are rare; but very few of them are requisite to convince any man, capable of feeling for others as he would for himself that the aggregate of happiness, amongst the lower species of our fellow-creatures, does not bear a just proportion to that of pain, and that their condition is capable of very essential improvement. Under the pressure of poverty and misfortune, the mind oftentimes forgets its noble nature, and the proper degree of estimation with which it should regard its own existence: and this is the case with that description of men here spoken of. To remove then this evil, by doing away the cause of the complaint (viz. Oppression), would be a work well worthy the attention of every friend of mankind. Under whatever circumstances of poverty and inferiority many of our fellow-creatures may be placed, yet they have a just claim upon our protection and support; for though habit, and the hard hand of oppressive want, may have contracted the modes of thinking amongst them, yet they undoubtedly possess intellects, which, if properly cultivated, might equally adorn a senate, or a forum, with those who are called their superiors, from the mere accidental circumstances of wealth, or hereditary distinctions. A human being, as he comes originally from the hand of nature, is every where the same; the capacity of improvement, the talents and virtues which the mind is capable of acquiring and exercising, are to every state of society alike inherent. Surely then all must rejoice in the melioration of that state, since to contribute to its improvement is the noblest pursuit of individuals, and ought to be the sole end of all governments; but the sacred principles of the social compact are no longer regarded, and that which should be the first is now become the last care or consideration of legislative science. To say that the state of society cannot be improved, is either to assert its perfection, to confess that all exertions to improve that state would be vain, or that these political evils are either necessary or irremediable. To the first of these arguments, if they can be deemed worthy of such a denomination, there is no necessity to reply, because it carries with it its own conviction; and with respect to the last, no one will hesitate to pronounce it an impious reflection upon the benevolence of the Creator, whose intention could never be to subject man to any species of political tyranny whatever; and well indeed might this fair creation and celestial harmony be called a Manichean system, or work of a malevolent being, if he could sanction upon this globe the detestable crimes, and abhorred impieties committed under the patronage, and often the immediate consequence, of vicious and corrupted governments; or if he could fix so narrow and confined a boundary to human happiness.

J. Hucks, A pedestrian tour in
North Wales in a series of letters, 1795

Joseph Hucks (1772-1800) as an Oxford Undergraduate in July 1794, accompanied Samuel Taylor Coleridge on a walking tour through Wales. They were school friends at Christ's Hospital, London. In 1800 he contributed three poems to Robert Southey's Annual Anthology but died of TB later that year.

....

"It has little to entice the attention of the tourist"

....

Not all of Wales was regarded as being of equal beauty. For those drawn to the South, admirers of the picturesque, or the statistical enquirer, historian and antiquarian, there was little worth in visiting beyond the southern extremity and a few spots in Ceredigion and Pembrokeshire.

IN making the Tour of South Wales and Monmouthshire, the *Admirer* of *picturesque beauty* dwells with peculiar pleasure on a tract of country comprising the greater part of Monmouthshire, and bordering the Severn and Bristol channel, to the western limits of Pembrokeshire. In this enchanting district, a succession of bold hills, clothed with wild forests, or ornamental plantations and delightful valleys, present themselves in constant variety: many fine estuaries and rivers, picturesque towns, and princely ruins, also adorn the scene, whose charms are inconceivably heightened by the contiguity of the Bristol channel, which washes the coast; in some places receding into capacious bays; in others, advancing into rocky promontories of the most imposing grandeur.

The Statistical Enquirer finds equal subject of gratification, in the uncommon fertility of several valleys, and the woody treasures of numerous hills, bearing myriads of oaks, and other first-rate timber-trees. The mineral wealth of the country, and its convenient coast for traffic, are likewise subjects of high consideration; and, while the statist applauds the late rapid strides of manufactures and commerce in this district, he may discover sources hitherto latent for their increase.

The Historian cannot fail of being interested while

treading on the ground where Britons made their latest and most vigorous efforts for independence, against successive invaders; nor *the Antiquary,* while traversing a country, replete with Monuments of the Druidical ages, military works of the Romans, Britons, Saxons, and Normans; and the venerable relics of numerous religious foundations.

Beyond this stripe of country, from ten to twenty miles in width, forming the southern extremity of Wales, and an intermixture of rich scenery (particularly in the neighbourhood of Brecon), with prevailing dreariness on the eastern frontier, South-Wales exhibits a tedious extent of hills without majesty, Valleys over-run with peat bogs, and unprofitable moors. Beside the superb ruins of St. David's, the course of the Tivy near Cardigan, and the scenery about the Devil's Bridge, it has little to entice the attention of the tourist: the towns, for the most part, are miserably poor, and travelling accommodations very uncertain; the roads, too, are wretched beyond any thing that a mere English traveller ever witnessed. It is, therefore, a subject of no small gratification, that the chief beauties of South-Wales are found in a compact route; abounding with good towns, respectable accommodations, and very fair roads. This part of the country maybe explored in a close carriage, though the better mode of travelling is, certainly, on horse-back. The pedestrian may claim peculiar advantages in his way of getting on; but I do not conceive, that a man enduring the fatigue of trudging day after day through miry roads, can maintain an exhilaration of spirits congenial with the beauties that surround him.

J. T. Barber, A tour throughout South Wales and
Monmouthshire, 1803

John Thomas Barber (1774-1841) was born in Marylebone (Middlesex at the time) and made his early career painting miniatures for the royal family. He visited Wales in 1802 and subsequently became involved in the insurance industry with great success. He launched the Provident Life Office, and the County Fire Office which over time became Royal Sun Alliance. He changed his name to John Barber Beaumont in 1812.

....
"An unlimited command of time"
....

The mode of travel excited the attention of many; to ride or to walk? The recommended clothing was also often intriguing.

Post-chaises and horses may he obtained at all the principal towns; and at most of them, cars capable of conveying three or four persons are kept. The price of posting is much the same as in England, a chaise and pair being usually charged Is. 6d. per mile, and a car and horse Is. per mile. The innkeepers, as in other parts of the kingdom, always charge any fraction of a mile as a whole mile; and the post-boys expect about 3d. a mile.

Those who are fond of riding on horseback may make the tour of Wales very pleasantly in this manner, and avoid the delays and fatigues incident to other plans of journeying. Their best mode will be, to proceed to Wales by the regular stages, and then buy a Welsh pony, which may be purchased at about six guineas and upwards. The surefootedness and caution exhibited by these animals can scarcely be imagined, except by those who have witnessed them mounting acclivities and descending steeps, amidst fragments of rocks and other obstructions, that appeared to render the mountain paths impassable. A pair of saddle-bags will contain the tourist's travelling apparatus. Those who journey on horseback must be cautious in passing fords after heavy rains, as the stream frequently swells suddenly to a great height, and renders the attempt very dangerous.

Many persons recommend walking; but this method can only be pursued with pleasure by male parties, who have health and strength, who are accustomed to the exercise, and who have an unlimited command of time. It certainly is the only mode in which *every* object can be visited, and a *thorough* acquaintance with the country obtained. "Apologies for walking," says the Rev. Mr. Freeman, in his "Sketches in Wales," "are not now needed. Reasoning people are agreed that there is neither disgrace nor impropriety in using one's limbs. I have wandered a good deal in my life, and have travelled in various ways, but I certainly prefer walking, when in an interesting country. A man may well be excused if he *hurries* over a district which he already sufficiently knows, or whose features are disagreeable; but the only way he has to make himself well acquainted with a country, is by passing through it leisurely, and on foot.

The pedestrian should provide himself with strong, pliant, and easy shoes, with short light gaiters, to keep out the dust. These are much better adapted for continued walking than boots or thin shoes. Blisters may be avoided by wearing fine soft flannel or woollen socks next to the skin, and by washing the feet previous to going to bed.

A change of linen, and a few articles necessary to personal comfort, maybe stowed in a knapsack, or case, made of brown dressed calf-skin, such as is used by saddlers, about twelve inches long and seven wide, lined with canvass, and having a flap and button. This should be made to fit between the shoulders, and attached to them by leather or list braces; or these articles may be put into a neat leathern bag, and carried in the same way as a shooting-bag, suspended under the left arm by a strap crossing the right shoulder. If two persons travel together, they will find it a good plan to have the case, or bag, made large enough for the articles of both, and to carry it alternately. Some pedestrian tourists have worn strong shooting jackets, with double pockets, for containing their luggage; but they have generally found this arrangement not so pleasant as the preceding.

[...]

Those persons who intend walking through Wales should arrange their tour so as to finish each day's excursion in some town, where they will generally be able to obtain good accommodation. The villages are seldom comfortable resting-places. If they propose to visit the various waterfalls and ascend mountains, they must recollect that the way is generally rugged and wet, and provide themselves with strong shoes. In the arduous ascents of Plinlimmon, Cader Idris, Snowdon, and other lofty mountains, some refreshment should be taken. The guides generally recommend spirits to be carried up, as an antidote against the effects of a raw and chilly atmosphere; but the use of these is rather dangerous, a very small quantity of them in these ethereal regions being sufficient to intoxicate. A bottle of milk and water, with a very small portion of brandy in it, will be found much more refreshing and agreeable than undiluted spirits. A pocket compass will be necessary, if the tourist intend traversing the mountains and penetrating the recesses of the country without a guide.

Samuel Leigh, Leigh's Guide to Wales & Monmouthshire, 1831

Samuel Leigh (1780-c1840) was a bookseller and publisher who published nine travel and guide books under his name between 1820 and 1837. He is most famous for 'Panorama of the Thames from London to Richmond', a 60 foot long sheet published between 1820-1830.

"The meagre journal of the day"

This is the first of several quotations from Samuel Pratt's adventures. He was taken to task in a review by 'Cymro' which can be read in Chapter 11.

If they are under the *necessity* to stay a night at any of these [intermediate stages] the most inquisitive of them stroll thro' the streets, or saunter round the ramparts, *while the supper is preparing.* The rest throw themselves on chairs and sophas, till arous'd by the return of their companions, who generally come back dissatisfied with their ramble; and, if they write at all, sit down, betwixt sleeping and waking, and insert in the meagre journal of the day a drowsy, yet splenetic, account of what they met with in their walk; depending on the sexton, as the historian of the buildings, and on some chance passenger as the intelligencer of the inhabitants, environs, police, &c. &c. At day break the next morning they are off, scarcely allowing time for swallowing a comfortless dish of coffee, squabbling with their host for extortion, cursing the country they are under the immediate protection of, and disgracing the manners of their own.

Samuel Jackson Pratt, Gleanings through Wales, 1795

Samuel Jackson Pratt (1749-1814) was variously a Clergyman, actor ('Courtney Melmoth'), poet, dramatist and novelist. His obituary in the Gentleman's Magazine (October 1814) notes he 'was one of the most prolific writers of his day'. His early life 'was marked by such indiscretions as too frequently accompany genius' while being 'particularly zealous in the cause of unfriended talents'.

....

"scarcely one person was capable of speaking English"

....

The traveller must be aware of the several perils that will await him.

At Caerphily we perceived a great change in the manners of the people; in the whole village, scarcely one person was capable of speaking English.

'The Author' (Allen Cliff),
The Cambrian Directory, 1800

Allen Cliff(e) anonymously wrote and published The Cambrian Directory, a guide for travellers to Wales. He was probably based in Worcester and the first edition of the Directory was published in Salisbury in 1800, with subsequent editions in 1801, 1802 and 1806.

....

"Now infested by an unawed banditti"

....

Cliff also notes that as well as the challenge of a strange language, the roads carried their own risks.

GREEN BRIDGE

It derives its name from an excavation in the rock, through which a little rivulet runs for a mile and a half. This cavity is completely concealed from the road, and impossible to be discovered unless pointed out by some neighbouring inhabitant. Let me, however, advise all Tourists to be cautious in their excursions to this natural curiosity, as it is a place evidently calculated for plunder, stratagems, and murder; and is now infested by an unawed banditti of smugglers, who have frequently practised the barbarous scheme of decoying vessels by false lights; and by whom we ourselves were insulted. Indeed, I would advise Travellers to alter their route from Swansea, and pursue the straight road to Caermarthen, and so to Tenby, by Narbeth. By these means they escape the unpleasant roads (and almost, indeed, inaccessible for carriages), leading from Oystermouth to Cheriton, and likewise from Llaugharne to Tenby. But should the Tourist be led by an invincible curiosity to inspect the ruins of Kidwely Castle, it may easily be accomplished, by pursuing the turnpike-road to Kidwely, and from thence to Caermarthen: in this last route you only omit visiting the seat of Mr. Talbot, of Penrice; though an object highly worthy of inspection.

'The Author' (Allen Cliff),
The Cambrian Directory, 1800

....

"Even Hannibal himself wou'd have found it impossible"

....

As a professional writer, Daniel Defoe visited Wales, as with the rest of Britain, looking for good copy. His books happily mixed his observations with whatever other material he came across. The following is from his second visit to Wales.

SIR, – My last from West Chester, gave you a full account of my progress thro' Wales, and my coming to Chester, at the end of that really fatiguing journey: I must confess, I that have seen the Alps, on so many occasions, have gone under so many of the most frightful passes in the country of the Grisons, and in the mountains of Tirol, never believ'd there was any thing in this island of Britain that came near, much less that exceeded those hills, in the terror of their aspect, or in the difficulty of access to them; But certainly, if they are out done any where in the world, it is here: Even Hannibal himself wou'd have found it impossible to have march'd his army over Snowden, or over the rocks of Merioneth and Montgomery Shires; no, not with all the help that fire and vinegar could have yielded, to make way for him.

The only support we had in this heavy journey, was, (1.) That we generally found their provisions very good and cheap, and very good accommodations in the inns. And (2.) That the Welsh gentlemen are very civil, hospitable, and kind; the people very obliging and conversible, and especially to strangers; but when we let them know, we travell'd merely in curiosity to view the country, and be able to speak well of them to strangers, their civility was heightened to such a degree, that nothing could be more friendly, willing to tell us every thing that belong'd to their country, and to show us every thing that we desired to see.

Daniel Defoe, A tour thro' the whole island of Great Britain, divided into circuits or journies, 1724

Daniel Defoe (c1660-1731) was the son of a London butcher and tallow chandler. After a disastrous career as a merchant resulted in his bankruptcy in 1692, he became a 'commissioner of the glass duty' and ran a brick and tile factory before publishing his first essays in 1697. As a dissenter, he was sentenced to three days in the pillory and prison in 1603, before being released by a patron. Later he was to work with Tory politicians. He wrote eight novels including Robinson Crusoe (1719) and Moll Flanders (1822), ten non-fiction books, 13 volumes of essays and two poems. Defoe's 'Tour thro' the whole island of Great Britain' consists of 13 letters published in three volumes between 1724 and 1726. Letters six and seven in the second volume include his visits to Wales.

....
"By some unaccountable neglect"
....

It was also a good idea to have somewhere to store your observations safely so as not to lose them. In fairness, Bingley was an enterprising traveller and a well regarded writer.

Near the road betwixt Llandudno and Eglwys Rhôs, *The Chapel in Rhos,* is a copper mine, which, though formerly not productive, is now worked to some extent. The miners here descend by shafts, and do not, as in most of the Welsh mines, enter through levels. — By some unaccountable neglect I have mislaid all the particulars that I had obtained respecting it...

William Bingley, North Wales, Vol. 1, 1804

William Bingley (1774-1823) was a clergyman and naturalist who visited North Wales in 1798 while an undergraduate at Peterhouse College, Cambridge. During this trip he and Peter Bailey Williams, who was Rector of Llanrug and Llanberis, made the first recorded ascent of Snowdon's Clogwyn Du'r Arddu while looking for arctic alpine flowers. His book 'Tour in North

Wales' was subsequently published in 1800. A second visit in 1801 resulted in 'North Wales' in 1804. He is best known for his 'Animal Biography' published in 1802. According to the Dictionary of National Biography 'his life [was] devoid of incident; his days were passed in compilation'.

3

THE JOURNEY

Rough roads and a long time spent on them meant that the actual journey could stir up mixed emotions. Some of this must have been for show, as can be seen from the marked contrast between the two private manuscript accounts by Johnson and Skinner and those intended for publication.

"Yet the retreat proved highly gratifying"

Falling for female travelling companions or witnessing a man falling off Swansea Castle made for a good trip, especially when decorum was seen to be maintained.

Among our female companions were two genteel young Welch-women of considerable personal attractions, whose vivacity and good nature had essentially contributed to the entertainment of the day: one of these was peculiarly bewitching[...]

These damsels preferring the certainty of a wetting upon deck to the chance of suffocation in the cabin, we made it our business to defend them as much as possible from "the pelting of the pitiless storm." Our travelling coats were fashionably large; so that each of us was able completely to shelter one, without exposing ourselves; a bottle of brandy too, that we had fortunately provided; helped to counteract the inclemency of the weather, and we were for some time thoroughly comfortable. The rain at length, penetrating our coverings, obliged us to seek a fresh resource; but to discover one was no easy matter; for the cabin had not a chink unoccupied, and there was not a dry sail on board to make use of. In this predicament it fortunately occurred to one of the ladies, that before the hatchway was closed she observed sufficient room in the hold for three or four persons who were not very bulky to lie down: to this place we gained admittance; and, although the angles of chests and packages formed a very inappropriate couch for the tender limbs of our friends, yet the retreat proved highly gratifying; and, after a short time spent in pleasing conversation, we enjoyed a refreshing sleep. — Unhallowed thoughts, be silent! voluptuous imaginations, conjure not up, from this pressure of circumstances, motives or actions that are unholy! It is true, the girls had charms that mighty warm an anchorite, and were filled with the glowing sensations of youthful passion; yet they were virtuous; nor had the tourists, although encountering temptation, a wish to endanger the possessors of qualities so lovely for a transitory enjoyment.

[…]

During my stay in Swansea, an intoxicated man fell asleep on the parapet of the castle, and, rolling off, fell to the ground at the depth of near 80 feet. The poor fellow was a servant in the castle: and, missing his room in winding up the turreted stair-case, unconsciously extended his journey to the summit of the castle. Nothing broke his fall (unless the roof of a low shed reared against the wall, and which he went clearly through, maybe considered as a favourable impediment), and yet, incredible as it may seem! the only effect produced on the man, was a slight broken head, and a restoration of his faculties. He bound up his head himself, made the best of his way to a public-house, took a little more ale, and then went soberly to bed. I should scarcely have believed this miraculous escape, had I not seen the broken tiles and rafters through which he fell, and heard the attestations of numerous witnesses of the accident.

J. T. Barber, A tour throughout South Wales and Monmouthshire, 1803

"French prisoners! French prisoners!"

At a time when foreign travellers were an unusual occurrence, there was always the chance that gentlemanly pursuits may be mistaken for something more dramatic.

Unable to unravel the intricacies of the way ourselves, we had recourse to the mistress of our inn for a guide, who put us under the direction of a young man belonging to the volunteer corps of the town. The company to which he belonged having been exercising that morning, the youth was still clad in his uniform; and as he carried a gun that Mr. H[amme]t had lent C. C—ll on the preceding day, he had every appearance of *being yet on duty.*

Accompanied by our guide, who marched before us with the fowling-piece thrown over his shoulder, we set off from Cardigan, but had scarcely reached the out-skirts of the town, before we found ourselves almost surrounded by a troop of women and boys, who followed us with huzzas and halloos, shouting as loudly as they could roar, "French prisoners! French prisoners!" an idea naturally enough suggested to them by the order of our march, our thread-bare appearance, and the news that had arrived on the preceding day of the French troops in Ireland having surrendered to Lord Cornwallis.

We thought that fancy had already exhausted herself in forming imaginary *characters* for us, and never apprehended we should have to add to the respectable list, (which comprised footpads, gaol-birds, militia-men, and acquitted felons) the reputation of being *Sans Culottes*.

Richard Warner, A second walk through Wales in
August and September 1798, 1799

Richard Warner (1763-1857) wrote forty-four books and papers, including three satires about Bath society, under the pseudonym Peter Paul Pallet. He spent most of his career as a vicar, first in Hampshire, then in Bath, and finally in Great Chalfield in Wiltshire where he died aged 93. He had a long standing interest in local history and antiquities. His first 'walk through Wales' was such a success that he repeated the exercise, first in Wales and twice more in England and Scotland.

"The honour that awaited us"

Richard Warner did have the knack of attracting attention.

The little bathing town of Abergelan afforded us some excellent London porter and Shropshire cheese. Whilst we were enjoying this repast, mine host, who seemed to regard our attacks upon his loaf with some astonishment, after begging pardon for making so bold, requested to know whether we were of *"the party."* The expression was of so *Proteus-like* a nature, (particularly in these days of difference and division) that we did not at all understand him, I therefore desired he would explain himself. "Why, gentlemen," returned he, "I wished to be informed whether you belonged to the set of *strolling players* who are lately gone to Bangor, because, if you had, I would have troubled one of you with an *old shirt* which a *gentleman of the party* left behind him instead of his reckoning, when he passed through here." We had already been taken for militia-men, plunderers, and recruits, but had no idea of the honour that awaited us, of being ranked amongst the itinerant sons of Thespis.

**Richard Warner, A second walk through Wales in
August and September 1798, 1799**

....

"Our souls seemed to partake of their purity"

....

Climbing the 'Welsh Alps' was a strenuous activity, offering simple pleasures for the body, and all kinds of enlightenment and exaltation for the soul.

I had long a desire of visiting the Welsh Alps, the summit of Snowdon. The curate was so much devoted to me, that I did not employ my rhetoric long, before I prevailed upon him to accompany me in the expedition. We set out from our hermitage, in the month of July; we arrived in the evening at a small thatched hut, at the foot of the mountain, near a lake which they call Llyn Cychwhechlyn, which I leave you to pronounce as well as you are able. At this hut we found a poor labouring man, with five or six children, the pictures of health and innocence. We had brought provisions with us for our journey, and we regaled ourselves in this situation, the family partaking of our feast, with more satisfaction and glee, than I have ever found at a nobleman's sumptuous entertainment.

We were determined to amuse ourselves, as well as we could in this dreary situation. For this purpose we sent for a poor blind harper, and procured a number of blooming country girls to divert us with their music and dancing. There is something very plaintive and affecting in the Welsh music, and the manner of their singing symphonious and responsive to the notes of the harp, renders it exceeding melodious. It gave me infinitely more pleasure to hear this rustic concert, than the finest airs of an Italian opera; and to see these rosy rural nymphs direct their mazy steps, without the needless sumptuous apparel of luxury and pride, than all the ladies at St. James's, in their artificial beauty and attire.

At the dawn of day, we began our journey up the mountain, which seemed to scale the heavens…We found a great change in the temperature of the atmosphere, as we ascended the mountain. When we had gone half way up, we found the wind rather high, attended with scudding clouds. But when we arrived at the summit, the air was calm and serene, and seemed much more subtle and rarified, less impregnated with vapors, and more agreeable for respiration.

[…]

As our situation was exalted above the globe, so were our ideas. And the nearer we were to the etherial regions, the more our souls seemed to partake of their purity. Our minds like the serene face of the sky, undisturbed with the storms of the passions became equal and composed. We were inspired with sentiments of commiseration and contempt, in contemplating the vain magnificence of human grandeur; and the pursuits of the world, for a few pieces of ore, which nature prudently concealed in the bowels of these mountains.

O my friend, why should we return to the busy haunt of men? why were we doomed to drag an existence in populous cities and the crouded forum! O that it had been our lot to live among these mountains, unenvied and unknown!

Joseph Cradock, Letters from Snowdon, 1770

Joseph Cradock (1742-1826) wrote a further travel book; An Account of some of the most Romantic Parts of North Wales (1777). Remarks on North Wales which appeared in Literary and Miscellaneous Memoirs, was published as four posthumous volumes in 1828.

. . . .

"Our memory is soon buried in oblivion"

. . . .

In contemporary travel writing it is usual to find that the author's interior journey is as significant as the places and people encountered. Most of the accounts in this collection are of a less introspective nature. Where there is self-expression, it is restricted to commenting on events that confirm the author's prejudices or allow their superior intellect to be exhibited. Here, though, is a splendid exception.

I arrived at this small village at four this afternoon, and the coach that I wished to proceed with being gone, I found myself obliged to stop here for the night, being eighteen miles short of where I intended. After taking a solitary walk across the fields, I came to a path which bent down to the banks of a rivulet, whose murmuring waters traced their way over broken fragments of rocks; sweet scented evergreen shrubs hung over the bank, and a deep grove of bending willows formed an inimitable shade, where contemplation may delight to linger ; the cooing of the dove was heard from the retirement of the forest, and the nightingale mingled its notes with the soft tones of the linnet; indulging myself by the stream of water, and the melody of the winged inhabitants of the wood, I continued to wander along the path, till at once appeared the ruins of a magnificent castle. O! said I, yonder are the relicks of ancient grandeur; those walls once vibrated to the voice of man, the sound of hilarity, or of grief and mourning, in their turns. I then turned off from the path, and directed my steps towards the ruins; when I entered I perceived the remains of stairs, which seemed not to be so much shattered as the rest. I ascended to the summit, which was an hundred steps, it then led me out to the top of an elevated tower, which commanded an extensive view, as it overlooked a considerable valley, the many windings of a beautiful river, and a long chain of hills.

It was near sun-set when I gained this situation, and I looked down with delight into the vale beneath, where I could see at a great distance the weary ploughman retiring from the toils of the day and turning the eye a little round, the cheerful shepherd descending from the hills, accompanied by his faithful dog, the companion of his steps and the partner of his toil. The irregular hills which encircled this place rose like an amphitheatre around, in some parts covered with an almost impenetrable wood, upon whose top the sun seemed to repose with lingering delight, and shone red upon the summit of the hills, which gave rural nature a glow, and filled me with enthusiastic rapture. I sat down upon this elevation, to contemplate at leisure the sublime scenery around me; the peaceful tranquillity of the valley, the beauty of the distant mountains, the slow declination of the sun, whose orb seemed to increase in magnitude as it verged to the edged the horizon, and the deep silence which forerun the night, entranced me upon the spot.

Alas! said I, where or what is become of the heirs of those that formerly lived here in splendour. Have they mistaken the beauties of these lofty hills, which the hand of man never formed, for the monuments and towers of the town, which have been erected by the hands of mortal man? or the beauty of the setting sun upon the dark-brown and green surface, for that of the gilded shops and variegated lamps? or the midnight parties for the sweet dew of the morning? or was the heir young and simple, and led astray by the luring looks and fair speeches of a worthless female, spent all his estate, and died in extreme poverty, and his posterity never been able to redeem the estate or title of their ancestors, but have been obliged to serve their fellow mortals, even them of low degree? or was it an heiress, a fair female, who has been seduced by a villain, who has robbed her of her honour, and degraded her name, and she become prostitute, and her heirs have never been heard of? or did a set of barbarians enter, and murder the inhabitants under their own roof, and burn their dwellings down? or did the heir turn rebel against his king? or hath he committed suicide, and forfeited his title and estate by the laws of his country? or was it contended between two near relations which of them was heir, and spent all their estate at law, and left this delightful dwelling standing in ruins? or further, hath thy wickedness been great, and thy iniquities infinite — "hast thou stripped the naked of their clothing, or hast thou not given drink to the weary, or withheld bread from the hungry; or hast thou sent widows empty away, or thy ear been deaf the cry of the fatherless children; or hast thou bowed down thyself to graven images, and thy iniquities been visited upon thy children, even unto the third and fourth generation?" or hast thou persecuted the servants of God, that all this evil is come upon thee?

As I sat in the silence of the evening, contemplating the sublimity of the scene around. I observed a venerable old sage at a little distance, whose head was silvered over with years; I hastened down to enquire of him the reason why the mansion was left in this dilapidated state, and never rebuilt again; as I approached him, his looks commanded respect. "Pray honoured father, (said I) canst thou tell me the cause of all this grandeur mouldering into ruins?"

[It transpired the estate had fallen into ruin after the English Civil war. Later, while in the graveyard, the author ponders mortality.]

Our best happiness on earth is short; we flourish as a flower to-day; but alas! to-morrow the taste can no more relish its delicacies, nor the ear be delighted with the eloquence of the lecturer; no more can the tongue express the pleasure or pain of the heart, the eyes open no more on sublunary scenes; the cheeks that now glow with health, shall then become pale; the feet shall decline their function, and the useless hands fall heavily down by the side! farewell then all the engaging and endearing scenes around me; for "as the shadow that departeth fleeth away, and its place is known no more," so we vanish from the earth, and our memory is soon buried in oblivion; to us little regard is any longer paid; our associates with usual gaiety and ardour pursue their several designs; still, as before, the business of life goes briskly on; the sun shines as bright; the earth blooms as gay; the flowers smell as sweet; the plants spring as green, and the world will proceed in its old course; the forest echoes sweetly with the music of its winged inhabitants; all things wear their accustomed form, while our neglected clay is mouldering in the dust.

William Black, Reflections on the Relicks of Ancient Grandeur, and the Pleasing Retirements in South Wales, 1823

I can find no information about Mr Black other than he was a gentleman from Bristol.

"With great fatigue and perseverance"

With contemporary maps only showing the main roads between towns and cities, asking the way was fraught with mutual incomprehension.

It was with much difficulty we found our way to Harlech. We made some enquiries at a small village, but in vain; for though we addressed ourselves to many, we could by no means make them understand us; all we received in return was a stare, immediately followed by a grin, and concluded with a "tin sarcenick," which signifies "no Saxon." We were obliged therefore to rely upon chance for our guide, which did not however upon this occasion befriend us; for, instead of keeping to the right upon the hills, we pursued the left path, that brought us into an extensive vale, or marsh, where, at the distance of about five miles, we first perceived the objects we were in pursuit of (viz.) the town and castle of Harlech. After some considerable exertions, we were obliged to abandon this valley, because it was so swampy, and so much intersected by ditches and drains, that it would have been, if not impracticable, at least extremely uncomfortable and difficult to proceed. With great fatigue and perseverance, we climbed up the almost perpendicular, and craggy sides of the mountain, which bounded that part of the vale, where we were reduced to the above perplexity, and at length reached Harlech; for the first time heartily fatigued.

The country people have no idea that a stranger can be ignorant of their roads; we have not unfrequently asked the way, and received for answer, "that it was as straight as we could go;" when, in a very few paces, we have been perplexed by two roads, one declining to the right, and the other to the left. — Nor have they much idea of distance; each measuring it by the rule of his own judgment and opinion. It is no unusual thing to be told, that the distance to such a place, may be about five miles, "and a pretty good step;" which pretty good step, generally proves to be about five miles more.

J Hucks, A pedestrian tour in North Wales
in a series of letters, 1795

"The bath is completely and indecently open"

Private journals did not need to sensationalise. Samuel Johnson visited Wales for several weeks, socialising, examining and ruminating. He kept a notebook of which even Boswell was unaware. "This Journal of Dr. Johnson exhibits his mind when he was alone, and when no one was looking on, and when no one was expected to adopt his thoughts, or to be influenced by them: in this respect, it differs from the conversations and anecdotes already published" wrote the editor, Richard Duppa, who published this account in 1816. Johnson started his journey on 5th July, 1774, returning on 25th August, with Mr. & Mrs. Thrale ("the Mistress") and their daughter. Johnson related to Boswell "that instead of bleak and barren mountains, there were green and fertile ones; and that one of the castles in Wales would contain all the castles that he had seen in Scotland." In a letter from Johnson to Boswell dated 1st October 1774, Johnson noted that "Wales is so little different from England, that it offers nothing to the speculation of the traveller."

We entered Wales, dined at Mold, and came to Lleweney…

In the lawn at Lleweney is a spring of fine water, which rises above the surface into a stone basin, from which it runs to waste, in a continual stream, through a pipe.

There are very large trees.

The Hall at Lleweney is forty feet long, and twenty-eight broad. The gallery one hundred and twenty feet long, (all paved.) The Library forty-two feet long, and twenty-eight broad. The Dining-parlours thirty-six feet long, and twenty-six broad.

It is partly sashed, and partly has casements.

[...]

We went to Dymerchion church, where the old clerk acknowledged his Mistress. It is the parish church of Bâch y Graig. A mean fabric: Mr. Salusbury [Mrs. Thrale's father] was buried in it. Bâch y Graig has fourteen seats in it.

As we rode by, I looked at the house again. We saw Llannerch, a house not mean, with a small park very well watered. There was an avenue of oaks, which, in a foolish compliance with the present mode, has been cut down. A few are yet standing. The owner's name is Davies.

The way lay through pleasant lanes, and overlooked a region beautifully diversified with trees and grass.

At Dymerchion church there is English service only once a month. This is about twenty miles from the English border.

The old Clerk had great appearance of joy at the sight of his Mistress, and foolishly said, that he was now willing to die. He had only a crown given him by my Mistress.

At Dymerchion church the texts on the walls are in Welsh.

We went in the coach to Holywell.

Talk with Mistress about flattery.

Holywell is a market town, neither very small nor mean. The spring called Winifred's Well is very clear, and so copious, that it yields one hundred tuns of water in a minute. It is all at once a very great stream, which, within perhaps thirty yards of its eruption, turns a mill, and in a course of two miles, eighteen mills more. In descent, it is very quick. It then falls into the sea. The well is covered by a lofty circular arch, supported by pillars; and over this arch is an old chapel, now a school. The chancel is separated by a wall. The bath is completely and indecently open. A woman bathed while we all looked on.

In the church, which makes a good appearance, and is surrounded by galleries to receive a numerous congregation, we were present while a child was christened in Welsh.

[...]

I dined at Mr. Myddleton's, of Gwaynynog. The house was a gentleman's house, below the second rate, perhaps below the third, built of stone roughly cut. The rooms were low, and the passage above stairs gloomy, but the furniture was good. The table was well supplied, except that the fruit was bad. It was truly the dinner of a country gentleman. Two tables were filled with company, not inelegant.

After dinner, the talk was of preserving the Welsh language. I offered them a scheme. Poor Evan Evans was mentioned, as incorrigibly addicted to strong drink. Washington was commended. Myddleton is the only man, who, in Wales, has talked to me of literature. I wish he were truly zealous. I recommended the republication of David ap Rhees's Welsh Grammar.

[...]

The Bishop and much company dined at Lleweney. Talk of Greek — and the Army. The Duke of Marlborough's officers useless. Read Phocylidis, distinguished the paragraphs. I looked in Leland: an unpleasant book of mere hints.

[...]

We went to visit Bodville, the place where Mrs. Thrale was born, and the churches called Tydweilliog and Llangwinodyl, which she holds by impropriation.

We had an invitation to the house of Mr. Griffiths of Bryn o dol, where we found a small neat new built house, with square rooms: the walls are of unhewn stone, and therefore thick; for the stones not fitting with exactness, are not strong without great thickness. He had planted a great deal of young wood in walks. Fruit trees do not thrive; but having grown a few years, reach some barren stratum and wither.

We found Mr. Griffiths not at home; but the provisions were good. Mr. Griffiths came home the next day. He married a lady who has a house and estate at [ ], over against Anglesea, and near Caernarvon, where she is more delighted, as it seems, to reside than at Bryn o dol.

I read Lloyd's account of Mona, which he proves to be Anglesea.

In our way to Bryn o dol, we saw at Llanerk a Church built crosswise, very spacious and magnificent for this country. We could not see the Parson, and could get no intelligence about it.

[...]

We came to the house of Dr. Worthington, at Llanrhaiadr.

Our entertainment was poor, though the house was not bad. The situation is very pleasant, by the side of a small river, of which the bank rises high on the other side, shaded by gradual rows of trees. The gloom, the stream, and the silence, generate thoughtfulness. The town is old, and very mean, but has, I think, a market.

In this town, the Welsh translation of the Old Testament was made. The Welsh singing Psalms were written by Archdeacon Price. They are not considered as elegant, but as very literal, and accurate.

We came to Llanrhaiadr, through Oswestry; a town not very little, nor very mean. The church, which I saw only at a distance, seems to be an edifice much too good for the present state of the place.

We visited the Waterfal, which is very high, and in rainy weather very copious. There is a reservoir made to supply it. In its fall, it has perforated a rock. There is a room built for entertainment. There was some difficulty in climbing to a near view. Lord Lyttelton came near it, and turned back.

Samuel Johnson, A Diary of a Journey into North Wales, in the year 1774, 1816

Samuel Johnson (1709-1784) was the outstanding man of letters of eighteenth-century Britain. His legacy chiefly rests upon his 'Dictionary of the English Language' (1755) which was the first English dictionary to trace the etymology of each word and provide illustrative quotations. 'The Plays of William Shakespeare' pioneered the use of explanatory notes and intertextual analysis. By being the subject of James Boswell's (1740-1795) 'Life of Johnson' (1791) he inspired the creation of the school of biography that considered the entire person.

....
"But they have such a terrible way of *mending it*"
....

Mutual incomprehension can also arise at any turn, even in something as everyday as the way in which a road is maintained. This account was subject to 'Cymro's' attention (see Chapter 11).

The road from Malvern to Hereford was remarkably good; but from thence to Hay, and from Hay hither, it has been intolerably disagreeable. Not that it is in itself bad, but they have such a terrible way of *mending it.* Their custom is to throw down vast quantities of huge stones, as large as they come out of the quarry, the size of a man's head, and many of them four times as big. These are spread over the road in heaps, perhaps a mile distant from each other, covering a great many yards of it. You must either drive over them, or wait till the people, who are there with large hammers for the purpose, have broken them. This they only do into pieces the size of a pretty large flint. Though we had not these enormous masses to go over, which would have endangered our lives, yet our speed was retarded so much as to make me entirely lose my patience.

At the first heap we came to, the horse made a full stop, and tossing his head backward and forward, he turned his eye up towards us, as far as the construction of it would let him. Could he have spoken, I am sure he would have said, Am I not thine horse, and have I not carried thee in safety these many hundred miles? Why then hast thou brought me into these difficulties?

In the course of these last fifteen miles there have not been less than seven or eight of these heaps, each of which, when broken, and spread upon the road, extends a quarter of a mile in length. Over these stones it is impossible to drive faster than a foot pace. Yet notwithstanding this uncomfortable circumstance, it gave me the most pleasing sensation to hear two men, who were at work upon it, speak to each other in Welsh. You are sensible I do not know a word of the language.

I can account for my emotion only in this manner; that, hearing people converse together in the language of the country, convinced me I was fully arrived where I had so long wished to be.

**Mrs. Morgan, A tour to Milford Haven,
in the year 1791, 1795**

Mrs Mary Morgan (1749-1808) was a cousin to Elizabeth, Countess Winterton (1757-1841) and lived with her husband the Rev. Caeser Morgan D.D. in Ely. Caesar Morgan's first cousin Sir Henry Mathias lived at Little Milford House in Pembrokeshire. The book 'was printed by subscription; and the list is a very handsome one' according to the Monthly Review (October 1795) which notes that 'although this volume be not remarkable for elegance of style...it may be read with pleasure and advantage'.

....
"You may put up with a little extortion"
....

Several accounts consider the cost of goods in various towns and remark on the generally good value of what is on offer. Some always want more for less and Samuel Pratt bemoaned the effect his fellow travellers were having on prices in general. This earned a rebuke from 'Cymro'.

In the first place it is a settled usage, and custom, throughout the principality, for the trading part of the people to over-reach you in your little marketings, or bargains, with them; that is to say, they will ask all strangers of genteel appearance, about a third more than they would ask a native or countryman; but even allowing this, you will have almost all the necessities, and most of the luxuries of life, at least, by a third cheaper than, with very few exceptions in the cheapest parts of England: at first you may put up with a little extortion, which will diminish as you become residentiary. All places, as they get into reputation for any beauty or convenience, and are, therefore, the resorts of people that, since they can afford to travel, are supposed to be wealthy, grow dear, at first imperceptibly, till, in a few years, that commodity which you could procure for sixpence, is not to be obtained for a shilling, and so on in proportion. This is remarkably verified in Wales; ground, house-rent, and the necessaries of life, are so much raised in price since my first tour in this country, about twelve years ago, that were not the fact universally admitted, I should be afraid you would suspect me of profiting by the licence *expected* to be taken by travellers, were I to mention the comparative difference betwixt that time and the present, in both North and South Wales.

**Samuel Pratt, Gleanings through Wales,
Holland and Westphalia, 1795**

....
"Come shipmate, doff your jacket"
....

Other than considering coastal resorts or coracle fishers, the sea and sea fishing in particular have a surprisingly low profile in most accounts. This wonderfully over the top exception by Samuel Pratt earned him another rebuke from 'Cymro'.

I set off from a lone house, on a sandy heath, very properly called the barren island, about a mile on the Aberestdwith side of Aberavon, where I had passed a stormy night, rendered yet more troublous by there being every hour brought, to the Ferry-House, the dead bodies of fishermen, who had perished in a tempest, which a few nights before had wrecked a number of vessels on the coast of Wales. It was the season of the herring fishery, in progress of which there are many misfortunes of this sort, and of other kinds; for a bad season, or which is tantamount, bad luck, will ruin a whole family, sometimes a whole village the sole dependence of which are the herrings, the staple commodity of the inhabitants. At the time of my quitting the barren island the clouds made the faired promises, and a beautiful rainbow stretched its arch across the heavens to confirm them, but I had not gone a league, before all these fair promises were broken, and I was drenched to the skin, notwithstanding my horse did the best in his power, for both our sakes, to prevent it.

We took shelter at a most miserable looking hut, at the side of the heath, and accepted the protection it offered, with as entire good will, as if it had been an eastern palace. My horse was obliged to crawl into a kind of out-house, where a swine-driver and his pigs had the instant before taken refuge, and while I was reconciling my steed to this society, a Jew pedlar with his pack, and another traveller and his dog, crouded in. Necessity, as Shakspeare says, brings one acquainted with strange company: not that these are the words of that immortal Bard, and of course my memory has injured even the sentiment: but you, who have literally his works by heart, can do him justice.

A being, scarcely human in appearance, invited me to enter the hut. I enter'd. – Its inhabitants – How shall I describe them? Fancy something; which assembles the extremes of filth, penury, health and felicity – personify these amongst men, women, and children – give to each of them forms and features, which confer a sort of grace and beauty, on the household of the barber of Barmouth by comparison. Put all this filth, penury, health, and felicity into motion; and having formed your groupe, imagine that you see it unshod, unstockinged, uncapped, and nearly unpetticoated and unbreechcd. Young and old were busied in counting the finest and freshest herrings I ever saw, that instant brought in from the fishing-boat. The father of the family, to whom the boat belonged, declared he had never had so prosperous a voyage; and, though he was almost blown away, he would hazard twice as much danger for such another drag: look what a size they are of, and how they shine, my boys and girls – i'faith, they seem'd plaguily afraid of the hurricane, and came in shoals to the nets as if they took shelter in them – little thinking, poor fools, that this was a jump from the water to the fire; and now I talk of that, here put half a dozen of them into a pan, for I am deuced hungry, and mayhap this gentleman may be so too; and if so be that he is, he shall be as welcome to a fresh herring and a brown biscuit as myself. — What say you, my heart of oak? continued he, clapping me as familiarly on the shoulder as if I had been his messmate, and indeed treating me as hospitably as if I had been so, and we had both escaped from a wreck to his cabin. Perceiving my dripping situation, he said, "Come shipmate, doff your jacket, put on this rug, come to an anchor in that corner, warm your shivering timbers with a drop of this dear creature, which will make a dead fish speak like an orator – there – another swig – don't be afraid of it – one more – and now you will do while your rigging and canvas are drying.

All this time, mine host of the hovel stood in his sea-drench'd apparel, on my reminding him of which, he cried out smilingly, Ah ! you are a fresh-water sailor, I perceive, and would take a deal of seasoning, before you were good for any thing; but for me, all winds and weathers are alike to old Jack, while I can get good fish abroad, and good flesh at home; so fry away, Molly, for the wet has made me as hungry as a shark, and though I have drank like a whale, I shall now eat like a lion – and I hope you will do the same, messmate. By this time, mine hostess set before us our dish of herrings, which, with oatmeal cakes, potatoes, and buttermilk, furnished one of the heartiest dinners I ever ate; after which, the sailor made me partaker of a can of slip – sung a song, about the dangers, and hardships of the sea-faring life; and made me take notice, that he was the happy father of a cabin full of children, that I might see another was upon the stocks; and that if it pleased God to send him a dozen such pieces of good fortune every year, for a dozen seasons, he should be as able, as he was willing, to procure a snug birth for every one; and meantime, master, we will have another sip of grog to drink success to the herring fishery.

Our regale was interrupted by the sudden exclamations from without doors, of — "She's lost – she can't weather it – she must go to the bottom – there is not water enough for her to come in, and the wind blows like the devil in her teeth – she's sinking – the next sea will finish her." All the cottagers ran to the beach, which was within a few paces. I followed instinctively. The hurricane was again renewed, the seas ran mountain high, and a small coasting vessel was struggling with them. In a few minutes the strand was covered with spectators, but not idle ones. The whole of the villagers hurried to give assistance. Amongst the croud, I discovered both the pig driver, and the pedlar, whose situation, I had begun to relate to my kind hearted host: but the most assiduous, of the whole multitude, was a young woman, who, while the tears ran down her cheeks, was amidst the first to leap into a small boat, which had been anchored on the beach, and in which, the master of our cottage and three others, resolved to trust themselves, to offer such assistance as was in their power. The wind did not abate of its fury, but shifted a few points more in-shore; this, perhaps, in a vessel of greater burthen, might have been fatal; but was, in some sort, favourable to the little bark in distress. She had, by tacking, gained a station parallel to a part of the harbour, where she might run ashore, which she did, at length without much damage: and the only thing now to be apprehended, was the loss of the boat, that had gone out to her succour. The people on board the vessel, were almost instantly on land, and one of them being shewn the boat, and told, at the same time, that she went out to the relief of the crew, was amongst the most active to throw out a rope, and try to return the favour intended him in kind. The same circumstance, however, which brought in the vessel, presently befriended the boat, who venturing to set her sail, was, after a few desperate rolls, impelled over the billows, and driven as it were, headlong on shore: but not before the sailor, who had been handing out the rope, perceived the female in the boat, on which he threw himself on the ground, in the eagerness of catching her in his arms. You already feel they were lovers: they were more. The bands of matrimony had united them the week before. The very fishing boat, which was now driven on shore, was the mutual property of the two fathers, who had agreed to give up each his share, to their son and daughter, as the wedding portion: two of the men in the little skiff were the fathers: the profits of the herring season, were to be the childrens fortune. How thin are the bounds that separate the extremes of happiness, from the excesses of misery. The former, however, were now realized: the vessel brought in a good freight, the fathers were saved, and the children were happy. They all resided, and, were, indeed, natives of the village, but mine host, whose house was nearest to the place of landing, and had a heart sufficiently expanded to fill a palace with people that stood in need of hospitality, insisted, that as soon as the Little Sally and Jack, which, it seems, was the name of the fishing-boat, could be left for half an hour, they should pass it with him: this being agreed to, all hands went to work upon the Little Sally and Jack, and if I had not been apprehensive that my ignorance in what was to be done, would rather have confused than assisted, my poor aid should not have been with-held. Matters being put to rights, and less mischief done than might have been expected, the company set off for the hut of my generous host, who took a hand of each of the married lovers, walking between them, and told them, he hoped, that as they had so well escaped Davy's Locker this time, they would tumble in a hammock together these fifty years. A fresh supply of fish, was immediately ordered into the pan, my landlord, swearing a terrible oath that on this occasion, (for there was a strict friendship between him and the parties preserved) the old saying should be verified, as to their swimming thrice: accordingly, for their second ocean, it was determined that the bowl, which, some years before, had commemorated an escape from a shipwreck in his own fortunes, should now be filled to the brim, to celebrate the success of the Little Sally and Jack. I was pressed to stay and take my share, on pain of being deemed too proud to be happy, amongst poor people, and on observing, that my steed all this time was in a state, which reproached me for faring so sumptuously, he started up, declaring, that though he could not ride, he loved a horse next to a man, and that if mine would put up with a mess of bran instead of hay, of which he had none, and a draught of ale, instead of water, he should be as welcome as his own foul. I took him at his word, and staid to witness and join in the festivities, till there was just enough of the evening left to reach Aberestdwith.

Samuel Pratt, Gleanings through Wales,
Holland and Westphalia, 1795

"So bad is the workmanship of the shoemakers"

As well as being properly equipped, travellers needed to keep their kit in good repair.

We could not leave the inn so soon as we intended on account of our boots not being ready so bad is the workmanship of the shoemakers in Wales that the repairs of one day were destroyed by the exertions of the next, and it was a business almost as regular as eating our dinner when we arrived at the inn to send our boots to get mended. Here I hope we have had them secured effectually as we ordered them to be studded with nails according to the fashion of the country. Although on our arrival we scarcely gained admittance at the inn as pedestrians yet on our departure we had to pay the bill calculated for equestrians of the first order so much had our consequence been raised by the loquacity of our attendant in the kitchen.

**John Skinner, Ten Days'
Tour through the Isle of Anglesea, 1802**

John Skinner (1772-1839) started his career as a barrister before taking Holy Orders and was a vicar from 1800 to 1839 who devoted himself to excavating Bronze Age barrows and Roman sites as well as visiting Celtic sites. His 98 volume collection of manuscripts was left to the British Library on condition they they were not opened for 50 years. He prepared a manuscript from a 50 day tour of Wales in 1835 which included 750 illustrations. The manuscript covering his visit to Anglesey was published in 1908 as a supplement to Archaeologia Cambrensis.

"He happened to be very intelligent"

Guides were often needed, which was something of a problem in places where they were not readily available. It appears likely that Henry Wyndham was among those unlucky travellers who suffered because of this lack of choice.

A Welsh guide blunders through his rout, and lest his knowledge should be suspected, will make no enquiry about it, till he himself is really alarmed; and then he becomes more terrified, than those he pretends to conduct.

This was the precise situation of our Harlech attendant, for we could not persuade him to advance a single step before us, either over the sands or through the waters of the Traeth Bychan, which is an arm of the sea, of considerable breadth, even at the lowest ebb.

This was the fourth guide which we had engaged: the first was from Caerphyli to the Pont y Prîdd, for which we had no occasion, if we had taken the most agreeable road: he happened to be very intelligent.

I took another from St. David's to the Maen sigl, for which too there was no occasion, as the thing itself was not worth seeing. But, though the distance was not more than two miles from St. David's, yet the guide could not find the stone, till he had left me within 200 yards of it, and enquired at a distant cottage after it.

The third voluntarily offered to attend my companion from St. David's to Fisgard, and this last lost the right track in such a manner, that I, though alone, arrived at Fisgard half an hour before him, notwithstanding the Maen sigl led me three miles about.

H. P. Wyndham, A Gentleman's Tour through Monmouthshire and Wales in the Months of June and July, 1774, 1775

Henry Penruddocke Wyndham (1736-1819) was educated at Eton and Wadham College, Oxford, becoming a Fellow of the Royal Society in 1783. He became Mayor of Salisbury in 1770-71 and was the High Sheriff of Wiltshire for 1772. He was the Whig MP for Wiltshire from 1795 to 1812, but took little interest in parliamentary politics. The first edition of his 1774 tour through Wales was published anonymously in 1775 but after revisiting Wales in 1777 and publishing it as a 'Tour Through Monmouthshire and Wales' he admitted being the author of the first volume.

....

**"When an intercourse with other
countries becomes easy or common"**

....

Easier communications led to less isolation and an erosion of difference. The rewards of real exploration sometimes demanded a suitable degree of difficulty.

OUR expedition becomes daily more interesting. We have entered the wildest part of the Principality, where the native simple manners of the people yet maintain their ground. We must not, however, expect to find this originality of character long amongst even the inhabitants of the Merionethshire mountains; the turnpike-roads, those means of communication, and, I may add, of corruption also, are excellent throughout North-Wales, and render a visit to its wildest and most beautiful parts easy even to the post-chaise traveller. The gentlemen of the northern counties, desirous of facilitating an access to their country, have directed their attention to the formation of public highways, and overcome the obstacles which nature opposed to them, carrying their roads through rock and over mountain with an unbaffled perseverance and unyielding spirit that do them infinite credit. But though these accommodations of ease may be desirable to the *lazy* traveller, they will subtract much from the pleasure of the speculative one. To him, the lofty mountain, the deep valley, the thundering cataract, and the beetling precipice, are but secondary objects; for he is not so much in pursuit of *natural* curiosities, as of *moral singularities,* original manners, ancient customs, local traditions, and national prejudices, which gradually fade away and disappear, when an intercourse with other countries becomes easy or common. Much of these, however, are still to be found in the parts of Merionethshire, which we have travelled within these two days, particularly during our journey of to-day. The scenery and manners are perfectly Highlandish, and the national language so universal, that scarcely a cottager whom we meet was able to give us a single word of English.

**Richard Warner, A second walk through Wales in
August and September 1798, 1799**

....
"Grace's prejudices against the English were rather violent"
....

It was useful to be on good terms with those who rowed you across the open waters.

Several ferries ply on this trajectus; we fortunately took that of Garth-Point, about half a mile from Bangor, which afforded us a very curious and singular character. It is worked by an old woman, by name Grace Parry, but more commonly called, from the place of her abode, Gras-y-Garth; a short, thick, squat female, who, though upwards of sixty winters have passed over her head, is as strong as a horse, and as active as one of her own country goats. Her excellence in rowing and managing a boat is unrivalled through the coast, but cannot be wondered at, as she served an early apprenticeship to the business, under her father and mother, who lived at the same little cottage which she inhabits, and worked the same passage for the better part of the past century.

[…]

As we found Grace's prejudices against the English were rather violent, and not knowing to what length they might carry her, particularly when she was under the influence of *cwrrw da,* we thought it necessary, for the safety of future Saxon travellers, to reward her labours with double the sum she demanded. This unexpected generosity so gratified the old woman, that she swore most bitterly we were the *greatest gentlemen* she ever met with; she declared, she should always like the English for our sake, and insisted upon shaking hands with us individually at parting. We indulged her wish, but (whether she meant it as a token of her kindness, or a proof of her strength, I know not) gave us each such a serious *gripe* as almost dislocated our fingers.

Richard Warner, A second walk through Wales in
August and September 1798, 1799

"A secluded but civilized country"

Good fortune favoured those who enjoy good company.

It was late before we reached Corwen, which is an insignificant village, but rather romantically situated at the foot of the Berwyn mountains. As we approached the inn we perceived two or three horses in the yard munching their corn, and seemingly just arrived from a journey. Sounds of hearty glee and conviviality issued also from the house, and two or three of the *femmes de cabaret* were hurrying to and fro, busily engaged in preparing for the entertainment of guests. We were somewhat fearful, from these signs, that the apartments of the inn, which is, by no means, large, were occupied for the night; and as we had no great inclination to extend our peregrinations any further that evening, we beheld these busy preparations with no great complacency. To ascertain, however, how matters stood, we entered the house, and learnt that we might have two very good beds and a sitting-room to ourselves of we wished, but that a party of gentlemen were just going to supper, and, most probably, would have no objection to our joining them. Both my friend and I am naturally of a social disposition, and the latter proposal was, by far, the most congenial to us. I, therefore, wrote on a card – "Two gentlemen from England, ramblers through Wales, would be particularly gratified by being admitted into your society for the evening;" and the landlord, Mr. Clark, immediately carried the note to the party in the parlour –

Alone he went – alone he came not on :- a fine and hearty-looking young man accompanied him, and accosted us with much cordiality. "Gentlemen," he said, "my companions will be all very glad of your company. Had we known that you were in the inn, we should before this have petitioned you to add to the glee of our little party; but we had no idea that there were any English strangers at this time of year at Corwen. Come, let me introduce you to my companions." – He opened the door of an adjoining room, as he spoke, and ushered us into the presence of a most goodly company. Round the table in the middle of the apartment were arranged seven or eight gentlemen in the most merry humour imaginable. A quantity of fishing-tackle, deposited in various parts of the room, indicated the manner in which the party had been occupied during the day: and we have since learnt, that these convivial meetings are by no means infrequent at Corwen, as the Dee in the neighbourhood affords the angler excellent sport. The ceremony of introduction was soon over, and we sat down at the table, altogether unknowing and unknown. But we felt none of that awkward restraint, which a person usually experiences when he is conscious of having intruded upon the privacy of others; because we were convinced from the manner of all present, that we were heartily welcome, and that reserve would have been but a sorry return for so much free and warm-hearted suavity. Nay, we soon found that it was the chief delight of the Welshmen to render us all those little nameless civilities, which are so gratifying to a stranger, and which – more than the most pompous and elaborate courtesy – impress him with a favourable opinion of the kindness of his entertainers. There was a total absence of that frigid formality, which is always repulsive, and which, in most instances, indicates a lamentable narrowness of mind; but there was abundance of that genial and attentive harmony, which is often to be found amongst the inhabitants of a secluded but civilized country. Our repast was excellent. Some very delicious salmon and trout from the Dee, with some prime mutton from the mountains, and some of the best fowls I have ever tasted, – washed down with no stinted allowance of capital sherry, – was fare not to be slighted by two tired, and, we will add, hungry travellers. But it was the charming spirit of good humour and conviviality, which cast so radiant a lustre over the whole. Never did I spent a happier evening than which I passed so pleasantly at Corwen; and it was with no trifling regret that we bade adieu to these social Cambro-Britons, when they mounted their horses to return home. What part my friend and I played in the occurrences of that memorable evening, it becomes not me to relate; but I will record the flattering farewell of the young man, who first introduced us to the company – "Thank you, gentlemen!" he exclaimed, as he shook us warmly by the hand, "thank you for one of the pleasantest evenings I have ever spent."

Anon, An excursion through North Wales, 1822

4

INNS, OUT AND ABOUT: EATING, DRINKING AND SLEEPING

The influence of William Gilpin rhapsodising the Wye (Chapter 5) meant that within a few years, there was a thriving network of inns and boats ready to cater for the seekers of the sublime.

....
"and every other necessary Refreshment"
....

Each town boasted its collection of inns, wines and cold collations.

INNS AT ROSS.
The Swan, — by Mr. Medhurst
The Inn for the London and South Wales Mail Coach.
The King's Head,-by Mrs. Howells.
[At the above Inns Carriages are kept.]
The George and Excise Office, by Mr. Potter.
Parties, making the Excursion down the Wye, may be provided with Pleasure Boats, at each of the above Houses; — cold Collation, the best Wines, and every other necessary Refreshment for the Voyage.

INNS AT MONMOUTH.
The Beaufort Arms, — by Mr. Avery.
The King's Head, by Mrs. Edwards.
The Crown and Thistle, by Mr. Barlow.
[At the above Inns Carriages are also kept.]

Boats, — cold Collation, Wines, &c.

Provided for Parties, the same as at Ross.

The Angel, by Mr. Williams.

Charles Heath, The excursion down the
Wye from Ross to Monmouth, 1796

Charles Heath (1761-1861) was born in Kidderminster and moved to Monmouth in 1791, setting up a printing press in the town that year. He wrote a variety of books, principally concerned with Monmouthshire subjects. He was elected Mayor of Monmouth in 1819 and 1821 opposed the effective appropriation by the Duke of Beaufort's family of the Monmouth Boroughs seat for Parliament.

As Mr. Donovan makes clear, a pleasant stay, as today, does not make for a good tale. The dismal dinner, ghastly repast or dreadful night needs to be recalled in minute detail. Although, a well-spent evening may also merit a mention, especially when blessed with good company.

....
"This was a serious disappointment"
....

The assumption that there was always room at the inn was not a safe one.

So much time was spent upon the coast below Kenfig, that night was hastily closing upon us as we drew near Taybach, which place we entered rather weary. Certain as we were that it would be inconvenient, if not impracticable, to bestow a visit on the copper works before the following morning, we designed in the way thither to rest in the town for the night. The dirty appearance of the place, and its inhabitants, as we walked up the main street, however, in a moment banished every favourable expectation we had conceived of the reception to be met with here, and but for the irresistible impulse of curiosity, had probably shaken our first resolves. Passing the smelting works we enquired for the inn to which our companion for the afternoon had directed us at parting: we found it, but it was full. This was a serious disappointment, from the anxiety of which we were relieved by the welcome intelligence that we had passed by the *best* inn of the place. To this we resorted immediately, and found it full too! — Our mortification was increased because there was no other. The hour was late, the night dark, and our only alternative seemed to be, to set out immediately for Neath, which being seven miles farther, we could scarcely hope to reach before midnight. The landlord seemed anxious to administer his advice in this dilemma. Indeed, gentlemen, said he, you should not have expected lodgings in a place like this. It is only a small town of coal miners and smelters, and my house, the best and only one, for public accommodation, except that you just left, always crowded with captains of vessels, and their mates, whose business brings them to the copper works. At the village of Aberavon, another mile on the road, are several good inns at which you may be certainly accommodated.

**E. Donovan, Descriptive excursions through South
Wales and Monmouthshire, in the year 1804,
and the four preceding summers, 1805**

Edward Donovan (1768-1837) wrote, drew, engraved and coloured eight books on natural history, including three on insects in India, China and Oceania, running to 39 volumes in total. He was born in Cork and spent most of his life in London, occasionally making excursions across Britain. He died in 1837 leaving his family destitute after not being paid for his later works.

....

"For a legion of fleas attacked us at all points"

....

A bad night is not good for the temper, but it may prove to be instructive.

CAREW. "Cold and comfortless", we knocked at the inn door (for inn is the name of every alehouse in Wales); when, to put a finishing stroke to the troubles of this eventful day, we learned that they had neither beds for us nor stabling for our horses; but we had previously heard, that the village boasted two inns, and accordingly went to the other: a similar information, however, awaited us here; with the additional intelligence, that there was not a stable in the village, and only one spare bed, which was at the other alehouse; there was no alternative; we were constrained to turn our tired and hungry horses into a field, and go back to the first house.

Here our apartment served not only "for parlour and kitchen and hall," but likewise for bed-room: every thing was in unison, the discoloured state of the walls and furniture; the care-worn looks of our host and hostess; our scanty fare, consisting of hard barley bread and salt butter; with nauseating ale, that even our keen appetites rejected; all betokened poverty and wretchedness: while in the bed, which extended from one side of the room to the other, two children were sending forth the most discordant yells; the one suffering a violent toothache, and the other crying because its brother cried. After enduring this scene of purgatory upwards of an hour, we were shewn to our bed: it was a recess built in an adjoining room, and furnished with a bag of straw, which was kept in its place by a couple of boards crossing the niche. In the same room was another bed, where two more pledges of our landlord's tender passion continued to torment us. Vexed with accumulating plagues, we threw ourselves half undressed on the bed; but our evil destiny had yet more troubles in store;— the sheets were wringing wet; so that we had reason to expect that on the morrow we should be laid up with colds or fevers; but this apprehension was soon superseded; for a legion of fleas attacked us at all points with such persevering ferocity, that we were kept in motion the whole night; a number of rats also, by gamboling among our straw, while others were busy in grating a sally port through the partition, held us in the fidgets; and thus the danger of obstructed circulation was avoided. We had just left off cursing rustic accommodation, and the itch for travelling which had led us to these sufferings, when the door opened; no light appeared, but the sound of footsteps, softly treading, passed near us. Suspecting foul play, we instantly sprang up, and caught hold of a poor ragged girl, who acted as maid of the inn, and was going to sleep with the children in the other bed.

This kind of rural accommodation may appear very diverting in a narrative; but to those accustomed to better fare, it will be found a very serious evil. Indeed, from this specimen we afterwards made it a rule to finish our day's journey at a good town; in consequence of which salutary resolution, except in one or two instances, we were never without a comfortable lodging. This caution is very practicable in South Wales, as the most interesting part of the country is well furnished with accommodation.

J. T. Barber, A tour throughout South Wales and
Monmouthshire, 1803

....

"Such a Noise and Confusion had some Simile with that of *Babel*"

....

Visiting a spa was meant to be about restoring one's health. For the poorly prepared pioneer, finding a place to stay was every bit as challenging as staying in what one found..

Employing a Guide here, and at this Time, might be attended with these bad Consequences; they might have taken us wrong, and, as we were; but a few, robb'd and murder'd us, by the Assistance of an Acquaintance or two; add to this, they might have made such an Agreement even before our Faces, speaking a Language we did not understand, therefore we thought it more proper to enquire than to be guarded, tho' my Cousin continually begg'd to have a Guide. Another Reason was, that the *Welch* have an universal Opinion that the *English* Travellers ask the Road though they know it quite well, which Notion answered our End extremely well. After riding a Mile through dirty Lanes, which were exceeding dark, we came at *Llanbadern* to the River *Ithon* again, which here runs almost Northerly ; its Turnings and Windings are so many between the Villages of *Bridge-End* and *Llanbadern*, which, as I said is but one Mile, yet I'm creadily inform'd it runs upwards of six to gain that much Ground; from hence it passes on below the *Llandrindod Wells,* to a Village call'd *Dysart,* and empties itself into the *Wye,* about three Miles below that Village. In some Places, the Current is strong, deep, and large enough to bear Vessels of Burthen; but the Descent being so, great, the Navigation would be attended with great Difficulties on it, provided it were in a Country that could support such an Expence; one Day's Rain making it overflow its Banks. It is well stored with Fish, Chub, Trout, Samlets, Roach, Dace, and Gudgeons, being very plentiful, and with a good Bait may be catch'd as many Fish as you please. I never had more Diversion of that Sort than at this River; no one is molested, for 'tis too patient a Sport, for the Natives, and turns, to small advantage to the Lord of the Manor.

[...]

It happened that a Man (fortunately for us) was going to Bed, whom we persuaded to direct us to *Llandrindod,* which he told us was a Mile and a half; tho' he had some Difficulty to persuade his Wife to let him attend us. It is reasonable to suppose we were much rejoiced, and gave him Sixpence, which was no small Sum to him. He told us it was a difficult Road, and being without Stockings or Shoes, he mounted behind Mr. *Jacome,* and on our saying we intended for the publick House, and enquiring how full it was, he told us that the House was full of Company, and that we were but a Quarter of a Mile from it, but to *Llandrindod* it was above a Mile; and, continued he, if you cannot have Lodgings here, I can provide you some at a neighbouring House, with the Man who lived at this publick House last Year, (where perhaps our being might have been more satisfactory.)

However we rode into the Yard, and enquired if we could have Lodgings; we saw a great many Lights within, and the Company made no small Noise. Though we were so much fatigued, and promised an Answer immediately, yet we were favoured with waiting almost half an Hour, before we could be resolved; at last the Landlady told us we might alight, and have good Accommodation. This was no Time to be inquisitive; accordingly we alighted, dismiss'd our Guide, and, weary as we were, went into the House.

I shall be as exact as possible in describing every particular Thing, and relate every Occurrence, with as strict a Regard to Truth, as Minutes and Memory will enable me, without any Intention to expose the Actions of any one particularly; but as Truth will oblige me to do Justice to all, I shall proceed thus,

We were introduced into a little nasty Room, by as nasty an old Woman, and were almost suffocated with Smoke. This old Creature got us a little Shrub; but a House in such Confusion, my Eyes never beheld: One cry'd, Cot rot you, why don't you fill the Mug; another, the Devil is in the Woman, do you hear the Shentleman call; one ran here, another there; such a Noise and Confusion had some Simile with that of *Babel*. Supper being just serv'd in, we chose to have something where we sat: We procured some Mutton Chops, though the greatest Part of them was Skin: My Cousin bless'd herself, declaring she never saw any thing like it; but, Circumstances considered, we were better than on a barren Mountain. While we were at Supper, we were interrupted by a Couple of lusty Girls, hauling a clumsy looking Fellow through our Room. We thought this something odd, and could scarce account for it, but, imagining they were Servants, and as I shall have frequent Occasion to speak of the whole Company more particularly, I shall say no more on that Head now. We finished a very bad Supper; the Cheese was indifferent, the Bread scarce half baked which, notwithstanding, these two Articles made the largest Share of our Supper; the Butter bad; Plates, Knives and Forks, enough to surfeit any ordinary Stomach; the Ale was good; the Wine indifferent; the Cyder the same. Being much tired, (after drinking a Glass or two) we desired to be shewn to our Rooms, (having given the necessary Order about our Horses, Clothes, &c.) but were told, my Cousin could not lie in the Room they intended; the Reason given to the contrary was, that she must have went thro' those modest young Ladies Room I have mentioned before. These, together with an old lecherous Fellow, which I shall describe, form'd so strong a Party, that notwithstanding we insisted on it, we were obliged to submit. Indeed had it been a whole Bed, Mr. *Jacome* and myself were resolv'd to have possess'd it; but a single Woman being in it before, and my Cousin being of a condescending Temper, we dropp'd the Affair, tho' not without some Reluctancy. She lay in a Garret, because it had a Lock on the Door, which ours had not. Our Room was just large enough for a Bed, and to go on one Side, and at the Bottom of the same: The Bed was without Curtains; we had a Coverlet, Blanket, and two Sheets, tho' they were wore almost to Tinder, and prodigious large Holes in them. Indeed my Cousin's Room was longer, but much colder. We resented this Usage, so that both our Landladies cry'd very much, that they were not able to prevent or remedy this Treatment: However we went to Bed, and being much tired, and not very curious, we slept soundly, notwithstanding the Fleas, (which were the most and largest I have seen) and some Fears of the Country Distemper.

'A Countryman', A Journey to Llandrindod Wells in Radnorshire, with a particular description of those wells, the places adjacent, the humours of the company there, &c., 1746

. . . .

"I found only one bed in the place that was not wretchedly bad"

. . . .

As an area opened to travellers, new inns and hotels were built, to the relief of the hard-bitten habitué of the old.

The *inn*, or rather public house, that I found at Beddgelert in both my journies, was one of the worst and most uncomfortable houses, in which necessity ever compelled me to take up my abode. In my first journey I found only one bed in the place that was not wretchedly bad. The room in which I slept for three nights (for the other two bed-rooms were occupied), was at the back of the house, and partly over the kitchen. The floor, the ceiling, and the boarded partition, were all so full of large holes, as to seem only an apology for separation from the rest of the house. I was so intolerably pestered by myriads of fleas, bred and harboured among the filth accumulated in every part, that had I not every night been fairly wearied out with my rambles during the day, it would have been altogether impossible for me to have taken any rest. After I had been here one night, I complained to the servant of the inexcusable negligence that had suffered these animals to become so numerous, as now to defy all attempts at their destruction: "Lord, sir, (said she,) if we were to kill one of them, ten would come to its burying." — Nothing, in this state of the house, could possibly have induced a traveller to remain here through the night, but the exquisite scenery around the place. In my second journey I found several very material improvements, in consequence of Mr. Jones of Bryntirion having begun to build a comfortable house for the reception of travellers, on the other side of the river, at a few hundred yards distance. This is now opened, and, I am told, affords excellent accommodations. It is called the *Beddgelert Hotel*. The sign over the door is of a goat clambering among the mountains of Snowdon, and, underneath it, is the motto *"Patria mea petra."* — The *guide* from Beddgelert to the mountains is William Lloyd, the village schoolmaster, whose boys, during the summer, are always engaged in rustic employments. He thus explains his summer occupations in a bill wafered on the inn door: "William Lloyd, conductor to Snowdon, Moel Hebog, Dinas Emrys, Llanberis pass, the lakes, waterfalls, &c. &c. Collector of crystals and fossils, and all natural curiosities in these regions. Dealer in superfine woollen hose, socks, gloves, &c."

William Bingley, North Wales; including its antiquities, customs, and some sketches of its natural history; delineated from two excursions through all the interesting parts of that country, during the Summers of 1798 and 1801, 1804

....

"The pleasure of social harmony"

....

An evening at the inn could have unforeseen consequences.

At Aberavon we succeeded better. We obtained admittance into what is esteemed the principal house of public entertainment in the village, with a promise of excellent beds for the night. And further still, we could perceive by the conduct of mine host of the "globe inn," that he considered us, his new visitors, of sufficient consequence to engross his sole attention. While his fair partner was assiduously engaged in providing our frugal repast for supper, he did us the honour to stand in waiting, fixing himself for this purpose against the wall, with his arms folded across, his eyes stedfastly fixed upon us, his features composed, and his whole body so perfectly motionless that he literally personated the statue of silence. — In this posture he remained so long that we began at last to suspect he intended waiting till we retired to rest. And perhaps we were not mistaken. But his presence becoming more and more necessary in the adjoining room, to settle some disturbances that prevailed there, he ventured occasionally towards the end of the evening to peep out at the door for that purpose. We were at last anxious to know the cause of it. — "Nothing material," said the landlord in answer to our enquiry, and resumed his former station. But the busy imp of discoid began at length to reign triumphant, the clamour was violent, the door of our apartment was broke open in a trice, and before we could be apprized of danger, we were huddled pell-mell into the vortex of men, women, and furniture that laid promiscuously sprawling upon the floor.

The occasion of this ridiculous affair we learnt afterwards. It appeared that the blacksmith of the village, and a few of his pot companions, had assembled in the evening to enjoy the pleasure of social harmony over their mugs of *Cwrrw*, when some unlucky word escaped from one of the party. Blows ensued, and in a moment the mugs, the candlesticks, and stools, flew about the room with the velocity of lightning. At the instigation of the landlord, peace was once more restored among the combatants, and the wonted hilarity prevailed again, when the uproar suddenly recommencing, the delinquent was hurled by main force into the street; but he was a powerful man, and his struggles were attended with all the disorder in which we had been involved. — Such are too commonly the effects of indulging in this favourite beverage among the lower orders of society in Wales, as well as the contaminated regions of the metropolis. — The sequel was more remarkable. The poor blacksmith enraged, and burning with fury for the insult, after many a strenuous effort to burst through the barricadoed door-way, but in vain, gave vent to his fury in poetic ire, in a style so truly characteristic of an ancient Briton, as could not fail to afford us some diversion. For one whole hour at least, at midnight, he loitered at the door, modulating his hoarse throat to the tunes of certain Welsh airs, to which he adapted the words, extempore, for the occasion, in his native tongue; reflecting on the disgraceful conduct he had just experienced, and soliciting to be re-admitted, or vowing vengeance against his unfeeling comrades, if they persisted to refuse him entrance.

E. Donovan, Descriptive Excursions through South Wales and Monmouthshire in the year 1804, and the four preceding summers, 1805

"Harpers sit in the hall, and play a variety of national airs"

By the 1830s, travel in North Wales had seen a well developed network of inns emerge, with harpers laid on for the authentic touch. Local beers and perries were also to be welcomed.

The inns are generally clean and comfortable; and some of them, such as the Penrhyn Arms at Bangor, and the inn at Capel Curig, splendid. In most of the principal inns throughput Wales, harpers sit in the hall, and play a variety of national airs, for the entertainment of the visitors. Many of them also act as guides to the vicinity.

The waiters are usually females: "a circumstance," says Mr. Warner," which immediately puts the traveller in a good humour with all that he meets with at a Welsh inn. Exclusive of the pleasure one naturally feels from the presence of female beauty, there is also a minute attention and kindness in the manners of women which give weight to the most trivial offices they perform for one, and add the force of an obligation even to a common act of servitude."

Wales has been famous, from time immemorial, for the excellence of its ale, here called *cwrw*. It is made from barley, but the grain is dried in a peculiar way, which gives it rather a smoky taste. The Llangollen ale is perhaps the most celebrated. The peasantry in some parts of Wales gather the berries of the mountain-ash,

and brew from them a liquor which they call *diod grigfol*.
Its flavour bears some resemblance to that of perry.

Samuel Leigh, Leigh's Guide to Wales &
Monmouthshire, 1831

"Their hospitality, and indeed kindness, towards strangers"

*Even the most hard-headed visitor could be taken aback by the
kindness shown to strangers in distress.*

The lower class here [Barmouth], as in many other parts
of Wales, indiscriminately dress and undress on the
sands, and pay very little distinction to their sex.

The board and lodging is regulated on the same
excellent plan here as at Tenby, with very little difference
in respect to the expence. The town itself is very dirty,
and so irregularly built, on the declivity of a rock, that
the windows of one house not uncommonly look down
on the neighbouring chimney. We could not avoid
observing the number of pigs, which are esteemed in
this part of the country far superior to any in England,
lying in every corner of the street; and these pigs, I
rather imagine, consider themselves, during the night,
inmates of the peasant's cottage: yet these hardships, if
they may be distinguished by that name, the inhabitants
of the hovel suffer without complaint, and deem
themselves perfectly happy as long as they possess a
pile of turf to keep off the inclemency of the winter's
blast, a small strip of ground, well stocked with
potatoes, some poultry, and a fat pig; though one hovel
protects them all. Though to appearance, their situation
is most miserable, yet it has no effect on their tempers
and dispositions; their hospitality, and indeed kindness,

towards strangers in distress, is an interesting trait in their character: to instance this, I am induced to mention an anecdote, which took place at Hubberstone, not long ago. A lady anxiously waiting the arrival of her husband, from Ireland, at the miserable village of Hubberstone, soon interested even the meaner inhabitants of the place in her behalf; who, willing to render her situation as comfortable as possible, seemed to vie with each other in producing the most delicious fruits, and the choicest garlands of flowers, to present them to the unhappy consort; and not content alone with this, she was generally greeted in the streets, with the phrase, "There goes poor Mrs. L-." The lady, at last, impatient for the arrival of her husband, determined to sail for Ireland. The faithfulness of the little group that accompanied her to the shore, can better be imagined than described; the last farewell, with tears of artless innocence, and the beseeching that Providence "who governs the waves, and stills the raging of the sea," to grant her a prosperous voyage; all this seemed to come so thoroughly from the bottom of their hearts, that we cannot avoid feeling ourselves interested in their behalf.

'The Author' (Allen Cliff), The Cambrian Director, 1800

"We accidentally met with a well-informed man"

People encountered in the more outlying areas were not supposed to be literate.

At the public-house, we accidentally met with a well-informed man, who minutely delineated every part of the castle and, beginning with the founder, in the true characteristic style of a Welchman, ran through his pedigree several generations: this, however, did not interest us, cursory pedestrians; and with little persuasion we soon induced him to write down, in as concise a manner as possible, any information he was acquainted with respecting the castle: "The founder of Harlech Castle, A.D. 552, was Maclegwynn; Gwynead made Caer Dugoll (Shrewsbury;) Caer Gyffin (Aber Conway;) Caer Gollwyn (Harleck;) supposed to be buried in Cirester, and reigned thirty-four years." Whether this information is correct, I will not take upon me to assert; but meeting with a Welchman, in this part of the country, capable of writing, rather surprised us, and induced me to transcribe this short paragraph.

'The Author' (Allen Cliff), The Cambrian Director, 1800

"Where kindness and humanity were so predominant"

Sometimes, it surprised visitors to alight at country houses in the more remote places.

We alighted, wet and numbed with cold, and found, as they told us, a charming fire, in a very spacious old-fashioned parlour. The damsels ran about with all the chearfulness and alacrity imaginable to dry our cloaths, and get us some refreshment. We supped upon a very large ham, which was rather salt, and not very delicate. Neither did I much relish the bread and butter. But it was the best they had; and it would be the height of ingratitude to find fault with any thing, where kindness and humanity were so predominant. I was so fatigued last night, that I could scarcely speak, to express my satisfaction at their treatment of us. But this morning I did not omit to admire a fire-screen in my bed-room, that was composed of feathers the good girls had put together with great pains.

The walls were ornamented with some very old portraits. The communicative girl told me they were likenesses of the former possessors of the house, which in days of yore belonged to a great and rich Welsh family. This was probably fact, and that they lived in solitary dignity, hemmed in on all sides by mountains and precipices, having a little principality within their own jurisdiction, and lording it over the poor simple peasants, their humble tenants and neighbours. This mode of living in voluntary seclusion from the society of their equals, was by no means peculiar to Wales, but prevailed over every part of this island.

**Mrs. Morgan, A tour to Milford Haven,
in the year 1791, 1795**

....

"Speedily regaled with a sumptuous supper"

....

The good inn catered for all tastes, satisfying the gourmand as well as the ascetic.

This very *agreeable* amusement continued till half past nine o'clock, when we were blessed with the sight of a rush-light glimmering through the window of the Angel inn, which we entered about two hours ago. Our first appearance was made in the kitchen, where a scene was exhibited that would have afforded an admirable subject for the pencil of Hogarth. A large table covered with rounds of beef, loins of pork, fragments of geese, &c. &c. appeared at one end, round which was seated a motley groupe of noisy Welsh rustics, who voraciously devoured the good things before them. Opposite to these were two Scotch pedlars, eating their frugal repast in silence, an oaten cake, and rock-like cheese, and diluting it with "acid tiff;" their eyes rivetted in wistful gaze, on the substantial fare which smoked on the adjoining table. The middle of the kitchen was occupied by a number of sportsmen just returned from growse-shooting on the mountains, cleaning their guns, and preparing them for the morrow's amusement. In the back ground flamed an enormous fire, where a counterpart of dame Leonarda was preparing another set of joints, for a second party of sportsmen who were just arrived. Tired pointers and snoring spaniels were scattered over the floor, and completed the picture. Notwithstanding the disadvantageous figure we made, (for to confess the truth we were marvellously foul) and the numerous guests who called on the mistress of the house in all directions, we met with an attention and civility from Mrs. Evans (the hostess) that will always claim our grateful remembrance. We were shewn into a snug little room, and speedily regaled with a sumptuous supper. To check, however, in some measure, the pleasure which arose from the comparison of our present situation with what we had experienced in the last six miles of our walk, we were given to understand, that only one of us could be accommodated with a bed in the house, and that the other must sleep at a cottage a quarter of a mile distant from it. Sad news this, to tired travellers, on a stormy night! Something, notwithstanding, was to be done, and one of us must brave the pelting of a pitiless storm that rattled against the casements. — *Jacta sit alea.* — We determined to toss up for the chamber at the Lion, and fortune has just declared in favour of C-.

I am not apt to grieve at the success of another, but I confess I never felt more inclined to quarrel with the fickle goddess for her decision, than on the present occasion, when a long walk through execrable roads has almost deprived me of the faculty of loco-motion.

Richard Warner, A walk through
Wales in August 1797, 1798

··
"For all the luxury of Lucullus"
··

A good walk deserved a good dinner.

Having ordered dinner and secured beds at the village inn, the Crossed-Foxes, we passed the bridge I have described, in order to ascend the mountain Camlin, and contemplate the effect of the setting sun on the contiguous hills. It was a most laborious effort, but more than repaid by the glorious scene which opened on our reaching the summit. The Arran, a mountain of peculiar form, and three thousand feet in height, rose two or three miles to the northward of us; its sugar-loaf head resplendently illuminated, while the *cwms* and precipices of the adjoining mountains, in the shade, were rendered still more dark and horrible by this brilliant contrast. Behind, the whole vale of Dovey, which we had just traversed, was spread under our eye, with its river, villages, and seats, lighted up by the rich rays of a retiring sun. On each hand was "a tempestuous sea of mountains," of different heights and distances, exhibiting a variety of beautiful tints, lessening in vividness and splendour by imperceptible graduations, till they were lost in distance, and melted with the sky.

Our host, Mr. David Lloyd, who holds a considerable farm in the neighbourhood, (a practice with all the Welsh publicans, who, by these means, are in general more opulent and respectable than the English landlords) had provided for us a most substantial meal of mutton-chops, bacon, and plumb-pye, beans, and peas, at which his daughters, two girls of pleasing persons, formed manners, and good education, did us the honour of attending. With these circumstances, and a mountain appetite to-boot, we felt ourselves as great as kings; and agreed *nem. con.* that we would not relinquish the pastoral scenery of Mallwyd, our excellent meal, and pretty attendants, for all the luxury of Lucullus, and the costly delicacies of his Apollo's chamber.

Richard Warner, A second walk through Wales in August and September 1798, 1799

"This is the rustic mode"

An inn needed its beer.

Shaping our course towards the Towy, we observed a number of females employed upon the margin of a meandering stream; and found, to our no small surprize, they were occupied in manufacturing the best and boasted liquor of the country, *cwrw*. As we had often refreshed our way-worn spirits, after many a toilsome day, with this incomparable beverage, it was natural to make inquiries into the process of making it. To you, who have witnessed the complicated and expensive apparatus of an English brewery, with furnaces, pumps, coolers, vats, &c. &c. the description of a Welsh brewery will appear singular, if not amusing. These persons were here with their tubs and barrels, placed on the banks of the stream: as it is a maxim with them to bring their utensils to the water, rather than the water to the utensils. Provided with wide and flat brazen pans, and an iron tripod, they kindle a fire with wood, over which they place the tripod, with the pan upon it; here they boil their water, rinse their vessels, mesh, boil their wort, and tun their beer, adding yest and letting it ferment in the casks, filling up as the ferment comes over. They place the casks for this purpose with a little inclination of the bung-hole towards the left hand; by this method the fermenting liquor, which has a rotatory motion, discharges its feculence with greater facility.

This is the rustic mode. In large towns they have utensils, as in England; but they ferment the worts in tubs, till a fine head arises, when they mix up both the body of the wort and the head, and tun it into casks, still leaving the bung aperture open for further fermentation; they then add wheat meal and hops, and stop it up for use. By this excellent method they produce a transparent salubrious liquor, fit for drinking in the course of a few weeks. Nor is it wonderful they should excel in the production of a liquor, which for ages has been the favourite beverage of the country. The ancient Britons ordinarily drank water or milk; but at their feasts, and on other extraordinary occasions, metheglin, or a liquor they denominated curmi, now degenerated into cwrw, and by the English ale. They sometimes incorporate with it spice and honey, forming a liquor they term bragawd.

John Evans, Letters written during a tour through South Wales, in the year 1803, and at other times, 1804

John Evans (1768-c1812) was the son of Benjamin Evans, a clergyman in Lydney Gloucestershire. He went to Jesus College Oxford in 1789-92, which at the time predominantly taught Welsh undergraduates. After being a schoolmaster, he took Holy Orders and wrote four books about Wales, mainly using secondary sources. His account of coal mining in Pembrokeshire written in 1804 is a rehash of George Owen's description from 1603. He died before the publication of his final book in the 'The Beauties of England and Wales' series (1815); 'South Wales' Vol. 18.

....

"The domestic concerns of the peasantry"

....

The statistical traveller will always take care to enquire as to the local people's lot and to compare what is consumed in their homes and at their inns.

The peasantry upon this coast find some employment in the increasing demand for limestone, of which there is abundance in this neighbourhood, since the value of this useful manure has become more generally known in the interior of the country. A number of workmen are employed about the rocks in the various process of boring, blasting, and quarrying the stone, after which it is conveyed away by water in that state; or burnt upon the spot, and thus prepared for use. In either case the value of the stone is estimated in the *rough*, and three shillings in the pound, or about one seventh of the net produce is paid to the proprietor of the land for it. The labourers receive from twelve, to fourteen, or fifteen pence per day, a sum not very adequate to the ordinary purposes of life, even in an oeconomical country, and a very humble station. Curiosity prompted us to make various enquiries into the domestic concerns of the peasantry about this spot, with the view of ascertaining the mode of life which those poor people are compelled through necessity to pursue. The common food of the cottager appears to be potatoes, for the conveniency of rearing which, a scanty patch or strip of land is considered as a necessary appendage to every little habitation. Oaten cake, and cheese of their own making, are likewise among the principal articles of their provisions. They have eggs in some plenty, because they can keep chickens at a small expence, but the temptation to increase the brood, or to dispose of them at a ready money market in the contiguous towns, prevails too strongly to permit them to consume many in their own families. Salted herrings are almost the only fish they eat, for although they live close to the sea, they seldom take the trouble to procure it, and yet they are remarkably partial to cockles, which they dig out of the sands with much more assiduity than would be requisite with the net to take fish in plenty a few score paces further: Meat is indeed a luxury which they seldom taste, except now and then, when they are able to purchase a small joint of mutton with the produce of their eggs and poultry. If at the expiration of a year spent in industry, they are fortunate enough to have reared a "*bacon*," or two, fit for killing at Christmas, that they may have pork for dinner, and the remainder salted for future occasions, it must be considered as no small proof of their oeconomy. Strange as it must appear in this abstemious course of life, sobriety is not one of the most prevailing virtues among this people. It were idle and absurd to talk about the store of ale in the cellars of the cottager; their most common beverage is buttermilk, and sometimes only water. But the truth is, there are many petty ale houses about the country, where the men of this description will too frequently indulge in stronger liquors, to the injury of their industrious wives and children. The heavy, viscid, intoxicating *Cwrw dha*, a sort of ale peculiar to the Principality, they are passionately fond of; and when the opportunity offers, will drink of it to excess. The average price of this liquor is six pence the jug, denominated a quart, but really containing rather less than a pint and a half of the Winchester standard, so that on those occasions, they not unfrequently spend more money in a few hours, than the penurious savings from a week's labour can conveniently reimburse.

E. Donovan, Descriptive Excursions through South Wales and Monmouthshire in the year 1804, and the four preceding summers, 1805

5

THE SUBLIME, ROMANTIC AND PICTURESQUE

It is reasonable to say that there were two aesthetic movements amongst visitors to Wales in the Eighteenth Century. In North Wales, the Romantics disdained to regard mountains as bleak wastes, recasting them as places of awesome grandeur. In South Wales, Gilpin inspired a generation or two to seek and classify the sublime. There is a fair degree of cross-over between the two.

....
"There are orders of architecture in mountains, as well as in palaces"
....

For Gilpin, the vales were the crowning glory of Wales.

If the Welsh counties, distinguished for so much beauty of scenery of various kinds, are remarkable for pre-eminence in any mode, I think it is in their *vales*. Their lakes are infinitely exceeded, both in grandeur and beauty, by those of Cumberland, Westmoreland, and Scotland. Nor are their mountains as far as I have observed, of such picturesque form, as many I have seen in those countries. They are often of a heavy lumpish kind: for there are orders of architecture in mountains, as well as in palaces. Their rivers I allow are often very picturesque; and so are their sea-coast views. But their *vales* and *vallies*, I think, exceed those of any country I ever saw.

William Gilpin, Observations on the River Wye, and several parts of South Wales, &. Relative chiefly to picturesque beauty; made in the summer of the year 1770, 1782

William Gilpin (1724-1804) was born in Carlisle, Cumberland where he fell in love with the scenery of the Lake District. After attending Queen's College, Oxford, where he wrote a book about Stowe's landscape, he became a curate. He was subsequently appointed a master and then headmaster at Cheam School, using the long holidays to visit parts of Britain as he developed his theories of the picturesque. In 1777, he became the Vicar of Boldre in the New Forest. This gave him the time needed to write up his manuscripts. In all, he wrote eleven books on the picturesque, five biographies and seven theological tomes.

Gilpin is an engaging example of the English eccentric happily employed on a journey of instruction. Utterly harmless, suffused by a desire to enlighten people towards a correct appreciation of the picturesque, he probably had no idea of how unintentionally hilarious his accounts could be. He was mercilessly satirised by William Combe in his poem 'The Tour of Dr Syntax in Search of the Picturesque', published with Thomas Rowlandson's droll cartoons in three parts for The Poetical Magazine in 1809-1811 and as a book in 1812. In the poem, Dr Syntax never specifically makes it across the Wye, but Rowlandson's cartoons depict an Englishman hopelessly lost at home and abroad. Jane Austen was a gentler critic in Northanger Abbey and Pride and Prejudice.

....
"And filled my mind with religious awe"
....

George Lyttleton wrote one of the earliest Romantic tourist accounts of Wales, containing a notable description of Mount Snowdon's sublimity.

Nothing remarkable occurred in our ride, until we came to Festiniog, a village in Merionethshire, the vale before which is the most perfectly beautiful of all we had seen. From the height of this village you have a view of the sea. The hills are green and well shaded with wood. There is a lovely rivulet which winds through the bottom; on each side are meadows, and above are corn-fields along the sides of the hills; at each end are high mountains which seemed placed there to guard this charming retreat against any invasions. With the woman one loves, with the friend of one's heart, and a good study of books, one might pass an age there, and think it a day. When we had skirted this *happy vale* an hour or two, we came to a narrow branch of the sea, which is dry at low water. As we passed over the sands, we were surprised to see all the cattle prefer that barren place to the meadows. The guide said it was to avoid a fly which in the heat of the day came out of the woods, and infested them in the vallies.

The view of the said sands is terrible, as they are hemmed in on each side with very high hills, but broken into a thousand irregular shapes. At one end is the ocean, at the other the formidable mountains of Snowdon, black and naked rocks, which seemed to be piled one above the other; the summits of some of them are covered with clouds, and. cannot be ascended. The grandeur of the ocean, corresponding with that of the mountain, formed a majestic and solemn scene; ideas of immensity swelled and exalted our minds at the sight: all lesser objects appeared mean and trifling, so that we could hardly do justice to the ruins of an old castle, situated upon the top of a conical hill, the foot of which is washed by the sea, and which has every feature that can give a romantic appearance. The morning being fair, we ventured to climb up to the top of a mountain, not, indeed, so high as Snowdon, which is here called Moel Guidon, i.e. the nest of the eagle; but one degree lower than that called Moel Happock, the nest of the hawk, from whence we saw a phenomenon new to our eyes, but common in Wales; on the one side was midnight, on the other bright day: the whole extent of the mountain of Snowdon on our left, was wrapt in clouds from top to bottom: on the right the sun shone most gloriously over the sea coast of Caernarvon. The hill we stood upon was perfectly clear, the way we came up a pretty easy ascent; but before us was a precipice of many hundred yards, and below a vale, which, though not cultivated, has much savage beauty the sides were steep, and fringed with low wood. There were two little lakes, or rather large pools, that stood in the bottom, from which issued a rivulet that serpentined in view for two or three miles, and was a pleasing relief to the eyes; but the mountains of Snowdon, covered with darkness and thick clouds, called to my memory the fall of Mount Sinai, with the laws delivered from it, and filled my mind with religious awe.

George Lyttelton, Account of
a Journey into Wales, 1756, 1774

George Lyttelton (1709-1773) was the son of the 4th Baronet Lyttelton and he was in turn created first Baron, Lord Lyttelton. After Eton and Christ Church, he became MP for Okehampton for 21 years from 1735, declining the 'Rotten Borough' seat of Old Sarum in 1741. After serving the Prince of Wales in 1737 and being Commissioner of the Treasury from 1744, he was appointed Chancellor of the Exchequer in 1755. He was a patron of the arts, supporting Henry Fielding, Alexander Pope and James Thomson amongst others.

"A *speck* of white is often beautiful"

Gilpin's greatest concern was that matters were in order. Here he berates the injudicious use of white paint.

In general, the Welsh gentlemen in these parts, seem fond of whitening their houses, which gives them a disagreeable glare. A *speck* of white is often beautiful; but white, in *profusion*, is, of all tints, the most inharmonious. A white seat, at the corner of a wood, or a few white cattle grazing in a meadow, inliven a scene perhaps more, than if the seat, or the cattle, had been of any other colour. They have meaning, and effect. But a front, and two staring wings;, an extent of rails; a huge, Chinese bridge; the tower of a Church; and a variety of other large objects, which we often see daubed over with white, make a disagreeable appearance; and unite ill with the general simplicity of nature's colouring.

William Gilpin, Observations on the River Wye, and several parts of South Wales, &. Relative chiefly to picturesque beauty; made in the summer of the year 1770, 1782

"And disgrace the noble object, you wish to adorn"

Likewise, plants were meant to have their place, so that any flora added to a scene was laid out in a suitably informal manner.

It is a pity, the ingenious embellisher of these scenes could not have been satisfied with the grand beauties of nature, which he commanded. The shrubberies he has introduced in this part of his improvements, I fear, will rather be esteemed paltry. As the embellishments of a house; or as the ornament of little scenes, which have nothing better to recommend them, a few flowering shrubs artfully composed may have their elegance and beauty: but in scenes, like this, they are only splendid patches, which injure the grandeur, and simplicity of the whole.

It is not the shrub, which offends: it is the *formal introduction* of it. Wild underwood may be an appendage of the grandest scene: It is a beautiful appendage. A bed of violets, or lilies may enamel the ground with propriety at the root of an oak: but if you introduce them artificially in a border, you introduce a trifling formality; and disgrace the noble object, you wish to adorn.

**William Gilpin, Observations on the River Wye, and
several parts of South Wales, &. Relative chiefly to
picturesque beauty; made in the summer of the year
1770, 1782**

....

"A very inchanting piece of ruin"

....

Gilpin's description and evaluation of the Wye near Tintern Abbey deserves to be reproduced at length.

After we had passed a few of these scenes, the hills gradually descend into Monmouth; which lies too low to make any appearance from the water: but on landing, we found it a pleasant town, and neatly built. The town-house, and church, are both handsome.

The transmutations of time are often ludicrous. Monmouth-castle was formerly the palace of a king; and birth-place of a mighty prince: it is now converted into a yard for fatting ducks.

The sun had set before we arrived at Monmouth. Here we met our chaise: but, on enquiry, finding a voyage more likely to produce amusement, than a journey, we made a new agreement with our bargemen; and embarked again, the next morning.

As we left Monmouth, the banks on the left, were, at first, low; but on both sides they soon grew steep, and woody; varying their shapes, as they had done the day before. The most beautiful of these scenes is in the neighbourhood of St. Breval's castle; where the vast, woody declivities, on each hand, are uncommonly magnificent. The castle is at too great a distance to make any object in the view.

The weather was now serene: the sun shone; and we saw enough of the effect of light, in the exhibitions of this day, to regret the want of it the day before.

During the whole course of our voyage from Ross, we had scarcely seen one corn-field. The banks of the Wye consist, almost entirely either of wood, or of pasturage; which I mention as a circumstance of peculiar value in landscape. Furrowed-lands and waving corn, however charming in pastoral poetry, are ill-accommodated to painting. The painter never desires the hand of art to touch his grounds. — But if art *must* stray among them — if it *must* mark out the limits of property, and turn them to the uses of agriculture, he wishes, that these limits may, as much as possible, be concealed; and that the lands they circumscribe, may approach, as nearly as may be, to nature — that is, that they may be pasturage. Pasturage not only presents an agreeable surface:; but the cattle, which graze it, add great variety, and animation to the scene.

The meadows, below Monmouth, which ran shelving from the hills to the water-side, were particularly beautiful, and well-inhabited. Flocks of sheep were every where hanging on their green steeps; and herds of cattle occupying the lower grounds. We often sailed past groups of them laving their sides in the water: or retiring from the heat under sheltered banks.

In this part of the river also, which now begins to widen, we were often entertained with light vessels gliding past us. Their white sails passing along the sides of woodland hills were very picturesque.

In many places also the views were varied by the prospect of bays, and harbours in miniature; where little barks lay moored, taking in ore, and other commodities from the mountains. These vessels, designed plainly for rougher water, than they at present incountred, shewed us, without any geographical knowledge, that we approached the sea.

From Monmouth we reached, by a late breakfast-hour, the noble ruin of *Tintern-abbey;* which belongs to the Duke of Beaufort; and is esteemed, with its appendages, the most beautiful and picturesque view on the river.

Castles, and abbeys have different situations, agreeable to their respective uses. The castle, meant for defence, stands boldly on the hill; the abbey, intended for meditation, is hid in the sequestered vale.

[...]

Such is the situation of *Tintern-abbey.* It occupies a great eminence in the middle of a circular valley, beautifully screened on all sides by woody hills; through which the river winds it's course; and the hills, closing on it's entrance, and on it's exit, leave no room for inclement blasts to enter. A more pleasing retreat could not easily be found. The woods, and glades intermixed; the winding of the river; the variety of the ground; the splendid ruin, contrasted with the objects of nature; and the elegant line formed by the summits of the hills, which include the whole; make all together a very inchanting piece of scenery. Every thing around breathes an air so calm, and tranquil; so sequestered from the commerce of life; that it is easy to conceive, a man of warm imagination, in monkish times, might have been allured by such a scene to become an inhabitant of it.No part of the ruins of Tintern is seen from the river, except the abbey-church. It has been an elegant Gothic pile; but it does not make that appearance as a *distant* object, which we expected. Tho the parts are beautiful, the whole is ill-shaped. No ruins of the tower are left, which might give form, and contrast to the buttresses, and walls. Instead of this, a number of gabel-ends hurt the eye with their regularity; and disgust it by the vulgarity of their shape. A mallet judiciously used (but who durst use it?) might be of service in fracturing some of them; particularly those of the cross isles, which are not only disagreeable in themselves, but confound the perspective.

But were the building ever so beautiful, incompassed as it is with shabby houses, it could make no appearance from the river. From a stand near the road, it is seen to more advantage.

But if *Tintern-abbey* be less striking as a *distant* object, it exhibits, on a *nearer* view, (when the whole together cannot be seen, but the eye settles on some of it's nobler parts,) a very inchanting piece of ruin. Nature has now made it her own. Time has worn off all traces of the rule: it has blunted the sharp edges of the chissel,; and broken the regularity of opposing parts. The figured ornaments of the east-window are gone; those of the west-window are left. Most of the other windows, with their principal ornaments, remain.

To these were supperadded the ornaments of time. Ivy, in masses uncommonly large, had taken possession of many parts of the wall; and given a happy contrast to the grey-coloured stone, of which the building is composed. Nor was this undecorated. Mosses of various hues, with lychens, maiden-hair, penny-leaf, and other humble plants, had over-spread the surface, or hung from every joint, and crevice. Some of them were in flower, others only in leaf; but all together gave those full-blown tints, which add the richest finishing to a ruin.

Such is the beautiful appearance, which Tintern-abbey exhibits on the *outside*, in those parts, where we can obtain a near view of it. But when we *enter it*, we see it in most perfection: at least if we consider it as an independent object, unconnected with landscape. The roof is gone: but the walls, and pillars, and abutments which supported it, are entire. A few of the pillars indeed have given way; and here and there, a piece of the facing of the wall:; but in corresponding parts, one always remains to tell the story. The pavement is obliterated: the elevation of the choir is no longer visible: the whole area is reduced to one level; cleared of rubbish; and covered with neat turf, closely shorn; and interrupted with nothing, but the noble columns, which formed the isles, and supported the tower.

When we stood at one end of this awful piece of ruin; and surveyed the whole in one view— the elements of air, and earth, it's only covering, and pavement; and the grand, and venerable remains, which terminated both— perfect enough to form the perspective; yet broken enough to destroy the regularity; the eye was above measure delighted with the beauty, the greatness, and the novelty of the scene. More *picturesque* it certainly would have been, if the area, unadorned, had been left with all it's rough fragments of ruin scattered round; and bold was the hand that removed them: yet as the outside of the ruin, which is the chief object of *picturesque curiosity*, is still left in all it's wild, and native rudeness, we excuse—perhaps we approve—the neatness, that is introduced within: it *may* add to the *beauty* of the scene—to its *novelty* it undoubtedly *does*.

Among other things in this scene of desolation, the

poverty and wretchedness of the inhabitants were remarkable. They occupy little huts, raised among the ruins of the monastery; and seem to have no employment but begging: as if a place once devoted to indolence, could never again become the seat of industry. As we left the abbey, we found the whole hamlet at the gate, either openly soliciting alms; or covertly, under the pretence of carrying us to some part of the ruins, which each could shew; and which was far superior to any thing which could be shewn by any one else. The most lucrative occasion could not have excited more jealousy, and contention.

One poor woman we followed, who had engaged to shew us the monks' library. She could scarce crawl; shuffling along her palsied limbs, and meagre, contracted body, by the help of two sticks. She led us, through an old gate, into a place overspread with nettles, and briars; and pointing to the remnant of a shattered cloister, told us, that was the place. It was her own mansion. All indeed she meant to tell us, was the story of her own wretchedness; and all she had to shew us, was her own miserable habitation. We did not expect to be interested; but we were. I never saw so loathsome a human dwelling. It was a cavity, loftily vaulted, between two ruined walls; which streamed with various-coloured stains of unwholsome dews. The floor was earth; yielding, through moisture, to the tread. Not the merest utensil, or furniture of any kind appeared, but a wretched bedstead, spread with a few rags, and drawn into the middle of the cell, to prevent its receiving the damp, which trickled down the walls. At one end was an aperture; which served just to let in light enough to discover the wretchedness within. —When we stood in the midst of this cell of misery; and felt the chilling damps which struck us in every direction, we were rather surprised, that the wretched inhabitant was still alive; than that she had only lost the use of her limbs.

The country about *Tintern-abbey* hath been described as a solitary, tranquil scene: but it's immediate environs only are meant. Within half a mile of it are carried on great iron-works; which introduce noise and bustle into these regions of tranquillity.

The ground about these works, appears from the river to consist of grand woody hills, sweeping, and intersecting each other in elegant lines. They are a continuation of the same kind of landscape, as that about *Tintern-abbey*; and are fully equal to it.

As we still descend the river, the same scenery continues. The banks are equally steep, winding, and woody; and in some parts diversified by prominent rocks, and ground finely broken, and adorned.

But one great disadvantage began here to invade us. Hitherto the river had been clear, and splendid; reflecting the several objects on it's banks. But it's waters now became ouzy, and discoloured. Sludgy shores too appeared, on each side; and other symptoms, which discovered the influence of a tide.

MR. Morris's improvements at Persfield, which we soon approached, are generally thought as much worth a traveller's notice, as any thing on the banks of the Wye. We pushed on shore close under his rocks; and the tide being at ebb, we landed with some difficulty on an ouzy beach. One of our bargemen, who knew the place, served as a guide; and under his conduct we climbed the steep by an easy, regular zig-zag; and gained the top.

The eminence, on which we stood, (one of those grand eminences, which overlooks the Wye,) is an intermixture of rock, and wood; and forms, in this place, a concave semicircle; sweeping round in a segment of two miles. The river winds under it; and the scenery, of course, is shewn in various directions. The river itself indeed, as we just observed, is charged with the impurities of the soil it washes; and when it ebbs, it's verdant banks become slopes of mud: but if we except these disadvantages, the situation of Persfield is noble.

Little indeed was left for improvement, but to open walks, and views, through the woods, to the various objects around them. All this the ingenious proprietor hath done with great judgment; and hath shewn his rocks, his woods, and his precipices, under various forms; and to great advantage. Sometimes a broad face of rock is presented, stretching along a vast space, like the walls of a citadel. Sometimes it is broken by intervening trees. In other parts, the rocks rise above the woods; a little farther, they sink below them: sometimes, they are seen through them; and sometimes one series of rocks appears rising above another: and tho many of these objects are repeatedly seen, yet seen from different stations, and with new accompaniments, they appear new. The winding of the precipice is the magical secret, by which all these inchanting scenes are produced.

We cannot, however, call these views picturesque. They are either presented from too high a point; or they have little to mark them as characteristic; or they do not fall into such composition, as would appear to advantage on canvas. But they are extremely romantic; and give a loose to the most pleasing riot of imagination.

[...]

As you continue your rout to Bualt, the country grows grander, and more picturesque. The valley of the Wye becomes contracted, and the road runs at the bottom; along the edge of the water.

It is possible, I think, the Wye may in this place be more beautiful, than in any other part of it's course. Between Ross, and Chepstow, the grandeur, and beauty of *it's banks* are it's chief praise. The *river itself* has no other merit, than that of a winding surface of smooth water. But here, added to the same decoration from it's banks, the Wye itself assumes a more beautiful character; pouring over shelving rocks; and forming itself into eddies, and cascades, which a solemn parading stream through a flat channel, cannot exhibit.

An additional merit also accrues to such a river from the different forms it assumes, according to the fulness, or emptiness of the stream. There are rocks of all shapes, and sizes; which always vary the appearance of the water, as it rushes over, or plays among them: so that such a river, to a picturesque eye, is a continued fund of new entertainment.

The Wye also, in this part of it's course, still receives farther beauty from the woods, which adorn it's banks; and which the navigation of the river, in its lower reaches, cannot allow. Here the whole is perfectly rural, and unincumbered. Even a boat, I believe, is never seen beyond the Hay. The boat itself might be an ornament: but we would not give up for it such a river, as would not suffer a boat.

Some beauties however the smooth river possesses above the rapid one. In the latter you cannot have those reflections, which are so ornamental to the former. — nor can you have in the rapid river, the opportunity of contemplating the grandeur of it's banks from the surface of the water — unless indeed the road winds close with the river at the bottom, when perhaps you may see them with additional advantage.

The foundation of these criticisms on *smooth* and *agitated* water, is this. When water is exhibited in *small quantities*,it wants the agitation of a torrent, a cascade, or some other adventitious circumstance, to give it consequence. But when it is spread out in the *reach of some capital river* — in a *lake* — or an *arm of the sea* — it is then able to support it's own dignity. In the former case it aims at beauty: in the latter at grandeur. Now the Wye has in no part of it's course a quantity of water sufficient to give it any great degree of grandeur; so that of consequence the *smooth* part must, on the whole, yield to the more *agitated,* which possesses more beauty.

> **William Gilpin, Observations on the River Wye, and several parts of South Wales, &. Relative chiefly to picturesque beauty: made in the summer of the year 1770, 1782**

....

"Different kinds of rocks have different degrees of beauty"

....

For subsequent authors, Gilpin set the bar sublimely high. That did not deter them.

SCENERY of such inimitable beauty (says the intelligent Mr. SHAW), as that viewed down the river Wye, which is unquestionably UNIQUE, naturally requires a minute detail of its constituent parts:—these have been minutely defined by that celebrated comparer of natural and artificial landscape, Mr. GILPIN, in his tour down this river in 1770, a recapitulation of which we here deem necessary.

The beauty of these scenes arises chiefly from two circumstances—the lofty banks of the river, and its mazy course. From these two circumstances, the views it exhibits are of the most beautiful kind of perspective free from the formality of lines.

Every view on a river, thus circumstanced, is composed of four grand parts; the area, which is the river itself; the two side screens, which are the opposite banks, and mark the perspective; and the front screen, which points out the winding of the river.

If the Wye ran, like a Dutch canal, between parallel banks, there could be no front screen: the two side screens, in that situation, would lengthen to a point.

The views on the Wye, though composed only of these simple parts, are yet infinitely varied. They are varied, first, by the contrast of the screens. Sometimes one of side-screens is elevated; sometimes the other; and sometimes the front. Or both the side-screens may be lofty, and the front either high or low

Again, they are varied by the folding of the side-screens over each other; and hiding more or less of the front. When none of the front is discovered, the folding-side either winds round, like an amphitheatre, or it becomes a long reach of perspective. These simple variations admit still farther variety from becoming complex. One of the sides may be compounded of various parts, while the other remains simple; or both may be compounded, and the front simple; or the front alone may be compounded.

Besides these sources of variety, there are other circumstances, which, under the name of ornaments, still farther increase them. The ornaments of the Wye may be ranged under four heads — ground — wood — rocks — and buildings. The ground of which the banks of the Wye consist, affords every variety, which ground is capable of receiving, from the steepest precipice to the flattest meadow. This variety appears in the line formed by the summits of the banks; in the swellings and excavations of their declivities, and in the unequal surfaces of the lower grounds. In many places also the ground is broken, which adds new sources of variety. The colour too of the broken soil is a great source of variety, — the yellow or the red oaker, the ashy grey, the black earth, or the marley blue. And the inter-mixtures of these with each other, and with patches of verdure, blooming heath, and other vegetable tints, still increase that variety.

The next great ornament on the banks of the Wye, are its woods. The woods themselves possess little beauty, and less grandeur; yet, when we consider them as the ornamental, not as the essential, parts of a scene, the eye must not examine them with exactness, but compound for a general effect.

The chief deficiency, in point of wood, is of large trees on the edge of the water; which, clumped here and there, would diversify the hills, as the eye passes them; and remove that heaviness, which always, in some degree (tho' here as little as any where) arises from the continuity of ground. But trees immediately on the foreground cannot be suffered in these scenes, as they would obstruct the navigation of the river.

The ROCKS, which are continually starting through the woods, produce another ornament on the banks of the Wye. The rock, as all other objects, though more than all, receives its chief beauty from contrast. Some objects are beautiful in themselves. The eye is pleased with the tuftings of a tree; it is amused with pursuing the eddying stream; or it rests with delight on the shattered arches of a Gothic ruin. Such objects, independent of composition, are beautiful in themselves. But the rock, bleak, naked, and unadorned, seems scarcely to deserve a place among them. Tint it with mosses, and lychens of various hues, and you give it a degree of beauty. Adorn it with shrubs and hanging herbage, and you still make it more picturesque. Connect it with wood, and water, and broken ground, and you make it in the highest degree interesting. Its colour and its form are so accommodating, that it generally blends into one of the most beautiful appendages of landscape.

Different kinds of rocks have different degrees of beauty. Those on the Wye, which are of a greyish colour, are, in general, simple and grand; rarely formal, or fantastic. Sometimes they project in those beautiful square masses, yet broken and shattered in every line, which is characteristic of the most majestic species of rock. Sometimes they slant obliquely from the eye in shelving diagonal strata; and sometimes they appear in large masses of smooth stone, detached from each other, and half buried in the soil. Rocks of this last kind are the most lumpish, and the least picturesque.

Charles Heath, The excursion down the Wye from Ross to Monmouth, 1796

"Perplexed with contradictory and incompatible ideas"

Buildings could not be appreciated for what they were. Rules had to be satisfied if you were to derive aesthetic pleasure from them.

A lofty wall surrounds the buildings of Margam park, to protect the remains of ancient, and the specimens of modern art from public pillage. The gardener, however, attends to conduct company through the place. Its most remarkable features are the ruins of the old priory, and the sumptuous green-house built by Mr. Talbot, for the reception of his orange-trees. A curious, and we thought an unpleasant, effect arises on entering the place, from the contiguity of edifices, built in stiles of architecture so completely dissimilar as the chapter-house and the green-house; the one a simple Gothic structure, the other a splendid classical building. The emotions excited by the former are destroyed by the latter, and the mind is consequently perplexed with contradictory and incompatible ideas. It concerned us to see the beautiful circular chapter-house in a state of dilapidation, that must speedily reduce it to a heap of ruins; great part of the roof has fallen in, the ribs which support the remaining portion are giving way, and no care seems to be taken to repair what is already dilapidated, or to prevent future injuries. This chapter-house, and some unintelligible ruins adjoining it, are all that remain of the once-famous abbey of Margam, a Cistertian house founded by Robert earl of Glocester, grandson to Fitz-hamon, A. D. 1147.

On entering the green-house, we were immediately struck with the want of a due *proportion* between the length, breadth, and height of it. Every beauty is destroyed by an utter defiance of all its rules, for it is impossible there can be any beauty in a room one hundred and nine yards long, and only twenty-seven yards broad. It must be recollected, however, that the green-house was built for a particular purpose, to receive a fine collection of orange-trees, so numerous as rendered an unusual extension of the edifice necessary. During the summer the orange-trees are removed into the open air, so that we saw the green-house under the disadvantage of its being empty, which rendered the want of symmetry still more striking. At each of the extremities of this structure is a small room, containing a collection, not large but well chosen, of ancient marbles, and models of ancient buildings.

Richard Warner, A second walk through Wales in August and September 1798, 1799

In North Wales, the more rugged going meant that the physical sensation of traversing the uplands added a further dimension to the search for the romantic view. In the early modern era, wild nature was something the refined mind sought to tame or to hide from view. By the eighteenth century, wilder landscapes were being constructed around noble houses and what lay beyond was to be explored with awe.

"Enchanting to the inquisitive pedestrians"

Beauty could be made more rewarding by its situation within a rugged landscape, closed to all but the intrepid walker.

By a retrograde saunter we soon gained the Tan-y-bwlch road, and passing over the romantic bridge of Pont ar

Garfa, beautifully entwined with the rich drapery of ivy, we ascended a steep path over the slaty mountain of Tylyn Gwladys, two miles in extent. — Sublimity, indeed, gave place to elegance; behind us, the huge steeps of Cader Idris, lifting high above the rolling clouds its shaggy head, of which at intervals, we caught a glance through the thick mist which enveloped it; in front Snowdon, conscious of pre-eminence, rose in the distant perspective; these were the boundaries of our view. On the opposite side a barren mountain, dignified by the name of Prince of Wales, appeared scarcely accessible, but to the steps of the enthusiast; this formerly afforded a vast quantity of ore, but it has lately so much failed, as not to produce even a sufficiency to remunerate the miners. While traversing these barren mountains, it is not less singular than interesting, occasionally to meet the most delicious vallies, watered by some foaming river; these literally surcharged "with weighted rains, and melted Alpine snows."

Such is the true characteristic of the Welch scenery: the finest verdure, and the most enchanting vallies are discovered in the bosom of sterility, where natural cascades, precipitating themselves from their rude pinnacles, alone disturb the silence which reigns in that asylum, only to render it more enchanting to the inquisitive pedestrians, for these landscapes are only accessible to their steps: the distant swell of the cataract had now long proclaimed our proximity to the object in pursuit.

'The Author' (Allen Cliff), The Cambrian Directory,
1800

....
"And beyond, a long extent of *alps*"
....

The higher you climbed, the harder the going and the more rewarding the view.

Every flight of path presents new and grand objects: at first, of the great windings of the river towards *Llanrwst*, the lofty towers of *Conwy*, and the venerable walls of the town; and beyond, a long extent of *alps*, with *Moel Siabod*, the *Drúm*, and *Carnedd Llewelyn* and *Dafydd*, appearing with distinguished height. From a little higher ascent is opened to us the discharge of the *Conwy* into the sea, sublimely bounded by the lesser *Penmaen*, and the immense *Orm's Head*, or *Llandudno*; between which appear, a fine bay, the vast promotory of *Penmaen Mawr*, the isle of *Priestholm*, and the long extent *of Anglesey*. After gaining the summit, beneath is seen a considerable flat, with the estuary of the river *Conwy* falling into the *Irish* sea on one side, and the beautiful half-moon bay of *Llandudno* on the other: one of whose horns is the great head of the same name; the other, the lofty rock of *Rhiwleden*, or the little *Orm's Head*. A little farther progress brings us in sight of a great bay, sweeping semicircularly the shores; and beyond are the distant hills of *Flintshire*, and the entrances into the estuaries of the *Mersey* and *Dee*, frequently animated with shipping.

Thomas Pennant, A tour in Wales, 1778

Thomas Pennant (1726-1798) was born at the family seat, Downing Hall, Whitford. As a man of independent means, he dedicated his life to travel and writing, concentrating on natural history and local and Welsh history. He matriculated at Queen's College, later joining Oriel College, but did not take his degree. He was elected a Fellow of the Royal Society in 1767 and was awarded an honorary degree from Oxford for his work in Zoology in 1771. He was by reputation an improving landlord, who, for the time, showed an unusual degree of concern for his tenants. While not fluent in Welsh, he made sure he had the assistance of those who were. Pennant was one of the leading naturalists of the eighteenth century, writing six books on various aspects of zoology and having twenty-two species named after him. Gilbert White's 'Natural History and Antiquities of Selborne' (1789) is in part formed from a series of letters to Pennant.

"A noble mountain of a stupendous bulk"

The traveller in North Wales did not have to worry about which order of architecture these mountains ought to belong to.

The traveller who wishes to visit *Snowdon*, from this town, may have a very agreeable ride. After crossing the *Fai*, or *Gwyrfai*, at *Pont y Bettws*, about four miles and a half from *Caernarvon*, he will find about the village of *Bettws Garmon*, or *Is-Gwrfai*, a beautiful cascade fronting him, as he passes up a valley; which consists of verdant meadows, watered by the same river, and bounded by hills rising fast into *alpine* majesty. He will go under *Moel Elian*, a noble mountain of a stupendous bulk, cloathed with a smooth green turf, and most regularly rounded. He will pass on the right near *Castell Cedwm*, said by Mr. *Rowlands* to be one of the guards to the entrance into *Snowdon*: it is a great rock; which I did not ascend, so cannot certify whether it had any works like those of other *British* posts. The lake *Cwellyn* here almost fills the valley; a water famous for its Char, which are taken in nets in the first winter months, and after that season retire to the inaccessible depths. In former times, this water was called, from the steepness of its banks, *Llyn y Torlennydd*. Above, on the right side of the lake, soars the magnificent *Mynnydd Vawr*, smooth on the top, but the sides receding inwards in a semicircular form, exhibiting a tremendous precipice. Soon after this, the vale expands; *y Wyddfa* appears full in view. The traveller will pass by *LLYN Y CADER*, and join in my former tour at *Bedd Kelert*.

Thomas Pennant, A tour in Wales, 1778

"All our difficulties were forgotten"

When climbing a mountain – in this case, Snowdon – all the vexations of the ascent could melt away in the euphoria of standing at the peak and looking at the world anew.

We engaged the miner, as our Conductor over the mountain, who entertained us much with displaying, in strong colours, the tricks and impositions of his brother guides, and more particularly of the methodistical Landlord of our Inn, who is generally employed on these occasions. His pride too is not a little elevated, by having conducted *The Great Doctor* to its highest summit; this seemingly ridiculous phrase for some time puzzled us; but we have since found out, that our guide [Evan Thomas, works in the copper-works at Aber-Glaslyn, and lives at a place called Dous Coreb, about a mile and an half beyond Beddgelert] was talking of no less a man, than the present respectable and learned Dean of Christchurch, who ascended this mountain last year. Though our Guide was pompous, and rather too partial to the marvellous, yet I strenuously recommend him to all tourists.

At half past twelve, we started from our Inn, determined to see the sun rise from its highest summit. The night was now very dark, and we could just discover, that the top of Snowdon was entirely enveloped in a thick, impenetrable mist; this unpropitious omen staggered our resolutions; and we for some time hesitated respecting our farther progress; but our Guide assuring us, that his *comfortable* cottage was not far distant, we again plucked up resolution; and, quitting the highway about two miles on the Caernarvon road, we turned to the right, through a boggy unpleasant land, and in danger of losing our shoes every step we took. This soon brought us to the *comfortable cot*, the filth and dirtiness of which can better be imagined than described; a worm-eaten bed, two small stools, and a table fixed to the wall, composed the whole of his furniture, — two fighting cocks were perched on a beam, which Thomas seemed to pride himself in the possession of; the smoke of the fire ascended through a small hole in the roof of this *comfortable mansion*, the door of which did not appear proof against the "churlish chiding of the winter blast."

Such, indeed, was the situation of this Cambrian mountaineer; and though, in our own opinion, misery, poverty, and dirt personified, seemed to be the real inhabitants of this cottage, yet there was something prepossessing in his character; for frequently, with the greatest vehemence imaginable, and in the true stile of an anchorite, he declared, that "though he boasted not riches, yet he boasted of independence; and though he possessed not wealth, yet he possessed the home of happiness, an honest breast."

The morning appearing to wear a more favourable aspect, we again sallied forth; the bogs, however, still rendered it extremely unpleasant. But this inconvenience was only temporary: we soon came to a part of the mountain, entirely composed of loose stones, and fragments of rock, which, by affording a very treacherous footing, you are liable to perpetual falls. The mountain now became much steeper, the path less rocky, and our mountaineer, the higher we proceeded, more induced to exhibit feats of his agility, by occasionally running down a short precipice, and then, by a loud shout or vociferation, shewing us the obedience of the sheep, who instantaneously flocked round him, at the sound of his voice: it is singular, the caution implanted in this animal, by instinct, for the mutual protection of each other; from the liberty they enjoy, they seldom congregate in one flock, but are generally discovered grazing in parties from six to a dozen, one of which is regularly appointed centinel, to watch the motions of their inveterate enemies (foxes and birds of prey), which infest this mountain. A wider expanse of the hemisphere disclosed itself, and every object below us gradually diminished, as we ascended. The freshness of the mountain *whetted* our appetites; and our conductor, with very little persuasion, soon influenced us to open our little basket of provisions. The sun, the "rich-hair'd youth of morn," was just peeping from its bed; and having refreshed ourselves, with eager impatience we again climbed the rugged precipice, for we had still a considerable height to ascend. We now descended several steep declivities, by a narrow path, not more than three yards wide, with a dreadful perpendicular on each side, the sight of which almost turned us giddy. As we were passing this hazardous path, a thick mist enveloped us, and an impenetrable abyss appeared on both sides; the effect, indeed, can scarcely be conceived; our footing to us, puisne mountaineers, seemed very insecure; and a total destruction would have been the consequence of one false step. The air grew intensely cold, and by our guide's recommendation, we a second time produced our pistol of rum, diluted with milk; but this cordial must be used with caution, as a very small quantity of strong liquor affects the head, owing to the rarification of the air. On our reaching the summit, all our difficulties were forgotten, and our imaginary complaints overborne with exclamations of wonder, surprise, and admiration. The light thin misty cloud, which had for some time enveloped us, as if by enchantment, suddenly dispersed; the whole ocean appeared illuminated by a fiery substance, and all the subject hills below us, for they resembled *mole-hills*, were gradually tinged by the rich glow of the sun; whose orb, becoming at length distinctly visible, displayed the whole island of Anglesea so distinctly visible, that we descried, as in map, its flat and uncultivated plains, bounded by the rich and inexhaustible Paris Mountains, in the vicinity of Holyhead. The point on which we were standing, did not exceed a square of five yards, and we sickened almost at the sight of the steep precipices which environed us; round it is a small parapet, formed by the customary tribute of all strangers, who visit this summit, and to which we likewise contributed, by placing a large stone on its top: this parapet, indeed, sheltered us from the chilly cold, and protected us from the piercing wind, which this height must naturally be exposed to.

We remained in this situation for a considerable time, and endeavoured, without success, to enumerate the several lakes, forest, woods, and counties, which were exposed to us in one view; but, lost and confounded with the innumerable objects worthy of admiration, and regardless of the chilling cold, we took a distinct survey of the Isle of Man, together with a faint prospect of the Highlands in Ireland, which appeared just visibly skirting the distant horizon; but another object soon engrossed all our attention:

[...]

For we unexpectedly observed long billows of vapour tossing about, half way down the mountain, totally excluding the country below, and occasionally dispersing, and partially revealing, its features, while above, the azure expanse of the heavens remained unobscured by the thinnest mist. This, however, was of no long continuance: a thick cloud presently wet us through; and the point on which we were standing could alone be distinguished. As there appeared little or no chance of the clouds dispersing, we soon commenced our descent. — Respecting this Alpine excursion, suffice it to say, that though our expectations were raised exceedingly high, it infinitely surpassed all conception, and baffled all description; for no colour of language can paint the grandeur of the rising sun, observed from this eminence, or describe the lakes, woods, and forests, which are extended before you; for description, though it enumerates their names, yet it cannot draw the elegance of outline, cannot give the effect of precipices, or delineate the minute features, which reward the actual observer, at every new choice of his position, and by changing their colour and form in his gradual ascent, till at last every object dwindles into atoms: in short, this interesting excursion, which comprehends every thing that is awful, grand, and sublime, producing the most pleasing sensations, has left traces in the memory, which the imagination will ever hold dear.

[...]

The first two miles of our descent, we by no means found difficult, but wishing to take a minute survey of the picturesque pass of Llanberris, we changed the route generally prescribed to strangers, and descended a rugged and almost perpendicular path, in opposition to the proposal of our guide, who strenuously endeavoured to dissuade us from the attempt, alleging the difficulty of the steep, and relating a melancholy story of a gentleman, who many years back had broken his leg. This had no effect. We determined to proceed; and the vale of Llanberris amply rewarded us for the trouble. It is bounded by the steep precipices of Snowdon, and two large lakes, communicating by a river. It was formerly a large forest, but the woods are now entirely cut down. We here dismissed our Cambrian mountaineer, and easily found our way to Dolbadern (pronounced *Dolbathern*) Castle, situated between the two lakes, and now reduced to one circular tower, thirty feet in diameter, with the foundations of the exterior buildings completely in ruins.

'The Author' (Allen Cliff),
The Cambrian Directory, 1800

....

"In a rude and rugged region"

....

Another challenge faced the seeker of the romantic journey; that of the landscape becoming just too bleak for just too long.

This is a route not generally pursued by English tourists. Towyn is so dull and secluded a place, as to be very rarely honoured by foreign visitors, albeit the road thither from Dolgellau, – a distance of about seventeen miles, – is upon the whole replete with that romantic variety of landscape, so common in North Wales; and I would certainly recommend the *meritorious traveller* to ride there some morning and return the day following. Old Griffith Owen and his "matchless harp," are worth this, at least; but more on this subject hereafter. The traveller, who would visit Towyn from Dolgellau, must proceed in a direction extending south-westerly from the latter, leaving the mountain path to Cader Idris above him, on the left. He will then find himself in a tolerably good road, bounded on the one side by the woods of Bryngwyn and Brynadda, and, on the other, by some fertile meadow-land leading down to the brink of the Wnion. About two miles from Dolgellau, we arrive at Llyn y Penmaen, having previously passed a wide great bog on the right. Hence the Wnion has joined the Mawddach, and both together form a broad and beautiful estuary, having its opposite banks composed of meadow and woods, and heather hills. Hitherto the tract is smooth and easy enough – for a Welsh one; but beyond the Llyn an acclivity commences, leading to a district, which may be justly termed the Western Highlands of Merionethshire. Having ascended Penmaen Hill, we find ourselves in a rude and rugged region, with few traces of cheerfulness, and not many of cultivation; and where that inexpressible emotion, caused by the awful solitude of the hills, is experienced to its fullest extent. Here are no grassy glades swelling out in richness of verdure, – no waving corn-fields, or "dew-bespangled meads," and no mountain rivulet to lull the ear with the murmuring melody of its waters. Dreary, indeed, is the scene, and its deep stillness is only interrupted by the clatter of the horse's hoofs, as the traveller rides onwards on his way, or by the sharp, shrill, bleating of the "fair-fleeced wether," rising in alarm at the approach of the intruder on its solitude.

[...]

But this cheerless landscape is not more than a mile in extent. The valley, through which the road passes, gradually contracts, till it terminates in a spot "so beautiful, so green, so full of goodly prospect," that he must be a stoical dog indeed, who does not enjoy the glorious scene around him, presenting, as it does, so strong and pleasing a contrast to the sterility, which precedes it. This spot is at an old and weather-beaten mill, worked by the water from a river, which, falling into a small but troubled stream, through a deep wood above the road on the left, passes under a bridge of one arch, and pursues its course through the midst of a lovely glen to the mighty Mawddach, whose glistening surface is just described between an opening of the hills on the right. About two hundred yards above the bridge the river swells out into a broad and bright pool, the pebbly bottom of which is distinctly visible through the clear transparency of the water.

[...]

Beyond the mill, the country assumes a more smiling and cheerful aspect. The flourishing plantations of Garthynghared enliven the landscape, and evince, in the worthy proprietor of that estate, a commendable eagerness to clothe the sides of his rugged hills with something more valuable than gorse or heather. The improvement, which has been effected within these few years, under the encouraging auspices of Mr. Owen, must carry with it its reward; to say nothing of the gratification, which the "'squire" must experience as he views the declivities of his hills, once bleak and desolate, now well covered with oak, birch and fir.

'Mervinius' (Mr Harper), Walks around Dolgellau. Walk III Dolgellau to Towyn, 1820

Mr Harper is described by one of his companions as 'a gentleman from London' of whom nothing more is known.

6

THE COMFORT OF CLICHÉS: AMUSING ANECDOTES AND OTHER OBSERVATIONS

Writing about what other people do matters when you are on the road. It allows an author to display their wit, to show how enlightened they are, and to demonstrate their compassion towards lesser beings. Categorising customs and manners is not easy, since many topics may become conflated within a paragraph of two. Further, there is a degree of ritual in these pieces, they are often written as the traveller is about to leave a county or is nearing the end of their account and, thus, seem to feel the need to take a step back and make some broader observations. It is obviously not an easy task to accomplish. Some observations are facile, others carry a tint of the voyeur, and a few are pretty telling.

What does come across in many of these accounts is their authors' self-confidence. Their observations are made with little chance that the objects of their attention will know what has been written about them, and even less chance that they could do anything about it.

Here, I group their observations in eight subsets; politics, the piety of poverty, bed-chambers and bathing beauties, superstitions, dress, sundry amusement, the Welsh character, and, finally, the Welsh language.

POLITICS

<hr>

"May all *Demicrats* be *gullotin'd*"

<hr>

Politics and bowls of punch tended not to mix.

We were yesterday much diverted with a curious political conversation carried on at the inn, in the room which we in part occupied, at a table by ourselves; at another, were seated the clergyman, the exciseman, the attorney, the apothecary, and I suppose, by his appearance, the barber of the place, &c. these were met upon business over a bowl of punch, which seemed to constitute the chief part of it; whilst in an opposite corner of the room, two more decent looking people were enjoying themselves in a similar manner. The clergyman gave aloud "Church and King," as a toast, and soon after one of our neighbours at the other table, proposed "General Washington" to his friend; this created a great commotion amongst the large party; for the clergyman immediately standing up gave as his second toast "may all *Demicrats* be *gullotin'd*" when the other filling *his* glass, added, "may all fools be gullotin'd, and then I knows who'll be the first;" after this ensued a violent and dreadful battle of tongues, in which these people excel in an extraordinary degree. The clergyman defended his toast, on the grounds that it shewed his zeal in a good cause, forgetting that it was necessary first to prove the merit of the sentiment, as united by him, and after that, to shew that his zeal was best made known as a clergyman, by his benevolent and truly pious wish. But majors and minors were things which this zealous and humane defender of his church and king had little regard for. The clamour at length became so loud, that we soon withdrew ourselves from the scene of contention, and left the combatants to settle the point in the best manner they could; though it seemed to me that it required more sophistry than the clergyman had displayed, and more wit than the other possessed, to justify or even excuse themselves.

J. Hucks, A pedestrian tour in North Wales in a series of letters, 1795

....

"Such pretensions to right, and such perversions of it"

....

Justice at the Welsh Assizes was to some degree a matter of luck. John Evans makes an important point about the ease with which justice could be miscarried when English was the only recognised language in a country where most people were monoglot Welsh. The use of Welsh in courts was banned by the 1535 Laws in Wales Act. Welsh was only allowed to be used in courts after the Welsh Language Act of 1967. However, it did not gain equal judicial status until the Welsh Language Act of 1993.

The Justices of West Wales, as we were about leaving the town, had opened their commission of oyer and terminer for this part of the principality. The novelty of an assize, held in a language so different from our own, excited the curiosity of the company. Nor was it long before this was amply gratified: several criminal cases, and a numerous list of causes at nisi prius bar occupied the cognizance of the court, and engaged our attention for some days; nor could any thing exceed the ridicule excited by such a medley of solemnity and frivolity, of such pretensions to right, and such perversions of it, as was exhibited on this occasion: and every humane mind must feel an unusual degree of indignation at the mode in which justice is administered here, and reprobate in the strongest terms the melancholy consequences. The judges were men of the highest respectability: the one at the crown bar a native of North Wales, a man of the most unshaken integrity, and famed for the acuteness and solidity of his judgment; qualities you would at once suppose, with the assistance of an upright Jury, would ensure to the parties at issue the most fair and honourable decisions. Happy would it be for this country, if the upright intentions of the bench could at all times be crowned with the wished for effect: but the language of North and South Wales are so different, as scarcely for the people of the two counties to be able to understand each other. This gives rise to a considerable degree of confusion between the parties and the Judge. The counsel are principally English: the witnesses, unable to speak English, are examined by an interpreter, who, though he is sworn faithfully to interpret to the best of his judgment, is not always impartial between the parties; and if he be, is not always able to deliver extempore the exact sentiments of the witness: for it is well known how much of the spirit and meaning of testimony may be lost, or its nature changed, in translating it from one language to another, more especially in languages so opposite in their origin and construction as the Welsh and English; not to mention that the very same sentiments, delivered in a different tone of voice, will appear to have a different, and ofttimes a quite contrary meaning. The interpreter is generally some attorney of the court, and if he should be a person of respectable character, yet such is the nature of man that he must be more than human if he act without bias in the questions he puts, or the answers he gives; then add the influence he has over the poor ignorant witness, now not confronted to the Jury, but oft to a powerful tyrant of his neighbourhood, whose anger expressed or understood he momentarily dreads more than the displeasure of his God. It is not, I am sensible, peculiar to a Welsh court for the attorney in the cause to be admissible evidence at the bar; but it is more frequent and less noticed in these than in English courts: and it not unfrequently happens, from the confused account of a common witness, and the clearer detail which a man of education and technical knowledge is able to give, for the Jury to decide upon the last and most artful evidence....These essential points not being attended to as they ought, you will not be surprised to hear that the courts of judicature in Wales are less beneficial to the subject than those of England. The cases we heard were strongly illustrative of these remarks. I could detail — but I forbear. They made a strong and lasting impression upon my mind, and I could not help exclaiming in an audible voice on the occasion: if ever my life or property should be subject under the law to the decision of a Jury, O! may it be a Jury of my peers—a Jury impannelled to the east of the Severn!

John Evans, Letters written during a tour through South Wales, in the year 1803, and at other times, 1804

....

"But a classical scholar and a well-bred gentleman"

....

People you met by chance were not meant to be well read. Nor were they meant to be Epicureans.

As we entered the latter village [Llanrhystud], "the dark mists of night" fell over us. We therefore finished our day's journey at the Red Lion inn, a tolerably decent ale-house, where we were presently joined by a man in a labourer's habit, whom we had observed on the road in very gallant intercourse with a peasant girl, and had rallied on the occasion; yet were we not a little surprized at finding him not only a man of extensive information, but a classical scholar and a well-bred gentleman. On his leaving the room, we had an opportunity of enquiring who this character was, and learned from our landlord that he was a native 'squire, who lived about ten miles distant, who till lately had been in orders and officiated in London; but on the death of his father had thrown off the gown and become a man of pleasure. "Though he is so shabbily dressed," said our host, "it is only a frolic, for he is a very able man." Now, as the term *able* in Wales is synonymous, with rich in other places, we enquired the amount of his income, and found it to be *near a hundred a year.*

This gentleman proved a most agreeable and useful companion during the evening but we were sorry to observe in him a professed Epicurean; the gratification of his appetites he declared to be his great object, and defended his practice on what he termed the fundamental

principles of nature; nor was he in want of an ingenious
sophism against every point of attack.

J. T. Barber, A tour throughout South Wales and
Monmouthshire, 1803

THE PIETY OF POVERTY

....

"A hardy and desultory manner of life"

....

*There was little more reassuring to a traveller than to know that
people were content with their destitution, doubly so when they
were not distracted by 'the habits of thinking'.*

To sum up the advantages and disadvantages; I do not
hesitate a moment to say, that were I to make the same
tour again, or one through a similar country, I should
certainly perform it on foot, both from motives of
convenience and independency.

Upon the whole I have been as much charmed with the
manners of the people, as with the country which they
inhabit; there is a boldness and originality in all their
actions, which marked the conduct, and characterised the
features of their ancestors. A love of liberty and
independence is implanted by nature in their breasts, and
is cherished into maturity upon their mountains and sea
coasts by a hardy and desultory manner of life. With
respect to hospitality, they still preserve their original
character; the manner of it is undoubtedly much altered,
it is less magnificent but more pleasing; the stranger is
not conducted into a noble hall, and placed at the right
hand of the chief; no bards attend with the songs of times
that are past; the walls are no longer hung with the massy

spears of departed heroes, or decorated with the spoils of a vanquished enemy; the conch does not sound to war, nor is the bossy shield struck as the signal to meet the threatening foe. Strange ferocious manners were blended with the hospitality of those days; but, happily for mankind, such barbarous features of uncivilized ages are at length every where humanized into more refined and social enjoyments. Whether society has not arrived at an excess of refinement; whether a great degree of refinement is not the parent of vice and corruption; and if so, whether an age of barbarity with honesty and virtue, or an age of refinement, with effeminacy, vice, and corruption, is most desirable, or most calculated to produce the immediate and eternal happiness of mankind ? I leave to be determined by those who have leisure and inclination, to consider with attention so abstracted a subject.

[...]

In Wales, pride and poverty go hand in hand, and the disposition of the people is strongly blended with superstition. When we were at the top of Cader Idris (the etimology of which signifies the chair of the giant Idris), the guide shewed us the giant's bed, at which we could not help laughing; the honest fellow, however, rebuked us for such levity, and expressed his belief as to the identity and existence of the giant, at the same time justifying himself from the authority of a clergyman, who had lately made a pilgrimage to the same spot; and, immediately falling down on his knees, began to say his prayers in a devout manner, and an audible voice; without doubt to appease the manes of this tremendous giant, and breathe out a pious requiem to his soul.

The general character of the people is certainly amiable — their attachments are strong and sincere; their passions and resentments violent, but transitory, which is always the characteristic of an unpolished people. The ingenuousness of nature is shewn in its real colours, and displayed in all their actions. They do not trouble themselves with the politics of the times, or addict themselves to the habits of thinking, and the cares of the world they have little concern with; for they are free from those occupations, those tremulous solicitudes, which engross the attention of a commercial people. With respect to their language, I am not sufficiently acquainted to give any opinion; to my ear, I must confess, it is not very harmonious; but resembles rather the ravishing sounds of a cat-call, or the musical clack of a flock of geese when highly irritated. The dialects are extremely various, and the difference is often observable, even between adjacent counties; but in North and South Wales, there is so great a variation, that they may almost be said to be different languages. Yet, notwithstanding, I feel much pleasure whenever I hear it spoken, being the old Celtic dialect, which, together with the simplicity of the country people, brings back to my mind the memory of former times; but my ideas of them are so imperfect, and our knowledge in general, of the relative virtue and happiness of our Celtic ancestors, so confused, that I scarcely know whether to rejoice that those times are past, or wish that they may again return with respect to them, and the Welsh as they are at this day, there appears to me to be this material distinction: the former knew not what wealth (in the modern acceptation of the word) was; and consequently were strangers to many vices attendant upon it. The latter, from their intercourse with the rich and mercantile parts of Great Britain, have unfortunately acquired a relish for riches without the means of procuring them: hence arises that pride which prompts them to conceal their poverty, and that jealousy of their national character and situation, which breaks out almost upon every occasion. The children are remarkably beautiful, and usually well made, but this only continues during their infancy; for, from the age of ten and upwards, they begin to bear the marks of hard labour, and still more precarious subsistence. — A haggard countenance, a reduced appearance, and, in short, all the traces of a premature old age: sad proofs these of poverty and wretchedness; and but too true indications of misery and want, and of an inferiority of condition, justifiable upon no grounds whatever, either of revealed religion, or natural equity. The population of North Wales, compared with its extent, is very trifling, and unequal. This may be accounted for from a long chain of causes, but chiefly from the continual state of discord and warfare, in which the chiefs and princes were always involved, until the final subjugation of Wales by Edward the First, and even then, the inhabitants were treated merely as a conquered people, and admitted to few privileges of the conquerors; for it was not till the time of Henry the Eighth, that they were suffered to have the same advantages with English subjects. Secondly, from the situation of the country, which is too remote for the English land trader, and opposed to a very dangerous sea; added to which its ports are by no means so commodious and safe as those of England. Thirdly, and principally, the barrenness of the soil, together with the mountainous nature of the country, and consequently the great difficulty of land carriage, which is the chief obstacle to its internal trade. These are certainly serious impediments to the flourishing state and prosperity of the people; but they are not beyond a remedy, and it ought to become the duty of the legislature to provide every possible means of improvement, and to endeavour, by wisdom and attention, to remove or diminish those local inconveniences which are a bar to the happiness of the society of any particular district or tract of land over which that legislature has dominion; establish manufactures, hold out rewards for agriculture; in short, increase the population of the country by the most approved methods; wealth will follow of course, commerce will be extended, and the now desolated mountains of North Wales may, at least, repay the labour of cultivation, though they can never be so productive and flourishing as those of their southern neighbours.

J. Hucks, **A pedestrian tour in North Wales in a series of letters, 1795**

. . . .

"The children, though thinly clad, ruddy and smiling"

. . . .

A Welsh Cottage on Elenydd, near Teifi Pools showed the traveller that money mattered less than it did for the English poor.

After such an uncomfortable rencontre, conceive the gratification to us, as well as to this vassal of superstition, afforded, by a *cur*, whose barking announced that we were not far from a human habitation. It was one of those poor huts that are thinly sprinkled by the sides of the hills, inhabited by peaters and shepherds. As we approached, first one and then two more fine children, almost in a state of nudity, ran out to see what little *Twrch* could be so alarmed at. A stout fresh-coloured woman, with dark sparkling eyes and black hair, made her appearance, habited in a striped gown and flannel petticoat, who seeing our condition, welcomed us by the most inviting sounds in her language to her little cot. It was partly formed by an excavation in the slate rock, and partly by walls of mud mixed with chopped rushes, covered with segs, and having a wattled or basket-work chimney. The entrance was at the gable end, facing the south east, which was defended during the night, or in very cold weather, by a wattled hurdle, clothed with rushes. A wail of turfs for fuel served as a partition for the bed-room; furnished with a bed of heath and dried rushes in one corner. The furniture was such as necessity dictated: some loose stones formed the grate; two large ones, with a plank across, supplied the place of chairs; a kettle, with a back stone for baking oaten cakes, answered every culinary purpose; and two coarse earthen pitchers stood by for the preserving or carrying water and dodgriafel [diod griafol, a drink made from hawthorn berries], the usual beverage of the family. On our making some inquiries respecting the neighbourhood, she expressed a wish that her husband had been at home, as he would have been able to have given us the desired information. *You have a husband* then, said I? with a smile of approbation upon her face, she replied, Yes, blessed be God! he and his father before him were *born* here; and she was as happy as any of the *great folk,* for that he loved her and his children, and worked very hard, and they wanted for nothing he could get for them: he was a *peater*, digging peat in the adjoining moors, and curing it for sale. Asking what wages he might get, she said that depended upon the weather, sometimes six shillings in the week, and sometimes three or four; that they had a little cow on the lease, and a few sheep upon the hills. What assistance do *you* give? said I: she observed, shaking her head at the time, that she could do but very little; her work was knitting, at which, with the assistance of her two eldest girls, one five and the other seven, if not interrupted, they could earn five pence a day; but that the younger children engrossed much of her time, and she soon expected another. Now, my friend, collect what they had to maintain a *family of seven,* a man, his wife, and five children!! The mother looked in health, and the children, though thinly clad, ruddy and smiling.

[...]

Indeed, there did not appear any thing like the misery and filth observable in the dwellings of many of the English poor, whose weekly income is four or six times as great. Though the floor was formed of the native rock, it was regularly swept with a besom made of segs, bound with a band of the same; and the fuel was as regularly piled as bread on a baker's shelves. All appeared in order, and the air of content apparent in the looks of this humble peasant and her family put us all justly to the blush; and a series of superior blessings, too often abused or too often forgotten, rushed instantly upon our recollection, at witnessing so much reason and gratitude in the habitation of penury. If we had reason to be thankful that we were not constrained thus to earn our bread, and live secluded amidst these mountains; we had still more so for the education which had given us greater degrees of knowledge, and, if not lost to ourselves, of greater happiness. We were anxious to know in what school she had learned so *important a lesson*: Sir, says she, we regularly go to yonder church, pointing to the hills; and if it be bad weather, we stop at Mr. Jones's meeting by the way, where we hear much the same things: that all we have is the gift of God, and that if we possess health and strength, we possess more than we deserve; if sensible of our utter unworthiness we sincerely believe in the Redeemer, and, following his example, perform the duties enjoined us in his gospel, relying for assistance on his Holy Spirit; conducting ourselves with propriety in that state of life in which it has pleased God to call us, we shall, after death, change this poor uncertain life for a better, where we shall be for ever happy; and the frequent interment of our friends and neighbours informs us daily this event can be at no great distance. Astonished at so much good sense and piety, where I so little expected to find it, I exclaimed, *Just step into this humble cot, ye rich and gay,* and learn *that happiness* ye so earnestly seek in vain; a happiness neither wealth nor pleasure can bestow.

John Evans, Letters written during a tour through South Wales, in the year 1803, and at other times, 1804

"An honest Cambrian of a very respectable appearance"

Goodness was a simple thing.

The road from thence to Llanvilling is very intricate, and we contrived to lose our way more than once, notwithstanding we had been told it was as straight as an arrow; we wanted about five miles of the latte place, when we met with an honest Cambrian of a very respectable appearance — we did not fail to make some enquiry of him concerning our road; he stopped his horse very politely, and informed us that he was then returning from Llanvilling, the place of his nativity, which he had not seen for more than twenty years before; he added that we should find an excellent inn, and plenty of the best ale in Wales he then wished us a pleasant walk, assuring us we should meet with princely accommodations, and earnestly recommending the sign of the *goat,* at the same time advising us to make use of his name, for Owen ap Jones ap Evans was as well known as any name in Wales. I relate this little anecdote to you, because I think the character of a people is best delineated by their actions, and their leading features are as completely developed by an action, or an anecdote of themselves, apparently insignificant, as they could possibly be in five hundred philosophical pages upon the nature of climate, situation, or government, and the physical causes and effects they may have upon the human genius and disposition.

**J. Hucks, A pedestrian tour in North Wales
in a series of letters, 1795**

"But the lower classes seem to be in every respect poorer"

No connection was made between the observations that Brecknock had a high proportion of country houses, and that its peasants were poorer than those in Glamorgan.

With respect to the condition of the common people, it invariably strikes the eye, on entering this county from Glamorganshire, that the appearance of the cottages, and the condition of the cottagers, changes, for the worse. The pride of decorating them, and the comfort of keeping them in repair, seem no longer to enter into the scale of happiness. The gardens and potatoe grounds are not universal, and seem, where they are possessed, not to be very highly valued. Even in the town of Brecknock, the habitations of the labouring poor are in a much worse condition, than streets similarly occupied in the most insignificant town of Glamorganshire, in the vale. Yet Brecknock contains an unusual portion of accommodation for the rich. But the lower classes seem to be in every respect poorer, and to live more hardly. They have no large manufacturing establishments, so that agriculture is the principal object of attention; yet they make a considerable quantity of coarse cloth and stockings in different places. Provisions and labour are not so much advanced as in Glamorganshire, but are much higher than when you advance to the north or west.

Benj. Heath Malkin, The Scenery, Antiquities and
Biography of South Wales, from materials collected
during two excursions in the year 1803, 1804

Benjamin Heath Malkin (1769-1842) was educated at Harrow and Trinity College, Cambridge and became a Doctor of Civil Law at St Mary Hall, Oxford (now Oriel College). He was the Headmaster of Bury St Edmunds Free School for 19 years before being appointed the first Professor of History at the University of London in 1829. He married Charlotte Williams, the daughter of the Vicar of Cowbridge and died in Cowbridge in 1842. He pioneered the appreciation of William Blake by writing a brief biography in 1806 along with publishing a number of his lyric poems.

"With the appellation of a pig-stye"

Sometimes absolute poverty could lose its picturesque charms.

We now for many miles passed a barren, dreary country, completely encircled with hills, and we only climbed one, to observe still others rising in the distant perspective: not even a house or tree appeared to interrupt the awfulness of the mountains, which, after the copious fall of rain in the night, teemed with innumerable cataracts. According to our directions, we enquired at the foot of Plinlimmon for Rhees Morgan, as a proper man to be our Conductor over the heights of the "fruitful father of rivers." This man being absent, the whole family appeared thunderstruck at our appearance, and ran with all haste imaginable into their miserable cot, or which might rather be dignified with the appellation of a pig-stye; as that *filthy animal* seemed to claim, with the wretched family, an equal right to a share of the hovel. One apartment served for the inhabitants of every description, with only one small hole to admit the light; the entrance unprotected by a door, but with a blanket as a substitute, was exposed to the pitiless blast of the winter's storm. Reviewing this despicable hovel, I recalled to my mind a very just observation of Goldsmith's, "that one half of the world are ignorant how the other half lives."

'The Author' (Allen Cliffe),
The Cambrian Directory, 1800

....

"All these habits are favourable to health and long life"

....

Another benefit of being poor was that it ensured longevity.

The habits of living among the common people in Glamorgan are favourable to health. They generally wear flannel shirts; and most of those who wear linen have flannel waistcoats under it. Though we mould not suppose it at a funeral, or on any occasion of conviviality, there is habitually less malt liquor drank here than in any part of the kingdom, and less animal food eaten. Their drink is in general water, or milk and water. Tea is also very much used. Their food is chiefly good wheaten bread, with cheese, butter, and milk in farm-houses. They use vegetables of all sorts in large quantities, and many kinds of food prepared from apples, gooseberries, and other fruits. Flummery made with oat-meal is used frequently in the vale, and almost daily in the mountains. Broths made from all sorts of meat are much used; in which large quantities of potherbs and other vegetables form a principal ingredient; abundance of leeks, onions, shalots, parsley, savoury, pennyroyal, marjoram, thyme, cresses, beets, lettuces, spinage, and other productions of the garden. Herb broth, as it is called, is much used by the common people. It may be considered as the Welsh soup maigre. It is water, thickened a very little with oatmeal, into which they put large quantities of such herbs as may be at hand, or in season. They relish it with a little salt, put into it a little butter, and take it with bread. All these habits are favourable to health and long life.

Benj. Heath Malkin, The Scenery, Antiquities and Biography of South Wales, from materials collected during two excursions in the year 1803, 1804

....

"The yeomanry and peasants are very civil and obliging"

....

Joseph Craddock's survey of the indolence of the gentry and poverty of the peasants does not make for comfortable reading.

I will not say the 'squires in Wales, differ materially from those of the same rank in England, except that they are more devoted to the jolly god. For like the Thracïans of old, when a stranger comes among them, they will do him the honors of the house [In every house that I visited in Wales, they had a capacious horn, or other enormous utensil, which they obliged every man to drink that came, filled with Cwrw, the Welsh word for strong ale.], by obliging him to drink intemperately; and will at least expect him to make a compliment of his reason, in return for their hospitality. They have, however, some good qualities, in a greater degree than the English. They keep better houses, employ a greater number of poor, are less avaritious, and are more charitable.

The clergy are in general the only people that have any knowledge of letters; to qualify them for orders, they have the advantage of a good school education;

and spend a considerable time at the university. It is the general, and I believe well founded, complaint of the country, that they return from thence very little improved, in their morals or learning. A certain air of pedantry, accompanied with vain assurance, and the acquisition of some fashionable vices, are too often the only means of distinguishing such as have had an university education.

[…]

Most of the clergy have two or three churches each to serve, and consequently it is impossible the duty should be properly discharged. Evening prayers are seldom read, and in many places they scarce ever preach. The benefices are for the most part of pretty considerable value, being a decent maintenance for a clergyman. Except in a few towns, and on the borders of England, the service of their churches is performed altogether in the Welsh or old British tongue.

The yeomanry and peasants are very civil and obliging in their behavior. They have not the ferocious disposition, which characterises the English, flowing from that spirit of liberty and independence, which animates the soul of an Englishman. They are shrewd and artful in their dealings. They have an inveterate rooted antipathy to all foreigners, especially English and Irish. If a stranger is so unfortunate as to go and live amongst them, they look upon him with a jealous eye, as one who comes with an intent to deprive them of their subsistence.

The manner of living of the lower class of people, is extremely poor. The chief of their subsistence, being barley and oat bread. They scarce ever eat flesh, or drink any thing but milk. They are not of that passionate and choleric temper, as the English describe them, but slow, deliberate, and wary in their speech and conduct, and submissive in their disposition. I know not whether to attribute it to their manner of life, or to the great power the 'squires exercise over them. Certain it is, that the people of this country in general, have no greater idea of English liberty than the peasants of France.

Joseph Cradock, Letters from Snowdon, 1770

"They are on fire in an instant"

From an English perspective, this was a relatively classless society. That particular myth endures to this day.

I will not deny that the Welsh are tinctured with what is called their native warmth of temper. For if, by any inadvertent or ill timed observation, you reflect upon either their country or their manners, they are on fire in an instant: but even this heat may be as suddenly extinguished as it was kindled. The least concession on your part, or acknowledgment that you have wronged them, and are sorry for it, will restore their wonted good humour, and their face again resumes its natural tranquillity. I verily believe, they have not the smallest particle of resentment in their whole composition. Who then would wish to rob them of their harmless jealousy of the honour of their native land, and particularly since it is a land that charms every body? Happy, thrice happy would it be for these Welsh gentlemen who have spent their patrimony in imitating English follies and English extravagance, had they retained a little more of their national prejudices, and set a proper value on those charming woods, mountains, and rivers, where fertility unites with commerce to bring to their very gates all that is useful and valuable in life.

[...]

If this place is deficient in any thing that may be deemed a comfort or a luxury, it is in vegetables and fruit. These are neither plentiful, nor in great perfection. But people of fortune know very well how to remedy this defect in their soil. Almost every body has a hot-house. I never was in any place where there were so many, for it chiefly consists of people who have an independency. There are very few carriages kept here, which is easily accounted for by the roads being stony and unpleasant for wheels. The ladies ride a great deal on horseback; and who indeed, that had their health and the use of their limbs, would be shut up in a box, when they can delight their eyes with such a charming country every step they ride? Another reason may be given for their not feeling the want of carriages at Haverfordwest; which is, that they have a number of sedan chairs always at command.

There does not seem to be that distinction of ranks, which subsists in most large towns. The people mix with ease together, and particularly the men. You see them standing at shop-doors in a morning, talking politics, or hearing and communicating the news of the day; and in an evening they meet at an inn, and either play at billiards, or are jolly over a bottle. But this latter custom is wearing away very fast, and, I believe, is chiefly kept up by the elderly part of the community. The young and the middle-aged, particularly the married men, visit with their families. Their natural love for the sex, united to their desire of amusement, make them fond of joining in parties where there are females.

Those gentlemen who, by education, and an acquaintance with the world have got rid of their national heat, have a softness of manners, that is perfectly pleasing; yet they still retain enough of their native spirit to make them manly and unaffected. They do not perhaps improve as fast as they might. Like some stones they resist the chizel at first; but when the impression is once made, they take the finest and most durable polish.

**Mrs. Morgan, A tour to Milford Haven,
in the year 1791, 1795**

BED-CHAMBERS AND BATHING BEAUTIES

....

"These tender sabbatical preliminaries"

....

While there was an almost voyeuristic fascination with the bed-chambers and bathing habits of the Welsh, they were often described in the most circumspect language. 'Cymro' (Chapter 11) thought this was worthy of satire.

And here amongst the usages and customs, I must not omit to inform you, that what you have, perhaps, often heard without believing respecting the *mode* of *courtship* amongst the Welch peasants, is true. The lower order of people, do actually carry on their love affairs in bed, and what would extremely astonish more polished lovers, they are carried on honourably, it being, at least, as

233

usual, for the pastora's of the mountains to go from the bed of courtship to the bed of marriage, as unpolluted and maidenly as the Chloes of fashion; and yet, you are not to conclude that this proceeds from their being less susceptible of the *belle passion* than their betters: or that the cold air, which they breathe, has "froze the genial current of their souls." By no means; if they cannot boast the voluptuous languors of an Italian sky, they glow with the bracing spirit of a more invigorating atmosphere. I really took some pains to investigate this curious custom, and after being assured, by many, of its veracity, had an opportunity of attesting its existence with my own eyes, The servant maid of the family I visited in Caernarvonshire, happened to be the object of a young peasant, who walked eleven long miles every Sunday morning, to favour his suit, and regularly returned the same night through all weathers, to be ready for m,onday's employment in the fields, being simply a day labourer. He usually arrived in time for morning service, which he constantly attended, after which he escorted his Dulcinea home to the house of her master, by whose permission they as constantly passed the succeeding hour in bed, according to the custom of the country. These tender sabbatical preliminaries continued without any interruption near two years, when the treaty of alliance was solemnized; and so far from any breach of articles happening in the intermediate time, it is most likely that it was considered by both parties as a matter of course, without exciting any other idea. On speaking to my friend on the subject, he observed that, though it certainly appeared a dangerous mode of making love, he had seen so few *living* abuses of it, during six and thirty years residence in that county, where it, nevertheless, had always, more or less, prevailed, he must conclude it was as innocent as any other. – One proof of its being thought so by the parties, is the perfect ease and freedom with which it is done; no awkwardness or confusion appearing on either side; the most well-behaved and decent young women giving into it without a blush, and they are by no means deficient in modesty. What is pure in idea is always so in conduct, since bad actions are the common consequence of ill thoughts; and though the better sort of people treat this ceremony as a barbarism, it is very much to be doubted whether more *faux pas* have been committed by the Cambrian boors in this *free access* to the bed-chambers of their mistresses, than by more fashionable Strephons and their nymphs…in groves and shady bowers. The power of habit is, perhaps, stronger than the power of passion, or even of the charms which inspire it; and it is sufficient, almost, to say a thing is the *custom of a country* to clear it from any reproach that would attach to an innovation. Were it the practice of a few only, and to be gratified by stealth, there would, from the strange construction of human nature, be more cause of suspicion; but being ancient, general, and carried on without difficulty, it is, probably as little dangerous as a tete-a-tete in a drawing-room, or in any other full-dress place, where young people meet to say soft things to each other. A moon-light walk in Papa's garden, where Miss steals out to meet her lover *against the consent of her parents*, and, of course, extremely agreeable to the young people, has ten times the peril.

Samuel Pratt, Gleanings through Wales, Holland and Westphalia,Vol. I, 1795

....

"The indecent customs of the Welch"

....

Watching partially dressed bathers required some stamina, but it was a necessary duty in order to contemplate their morals.

At length we parted with this agreeable scenery; and soon after, on a sudden turn of the lane, came within view of the picturesque ruin of Llanstephan castle. A farming party also appeared at this instant, proceeding with goods for Caermarthen market. This group was opened by a robust young fellow driving a couple of cows; he wore the general dress of the country, a short blue coarse cloth coat, and breeches of the same open at the knees; but he also possessed the luxury of shoes and stockings. A sledge loaded with sacks of grain followed; drawn by a horse, on which a lusty wench sat astride, as the peasant girls generally do in Wales; cloathed in a brown jirkin and petticoat, but with her lower extremities uncovered. She urged on the horse by kicking him with her bare heels, while her hands were busied in knitting. Two other buxom bare-legged girls followed on foot, with their fingers similarly employed, and with large baskets of eggs and poultry on their heads. But a word on the sledge, the common farming carriage in Wales. — This is a most simple contrivance, consisting of two rude poles, between which the horse is placed; their ends trail on the ground, toward which extremity there are two or three cross bars; a few upright sticks from these complete the carriage. A comely dame, seated on horseback, and accommodated with a sort of sidesaddle made with cross rails, was probably the mistress; she closed the rear; and her superior condition was evident, in her dark blue worsted stockings, ponderous shoes, and small brass buckles.

[...]

We passed from this wild abode, and floundered among ditch-like tracks to recover the high road from Llandilo to Swansea. In a romantic hollow we were stopped by a branch of the Towey; which, though in ordinary times an inconsiderable rivulet, was now swelled to a deep and menacing torrent. Here we found a party of men and women peasants on the opposite side, in doubt whether it might be safely crossed; but at length one of the men stripped and waded over, thus satisfying us that the ford was practicable. The rest followed; the men first getting rid of the lower part of their dress; — a trouble avoided by the females, who, unused to the encumbrance of shoes and stockings, had only to hold up their clothes to the highest extent; and, thus prepared, the whole party moved toward us. Viewing this remnant of barbarity with disgust, we at the same time felt uneasy for the situation of the girls: but we might have spared ourselves that pain; their countenances proved them to be unembarrassed by the consciousness of shame; nor did their eyes wander from the precise line in which they were going. The transaction was to them a matter of perfect indifference.

It may reasonably be supposed, that the indecent customs of the Welch operate against the observance of chastity: yet seeing that the Welch are by no means deficient in that excellence, it may be supposed that were such scenes less frequent they would be so; but, as they are continually recurring, the imagination has no time to effervesce; it is at once saturated with naked facts, and on that principle the ebullitions of passion are kept under. On the one hand, those strong bulwarks decency and delicacy are done away; but on the other, the mind, fully informed, is not irritated by the conjurations of fancy; which may be a pretty fair set-off. Yet, without doubt, their strongest safeguard exists in the considerative defence; for the moral turpitude and political infamy of unchastity is recognized in Wales to an extent that can hardly be conceived in circles of modern refinement: even at this day, in districts not yet drawn within the imposing vortex of trade, a golden age of innocence may be discovered, where bastardy is unknown, or known but in recorded instances, in which the man is properly consigned to equal disgrace with the female offender.

J. T. Barber, A tour throughout South Wales and Monmouthshire, 1803

....

"Both sexes promiscuously enjoying themselves"

....

When watching, it was also necessary to remind the reader that this was not a pleasant undertaking.

Abergeley is a small watering place, about half a mile from the sea. — They have a strange custom there, that has an air of great indelicacy to a stranger; which is, that the inferior orders of people commonly bathe, without the usual precautions of machines or dresses; nor is it singular to see ten or a dozen of both sexes promiscuously enjoying themselves in the lucid element, regardless, or rather unconscious, of any indecency. Not being myself accustomed to this mode, I chose to retire farther up; but it is very unpleasant bathing, being a flat level beach, and necessary to wade a quarter of a mile into the sea before one can arrive at any comfortable depth.

**J. Hucks, A pedestrian tour in
North Wales in a series of letters, 1795**

···

"Gambols in the water with the utmost indifference"

···

Readers were reassured that no depravity arose from mixed naked bathing and that it was indeed beneficial to their health.

An incident of novelty, at least to strangers, and which may serve to exemplify, in a striking manner, one peculiar custom of the country, intervened in this walk. We were pacing our route slowly back [to Ogmore], to take advantage of the delicious coolness of the evening, rendered doubly grateful after the oppressive sultry heats of the day, which we had nearly spent in perambulating the burning sands, when we were unexpectedly overtaken by a merry party of barefooted females, amounting altogether to about thirty, including girls and women. Most of them being attired in dark blue striped clothes, with scarlet cloaks, and hats of black beaver, in the true style of the south wallian peasantry, their appearance at the first deceived us greatly. ... Having once overtaken us, the party hastened briskly along, greeting us at parting with a favourite Welsh tune, which they chaunted in chorus with such a vigorous exertion of vocal powers, as convinced us they were determined to banish care. We now perceived that some were on horseback, huddled in pairs or groups of three or four together, the foremost one of which invariably sat astride, to govern the poor little ponies on which they rode with more facility. Others suffered themselves to be drawn along the rugged road in sleds, a kind of vehicle without wheels, which the farmers use in the fields for gathering in the hay, and which, for this purpose, were suspended to the horse, by means of traces made of hay-bands; while the rest walked barefooted, carrying their shoes in their hands. The appearance of this formidable troop of females in such a lonely situation, and at such an hour, excited various speculations in our minds as to the motives they had in view, knowing the road they were pursuing would only lead to the dreary extent of sands we were to traverse in returning to the bathing house. But the whole mystery of their rambles was unravelled soon after. They were coming down from the adjacent villages, to enjoy the pleasures of bathing in the open sea in the cool of the evening, and when we crossed the sands, they appeared before us without disguise in the very same predicament as the chaste Diana and her attendant fair ... The sportive damsels were neither terrified nor amazed at our unexpected presence, and continued their gambols in the water with the utmost indifference and composure, when they found we had no intention of approaching nearer to them than was necessary to pursue our journey. —So far has custom given countenance to a practice not altogether consistent with the refined ideas entertained of female morals in populous towns, or even in the inland parts of Wales. But along this coast the custom of bathing naked in the sea is so prevalent with both sexes, that nothing amiss is thought of it. And surely while the mind remains undepraved by such procedure, the benefits arising from it are not to be disputed: the men along this coast are remarkably hardy, and the women, though not robust, are healthy, strong, and capable of enduring a vast degree of labour.

E. Donovan, Descriptive excursions through South Wales and Monmouthshire in the year 1804, and the four preceding summers, Vol. I, 1805

....

"This palpable inconvenience"

....

Barmouth was seen as better suited for riding than bathing as the bathing machines did not decorously reach the waves.

Barmouth, though considered as a bathing-place, is very inferior to Tenby, yet its situation for grandeur of rocks, has been frequently compared, by many Tourists, to Gibraltar; and by others, esteemed not unlike St. Kitts, in the West Indies, The vast sand banks, formed by the tides immediately in front of the town, are the only barriers which protect it from the inundations of the sea. The shore is extremely level, and affords, for many miles, excellent riding. In respect to the bathing, little can be said to recommend it; the machines are not drawn into the water, and by this palpable inconvenience, you are under the disagreeable necessity of walking a considerable way in, before the water is sufficiently deep for "plunging headlong in the briny flood." During our stay here, two gentlemen perceiving that the water was very much alloyed by a fresh water stream disemboguing itself into the sea, at Barmouth, persuaded Mrs. Lewis, the obliging landlady of the Cors-y-gedol Arms, to remove the machines farther from the town; and from them we were informed, that though the salt water was purer, yet they found it impossible to draw them sufficiently deep for good bathing: the machines being stationary on the sands, the ladies likewise find it remarkably inconvenient, being equally compelled to walk in. The folly of this method seems to be more striking, as the objection might be so easily obviated. The lower class here, as in many other parts of Wales, indiscriminately dress and undress on the sands, and pay very little distinction to their sex.

'The Author' (Allen Cliffe),
The Cambrian Directory, 1800

SUPERSTITIONS

....
"Hence the belief in fairies"
....

John Evans's reflections on 'Welsh Credulity and Superstition' focussed on an excessive zeal in the wrong form of religion.

Unbounded credulity is another prominent feature in the character of the Welsh. This subjects them to perpetual imposition: hence their faith in fynnon vair, or holy wells; and the confidence they place in those impudent charlatans in medicine vulgarly denominated *water doctors:* men who, Browne observes, endeavour to make us believe, that there is Aaron's breast-plate in urines; and to these they have recourse as to the oracle of life; make them the determinators of virginity, conception, fecundity, and all the inscrutable infirmities of the human frame; and pretend to resolve things at which the devil of Delphos would demur.

[…]

But credulity is the offspring of superstition, which is made up of an unreasonable degree of religious fear. As soon as religion began to lose its purity, it very fast degenerated; and instead of a comfortable sense of duty, there succeeded a fearful gloom; an unnatural horror, which was continually augmented, as men departed from the source of truth.

[...]

Hence the belief in fairies, the reappearance of departed spirits, supernatural appearances, and miraculous powers exercised by invisible agents during the peaceable time of night is pretty general through the country. What is called second sight in Scotland, here awnmawr, is confined to some districts; and in Cardigan and its borders the belief in canwyll corf, or the *corpse candle* is greatly magnified and extended. This is a light discoverable by some indifferent person previous to the death of another in the neighbourhood; and is looked upon as an infallible prognostic of fatality, in whatever house it is seen to enter: there it is supposed to remain till the time affixed for the interment of the person whose mortality it has presaged, when it moves slowly before the funeral procession; and when the body is laid in the grave it instantly disappears. This phenomenon may be accounted for from the frequent inflammation of hydrogynous gas mixing with atmospheric air, and enkindled by electric matter. Indeed, from the peaty and morassy soils of this district, such is its phosphorescent quality, that often sparks of fire will be seen under the feet of travellers, which, to persons unacquainted with the cause, must appear formidable, if not ominous. From similar causes proceed those luminous effects called, from the supposed shapes they assume, lanterns, flying dragons, dancing giants, &c. &c.

It is a custom in Caermarthenshire to repair at midnight, on the eve of All Souls' Day, to the parish church, to look into the book of fate, then supposed to be opened. After uttering certain prayers, and attending in silence till the awful hour, they suppose they hear distinctly whispered the names of all those that shall die in their neighbourhood during the following year. That this was an imposition practised upon the people during the time of popery, I can readily believe; and there can be little doubt, but the wantonness of the present age tends to support the farce.

During the Christmas holidays, till after twelfth day, it is a custom for persons to assume the shape of a horse, or bull, either clothed in the skin, or dressed in the shape of one of those animals, and attended by a company of idle people to enter the house of respectable people, neighing or bellowing in a hideous manner, and committing other acts of rudeness, to the great terror or annoyance of the inhabitants, who generally, by a gratuity of viands and money, purchase their deliverance from these invaders of their peace. Johnson mentions a similar custom practised in the Hebrides; as also another, very frequent here, that of bowing or courtesying, and blessing the *new moon*. Others, common to both parts of the principality, I have mentioned in my description of North Wales: many of them clearly relics of the impious rites and ridiculous ceremonies used in the *Saturnalia* of the ancient Romans. A spirit directly opposite to this has, however, of late years occupied the bosom of the Welsh. *A misguided and excessive zeal in matters of religion.* If superstition fears, enthusiasm presumes too much; and the danger from presumption is greater than from fear. The one is consistent with humility, the other is constantly accompanied by pride. Standing on the ground where Christianity was planted, at a very early period, and which had for ages been the theatre for the display of truth in greater purity than in many other places, we could not but lament to see the present humiliating state of the church and the ravages made in the flock of Christ. Methodism, as it is vulgarly termed, wears a very different aspect in the southern to what it does in the northern part of the principality. It does not however consist in heresy, but in fanaticism; not so much in perverse, or unscriptural doctrines, as a disorderly zeal for the propagation of truth; which produces irregularity, confusion, and many evil works.

John Evans, Letters written during a tour through South Wales, in the year 1803, and at other times, 1804

....

"A night thus spent in penitence must effect a cure"

....

Belief in the power of prayer amongst 'the lower orders' was frowned upon.

A second visit to Christ Church concluded this agreeable excursion from the Newport road to Caerleon. —On the evening before, we had toiled up the laborious ascent leading from the latter place to this venerable edifice, in order to survey its interior at our leisure; as well as at the same time to pay due attention to the ancient monument preserved here, whose miraculous virtues in the cure of all disorders, on a certain day of the year, is credulously believed amongst the country people. The preceding evening happening to be the eve of Trinity Thursday, we were unexpectedly present at the visitation of a large party of these poor deluded people to the very tomb-stone whose fame had awakened our curiosity; and the inspection of which, indeed, had been the chief motive of our journey thither. The old clerk of Caerleon accompanied us in our walk up the road, without recollecting the circumstance: we were even debating upon the propriety of borrowing the key of the Church from the sexton, who has a cottage hard by, when we perceived the doors were already open. Upon entering the aile, the sound of several voices assailed our ears, arising, as it afterwards appeared, from a group of persons assembled together in the chancel. We accordingly passed down the Church to the spot from whence it seemed to issue; and there, to our inexpressible astonishment, we beheld a young man of very creditable appearance, with his night cap on, laying upon the bare pavement, shivering with cold, his hands uplifted, and with many pious aspirations, muttering a prayer, for the cure of some affliction, under which he appeared to labour. – During this religious farce, his friends formed a spacious circle round him, some standing, some sitting, and others kneeling, as best accorded with their inclinations; but all were equally intent in watching the countenance and motion of the patient, to observe the progressive advancement of the miracle wrought upon him, in consequence of this superstitious ceremony.

Perceiving that at our approach those who were seated, rose up, I paused immediately. – "There is the old tomb-stone," whispered Jones to my fellow-traveller, pointing at the same time aside with his finger, to the stone on which the young man was laying; and so it proved to be on a nearer view. Curiosity, on this occasion, gave place to other, and I trust it will be accredited, to better feelings: the enormous magnitude of the slab, it is true, would have allowed us sufficient opportunity to trace the inscription on the stone, without disturbing this object of our pity, while the people, finding we were strangers, and learning from our conductor the purpose of our visit, might have permitted us to examine it, but it would have still been, in my mind, highly indecorous to indulge any such impertinent propensity at this crisis. After a few minutes spent in observing the ceremony, we therefore left him, regretting only that his piety had not been better directed, than to the reputed sanctity of the stone, or of the two frail mortals whose ashes reposed beneath it. — Or if custom, ignorance, or superstition had induced him to spend a night of penitence upon this stone, that the indulgence of a feather bed had been allowed, in addition to the pillow on which his head alone was permitted to recline.

"Well, do you really think, gentlemen, it will do the young man any service," enquired one who had been seated in the circle, eagerly of us, as he followed our footsteps out of the Church. There was something in his manner, and attentive eye, while he spoke, that seemed to imply no small share of confidence in the result of the answer he should receive, for what reason we knew not, but I was not disposed, whatever might be his opinion of us, to weaken his belief in the efficacy of this extraordinary remedy; to destroy his hopes would have been painful, to have flattered them imprudent: the question was unexpected, and the reply was cautious. From this dilemma we were, however, soon relieved by *Jones*, who very innocently remarked, that "the prayers of good people, such as these saints had been, availeth much;—yet he did not *know* that it would be of any service to lay upon the cold stone all night." "Besides," added he, "the young man being sick already, may catch cold, and be worse instead of better: he may get rid of one disorder, and have another overtake him:" to this *sound* reasoning we did not think proper to withhold our assent, and the conversation ended by the countryman rejoining, that he was afraid so too.

On the thursday morning, the stools and cushions remained about the grave-stone, as on the former evening. We were also given to understand, that the poor fellow had lain in the manner we had seen him, the whole night; together with a child of about two years of age, that had the rickets, in order to brace his solids and *strengthen* him. The nature of the young man's complaint could not be learned; they only knew that he was troubled with fits, and had come from the other side of the hills, in the firm persuasion, that after all medical aid had failed, a night thus spent in penitence must effect a cure.

The virtues of this remedy in the healing art, is happily for the interest of the village doctors in the district, restrained within very moderate limits. It is only during the night before the revel, or wake, held in the burying ground, by the country people, on Trinity Thursday, (an ancient custom, established in honour of the eucharist,) that the stone possesses this power of charming away diseases. The patients are placed upon it about sun set, and are allowed to depart about five or six o'clock on the following morning, being then assured that its miraculous virtues cease, and that the sick have derived all the benefit they can possibly receive from this act of superstition. We may conceive the number of poor deluded people, who formerly paid their devotions to this grave-stone, was very great: of late years even, so many as two and twenty persons, including both sexes, adults and children, have been known to lie either upon the stone, or the pavement round it, and in some manner touching it: a leg or an arm lying in contact with it, being thought sufficient to work the cure when the case is not very desperate. For the five preceding wakes this stone had been neglected, when the ceremony was revived last summer, in the instance adduced already. — Some time about, or rather before the middle of the last century, as I was told, a gentleman of this part of Monmouthshire, *Squire Van* of Lanwern, exerted his best endeavours to suppress this silly custom. With that view he forbade the meeting of the peasantry in the Church on the eve of Trinity thursday, and to ensure implicit obedience to his commands, ordered the doors to be securely locked, that no one should obtain admittance. This was performed accordingly, when, marvellous to relate, at the hour of midnight the bells began ringing of themselves, and continued to alarm the whole country with their deep, incessant peals, till the dawn of morning, after which they ceased. The delinquent, fully convinced that he had acted against the will of Heaven, from this awful warning, could not possibly believe that any wicked rogue had secreted himself in the Church to play the trick upon him, but expressing a due sense of his contrition for the offence, protested he would never more be accessary, in any manner, to the abolition of this tolerated practice. — Whether the fear of another midnight salutation of the bells, or some more serious prank of the invisible agents busy on that occasion, has been dreaded in latter days, or not, is doubtful: the fact is certain, that the people have never been prevented from assembling in the Church for the pious purpose before-mentioned since the belfry resounded so loudly in its vindication.

There are several persons of the Roman Catholic persuasion among the lower orders in this district, who have at least the credit of promoting this extraordinary act of devotion.

E. Donovan, Descriptive excursions through South
Wales and Monmouthshire in the year 1804, and the
four preceding summers, Vol. I, 1805

CLOTHING

....
"A necessary preservation against the damps"
....

In Little England beyond Wales, a Flemish flavour was detected.

There is a particularity in the dress of the Pembrokeshire women, which, because it differs from the rest of the Welsh, I will describe.

The women, even in the midst of summer, generally wear a heavy cloth gown; and instead of a cap, a large handkerchief wrapt over their heads, and tied under their chins.

On first seeing this fantastic head dress, I really

imagined that there was an epidemical swelling or toothache in the country.

It is possible that this fashion might originate from Flanders, as Pembrokeshire was formerly settled by Flemings. In that low country, this head dress might have been thought a necessary preservation against the damps, and a national prejudice may have continued it in Wales, for more than six centuries.

H. P. Wyndham, Gentleman's Tour through
Monmouthshire and Wales in the Months of June and
July, 1774, 1775

....

"Unvitiated by communication with polished life"

....

However, Richard Warner could only identify a 'national' dress.

The dress of the Welsh women is exactly similar throughout the principality, and consists of these particulars: a petticoat of flannel, the manufacture of the country, either blue or striped; a kind of bed-gown with loose sleeves, of the same stuff, but generally of a brown colour; a broad handkerchief over the neck and shoulders; a neat mob-cap, and a man's beaver hat. In dirty, or cold weather, the person is wrapped in a long blue cloak, which descends below the knee. Except when particularly dressed, they go without shoe or stocking; and even if they have these luxuries, the latter in general has no foot to it. The man's attire is a jacket, waistcoat, and breeches, of their country flannel, the last of which are open at the knees, and the stockings (for the men generally wear them) are bound under the knees with red garters. Both men and women are vivacious, cheerful, and intelligent, not exhibiting that appearance of torpor and dejection which characterize the labouring poor of our own country; their wants being few, are easily supplied; a little milk, which their own mountain goat, or the benevolence of a neighbouring farmer, affords them, an oaten cake, and a few potatoes, furnish the only meal which they desire. Unvitiated by communication with polished life, they continue to think and act as nature dictates. Confined to their own mountains, they witness no scenes of profusion and extravagance to excite envy or malignity, by a comparison between their own penury and the abundance of others. They look round and see nothing but active industry and unrepining poverty, and are content.

Richard Warner, A walk through
Wales in August 1797, 1798

AMUSEMENTS

....
"A well-proportioned fairy"
....

Thomas Pennant was introduced to a dwarf.

During my stay at *Penmorva,* I was desired to observe *Dick Bach,* a diminutive person, who casually called there. He was servant to a neighboring gentleman, about the age of thirty, and only three feet eleven inches high. He was pointed out to me only for the sake of describing his sister, *Mary Bach o Cwmmain,* or, little *Mary* of *Cwmmain;* a well-proportioned fairy, of the height of three feet four. Her virtues are superior to her size: she brews, bakes, pickles; in short, does every thing that the best housekeeper can do. Their parents live in these parts, have many children of the common stature of man; but nature chose to sport in the formation of this little pair.

Thomas Pennant, A tour in Wales, Vol. II, 1781

....

"That I am tolerably strong: you must confess it"

....

Near Llanberis resided a notably strong lady.

I was one day strolling with my friend Williams along the vale, when he pointed out to me a female well known in this village, and who, from the masculine tone of her voice, her manners, and appearance, might have been a descendant of the celebrated Margaret Uch Evan, called

Caddy Of Cwm Glas.

This athletic female does not often visit the town of Caernarvon; but, whenever she does, the boys run after, and call her, " the woman with a beard." Caddy resides in Cwm Glâs, a romantic vale, about two miles from Llanberis. She is accustomed to masculine employments of every description, and such is her muscular power, that no man of the village would dare to try a fall with her. Mr. Jones of the copper-mine had often rallied her on the subject of her great strength, and told her that he did not believe half the stories that he had heard related: she one day, in perfect good humour, came behind him, as he was standing on the bank of the pier, near the stamping mill, and lifting him from the ground, held him in her arm, though by no means a small man, with great apparent ease, over the water. "Now, Sir, (says she)

I suppose you will believe that I am tolerably strong: you must confess it, or I shall throw you in." He immediately acknowledged her powers, and was relieved from his predicament. — About eighteen months ago, a huge, raw-boned fellow, entered her cottage, during her absence, and had collected together some eatables and clothes, with which he was escaping, just as she returned. Though this cottage is in a very solitary situation, and she was entirely alone, she resolutely went up and insisted on his returning every thing he had taken. He opened his wallet, and gave up the eatables. Supposing these to be all, she returned with them to the cottage. But soon after discovering that a silk handkerchief, which she had left on the table, was gone, she immediately seized one of the bars of a small gate in her hand, and went in pursuit of the thief. She overtook him in the most solitary part of the vale, and, brandishing her cudgel about his ears, with the utmost courage, demanded restitution of the remainder of her property. An answer she did not wait for, but seizing the bag from the cowardly scoundrel, shook the whole contents, with the most contemptuous air, upon the ground. When she had selected her own property, she threw the bag in the fellow's face; and, after bestowing a hearty thwack with her cudgel on each of his shoulders, left her opponent to comfort himself with the idea of having escaped a more sound drubbing, which, as she afterwards declared, she would have inflicted, had she thought it necessary.

William Bingley, North Wales, Vol. I, 1804

"The amusements of the country"

Rural thespians provided some amusement for the cultured onlooker.

It is a custom likewise invariably observed to make a bonfire near every house on All saints eve. Whether this was originally owing to public rejoicing, or to some superstitious ceremony, I could never be informed.

Among the amusements of the country, the principal are the stage plays. You will smile, when I tell you that we have comedies and tragedies. King David and Solomon are often brought upon the stage, and are taught to speak pure Welsh. These entertainments are called ANTERLUTES, which seems to be no more than a corruption of the English word interlude.

My curiosity prevailed upon me to go and see one of these plays acted, the stage consisted of some boards fixed at the end of a barn; beneath it was the green room; for it was a small inclosure made up of furze. The play that was acted, was king Lear; but so mutilated and murdered, that I was told it had scarce any other resemblance to the play written by Shakespeare, than the name. It was not unentertaining to see these brawny ploughmen, act in the characters of Lear's daughters.

The two principal characters which they never fail to introduce into every play, are those of the fool and miser. The former uses all kind of indecent ribaldry, obscene gestures, and expressions, which generally prove highly entertaining to the audience.

Joseph Cradock, Letters from Snowdon, 1770

··

"Dogs pop their heads out of the oven-holes"

··

Ovens were used for keeping dogs in.

English is spoken pretty generally here, and the inhabitants are sufficiently courteous to strangers, though, we could not but remark, our welcome was the more hearty after Mrs. Jones, the hostess, had discovered that our companions, the Th-m-s's, could converse with her in her own dear native tongue. There is little interesting in the village itself, if we except one practice, which, indeed, is not peculiar to this place, but extends to all the hamlets through Cwm Neath; I mean the singular use to which the *ovens* of the cottages are applied. The peasantry all keep dogs, and are surprisingly attached to these domestic animals; in proof of their affection, they allow them to occupy the *ovens* when not engaged by a batch of bread, and actually make beds of straw within them for their better accommodation. The effect produced by this custom is odd enough to a stranger, the moment he enters a cottage, one, two, or three dogs pop their heads out of the oven-holes, and salute him in a manner as strange as unexpected.

Richard Warner, A second walk through Wales in August and September 1798, 1799

....

"For the hog ... is generally considered as *one* of the *family*"

....

Welsh pigs were better mannered than their English cousins and liked to rest in front of the fire.

The peasantry, indeed, in the neighbourhood of this country [Merionethshire], exhibit altogether a specimen of singular manners. Until the formation of the turnpike-road, which I have above described, the use of wheels was scarcely known here, the sled being the only vehicle made use of. The small patches of land amongst the mountains capable of cultivation, are not brought into tillage by the *plough,* or manured by the help of *carts;* the spade being used for the one purpose, and small hand-barrows for the other. But notwithstanding that nature has denied to these people a luxuriant soil, and productive harvests, they still live comfortably, and happily. Every cottager (almost, without an exception) keeps his poney and his cow, the one to assist his labours, the other to furnish him with food. Meat, indeed, he seldom tastes, but his diet is not contemptible—oaten cake, or bread made by a mixture of wheat and rye, hard cheese, potatoes, and excellent butter-milk, furnish a meal substantial and wholesome. The last article, however, is generally diluted with water, and when thus prepared, the beverage is emphatically called *glas ddu,* or *blue water.* Fortunately for these happy, simple people, the use of spirits is not known amongst them; and the high price and small measure of the *cwrrw* effectually prevent them from injuring their health, and ruining their families, by frequently intoxicating themselves even with this national liquor. I had almost forgotten to observe, that the

257

peasant generally adds to his establishment a sow or a hog; which, when fatted, he carries to market, and sells to assist in paying his rent. These are noble animals in Wales, of a large majestic breed, and much more tame and *gentle* in their *manners* than our English pigs. We attributed this, indeed, in a great measure to *education*; for the hog in these highland regions is generally considered as *one* of the *family*; and is very commonly seen reposing comfortably before the cottage fire, with the children of the peasant sporting around him.

Richard Warner, A second walk through Wales in August and September 1798, 1799

··

"The best and most active Country Dancers I ever saw"

··

Dancing was done with finesse through all strata of society.

At the End of a Mead, by this River Side, were a Company dancing in a Barn. They were about nine Couple, genteelly dress'd, and all People of Fortune and Fashion, and I may with Security say, the best and most active Country Dancers I ever saw. We observed that the Men were gay and genteel, handsome and well-shaped; the Women were genteel, without Pride; modest, without Affectation; beautiful, without Art; and free, without Fondness: The generous Hand of Nature appeared in every Face, unspotted with the artful Follies of this degenerate Age. It gave me a strong Idea of the Happiness and Simplicity of the ancient *Britons* before the *Roman* and other Corruptions overwhelm'd the now refined Part of the Island (as we are pleased to term it:) But these Zealots for Liberty maintained their Independency long, and under this happy Government they continue (and may they never end,) their innocent Customs, Manners, and Recreations. A favourite Dance (Bumpers 'Squire *Jones*) I saw them perform with the greatest Spirit, Order, and Exactness. Mr. *Percy* gave us a Sign to follow him, which we did; accordingly he lead us through a throng'd Lane to the Church-Yard, which, though large, was filled with people of almost all Ages and Qualities.

Near this was a little House, where we put off our Riding Coats, &c. The Church is a strong Building, and pretty large, against the Sides of which were a Dozen lusty young Fellows playing at Tennis, and as many against the Steeple at Fives. They play'd very well, but spoke (as indeed almost every one else did) in the *Welch* Tongue. One Side the Church were about six Couple dancing to one Violin, and just below three or four Couple to three Violins, whose Seat was a Tomb Stone. In short, the whole was something whimsically odd. We here saw common Games of Ball against the sacred Pile, and there the Musick playing over the Bones of the deceased. We were in the Middle of a merry noisy Throng, without knowing their Language, or indeed almost any Thing they said.

[...]

Things not pleasing us here, we walk'd up the Hill towards the Church-yard; here we found a large Concourse of People, and under a Yew-Tree, was about ten Couple Dancing to the Tune of an indifferent Fiddle: Against the Tower, were some of the most active Lads I've seen, playing at Fives; their Language was entirely *Welch*. Here we met, of Mr. *Percy's* Acquaintance, an old Clergyman, who is Rector of two neighbouring Parishes, and a young genteel Attorney: They led us from this Place farther in the Village, where we found an exceeding good Company of Dancers, among whom Was Mr. *Prothero's* Daughter of *Built;* before-mentioned, this Attorney's Sisters, &c. They had two Violins and a Harp; they dance'd in a Booth made of Poles and Boughs: We found in and about this Place, several Hundreds of People, all in their best, and, what is not a natural *Welch* Quality, were very clean. It was to me surprising to see here almost as many People as I thought was in the whole County of *Radnor.*

M. Cooper, A Journey to Llandrindod Wells in
Radnorshire, 1746

"All was idleness and noise"

The rural idyll could be disturbed by the distractions of a race-week.

Situated close upon the shore, *Towyn* has nothing to recommend it but a bold unbounded view of the ocean, with a fine level hard sand, well calculated for sea-bathing.

We did not continue long in the town, as it happens to be a race-week there, and the motley crew assembled to partake of these annual sports seemed to eye us with no very friendly glances. We could not but observe with regret, the consequences of this unnatural introduction of an amusement (the twin-brother of profligacy and licentiousness) into a place which nature seemed to have consecrated to quiet and retirement, to simplicity and peace. Instead of that appearance of industry and decency which characterise a sequestered country village, all was idleness and noise. Every proper avocation seemed to be forgotten. Collected together in little groups, the inhabitants were squabbling over the result of the last afternoon's race, or making bets for the match of the approaching evening; whilst others, less deep in the business of the turf, but, bitten by the genius of idleness that hovered over the village, were drowning their faculties in copious potations of *cwrrw,* or, like the Centaurs and Lapithae of old, were bruising over the inflaming goblets they had drained.

We quitted this scene, in which rustic simplicity and fashionable profligacy were united by an heterogenous combination, with the conviction, that there is no better, more speedy, or efficacious mode of corrupting the rural character of a country village, and converting simplicity and industry into dishonesty and idleness, than the institution of an *annual race-week.*

Richard Warner, A second walk through Wales in August and September 1798, 1799

THE WELSH CHARACTER

....

"A natural degree of characteristic pride"

....

Plenty of these accounts have included observations on the Welsh 'character'. Henry Skrine indulged in some detailed 'General Observations on Wales and its Inhabitants'.

Having thus fulfilled my design in making a thorough survey of the principality of Wales, I cannot properly conclude this work without recording a few observations on the manners of the people and the nature of the countries I have described, following nearly the same line which I pursued in my remarks on Scotland and its inhabitants.

The division of Wales into its two great districts of North and South, and the several counties contained in them, is supposed to have been marked formerly by as great a variation in the manners of their inhabitants, produced by local customs prevailing in each, and the systems of hostility which existed under their several princes. The frank and earnest temper of the Welch, aided by a natural degree of characteristic pride, kept up the spirit of these distinctions long after the causes of them had subsided, and few nations have shewn, in modern times at least, so strong an attachment to the customs, the traditions, and the long-traced descent of their ancestors. Insensibly, however, in the lapse of time are these points of variation from their neighbours sinking into oblivion, their asperities have been softened down by mutual intercourse, and what remains is far more pleasing and curious than offensive to a stranger. — The provincial divisions have long since ceased to present any material difference in manners, except where peculiar circumstances (as in almost the whole of Pembrokeshire, and a part of the coast of Glamorganshire) have introduced a totally different people. Even the greater separation between the inhabitants of North and South Wales has in a considerable degree disappeared, their manners being so blended that, except the uniform and almost exclusive attachment to the music of the harp, it is now difficult to distinguish the few traces of originality which have been so long boasted by the native of North Wales as proofs of his superiority. The intervention of a third nation has in great measure effected this, and the domineering influence of the English character has in a manner *amalgamated* itself with two collateral masses, which might perhaps, though not insimilar, have never otherwise thoroughly united with each other. English laws, English judges, and, above all, the constantly increasing connexion with English families, must in time do away every essential difference between the inhabitants of the two countries, and if another century is allowed to roll on in prosperity, even the language of Wales seems likely to be lost, and those traits of peculiarity, which we now find it difficult to collect, will vanish.

Refinement has not yet attained to so high a pitch in Wales, that the social virtues should be extinguished, or even much obscured by apathy; among these virtues may justly be reckoned that singular attachment of its inhabitants to each other, which prevails most eminently in private families, and universally in the whole community. Thus is the general band of union strengthened by reciprocal good offices between all orders of people, the rich assisting the poor with a kind of parental solicitude for their welfare, and the peasants exhibiting that veneration towards their great land-owners, which they have been accustomed to shew from age to age to their ancestors. So harmless a relique of the feudal dominion is productive here of much benefit to society, for instances of oppression and tyranny are very rare in modern times, nor perhaps are those in power more disposed to misuse it, than those under them to submit to an undue exercise of it. Yet is even this happy trait of character in danger of being lost as refinement increases, if the gentlemen of Wales, following the example of those of England, desert their proper stations, and lose once that high estimation which the imposing presence of an active and upright landlord has transmitted to posterity.— A more useful or dignified being indeed can hardly exist than a native man of landed property in Wales, living with credit in the mansion house of his ancestors, and exercising his talents for the general good as an upright magistrate, a friendly neighbour, and a liberal benefactor.

High spirit, energetic animation, and courage, may be accounted strong points of the Welch character; and these, when properly exhibited, cannot fail to create respect and admiration. That zeal which attaches the numerous branches of families to each other, and the tenants to their landlords, often calls these propensities of the mind into action, nor are there wanting examples, in which they have been displayed with a force and sentiment almost bordering upon romance. A striking instance of natural, as well as national intrepidity, was shewn in the spring of 1797, when crowds thronged together on the first rumour of the French invasion; peasants unused to military discipline, ranged themselves under the standard of Lord Cawdor, and even the women of Pembrokeshire contributed to dismay the enemy.

Hospitality, that engaging affection, which may take root in every nation, but which retreats in general from the seats of opulence and luxury, is peculiarly adapted to the disposition of the Welch, and wherever an opportunity has occurred, I have often witnessed its fascinating influence. This ever-blooming flower frequently adorns those rugged tracts which would seem almost impervious to the haunts of men, in the most dreary wilds it charms the wearied senses of the traveller, and it flourishes eminently in the remotest vallies of Cambria. — Open, ingenuous, and considerate, the native gentleman of Wales dispenses freely around him the benefits he receives from his position, and supports the character he derives from his predecessors by a well-timed and liberal attention to all who fall within his sphere of action. No aspersion can be more false than that which has described the Welch as averse to strangers, and well may those travellers contradict it, who coming into the country properly recommended, have been shewn its curiosities with all the energy of zealous attention, and entertained with that kind of impressive welcome, which may be sought for in vain in more polished districts.

Some few defects appear amidst the many valuable qualities of the Welch; but even these may frequently be traced to the excess of virtues, and as the general civilization increases they will no longer be observable. Hence has the natural character for animation sometimes partaken too much of warmth of temper, and a hastiness of expression has gained the Welchman the reputation of being quarrelsome. Conviviality in too great an extreme has in some societies led to habitual intemperance, the minute attention to ancient customs has often retarded improvement, and the veneration shewn to a long line of ancestors has occasionally degenerated into the stiffness of family pride. The higher orders of society have already, in great measure, emancipated themselves from these shackles, but the lower are yet slow in following so laudable an example. Among them the prevalent vice of drunkenness is apt to foster the seeds of every other evil; a litigious spirit, too often fomented industriously by the arts of chicane, supersedes frequently the natural tendency to fair dealing, an habitual idleness shuts up the sources of industry, and a want of attention to cleanliness, encumbering poverty, degrades it by the squalid appearance of want, raggedness, and disease. — These shades in the national character, which are by no means so general as they have been, already fading imperceptibly beneath the sunshine of prosperity, and the introduction of arts and manufactures, must ultimately yield to that enlightened spirit which arises from an enlarged intercourse with other countries, and the regular progress of improvement in every branch of industry.

Man has not alone been considered in the blessings so liberally bestowed, for the face of Nature must abundantly confess her benign influence, and Wales far exceeds all its neighbouring districts in romantic beauty. In cultivation and refinement it certainly as yet falls short of its powerful and polished mistress, but in the rude grandeur and unfettered sublimity of wild rocks, lofty mountains, and rapid torrents, few countries can surpass it. Its vales, fertile, picturesque, and well inhabited, frequently burst upon the sight of an astonished traveller with a charm difficult to be described, after he has traversed the long and dreary waste of the intervening mountains. Fine rivers, abounding in romantic scenery, pervade the principality in every direction, and issuing from their central mountains, form in their curves those vallies through which they disport themselves in their passage to either sea. These streams are mostly rapid in their origin, but many of them change their character, like the Severn, from the nature of the countries through which they flow; and some, like the Wye, after experiencing such a change, resume at last their pristine appearance, and become again engulphed in rocks and mountains.

Henry Skrine, Two successive tours throughout the whole of Wales, 1798

Henry Skrine (1755-1803) came from a gentry, the family seat being Warleigh Manor, Somerset. He was educated at Christ Church, Oxford and became a barrister at Lincoln's Inn in 1782. His second wife was Letitia Harcourt of Dan-y-Parc in Llangattock, Brecknockshire where she inherited the house and a 545 acre estate. In 1795 he was appointed the High Sheriff of the county and died in Walton-on-Thames in 1803. Much of his time was spent travelling across Britain, including northern Scotland.

"Sometimes bordering on the ludicrous"

Those of a sensitive disposition were to be warned about warm greetings and other displays of exuberance.

Their modes of greeting are unusually affectionate, sometimes bordering on the ludicrous, among the women particularly, who are constantly seen saluting each other at market, and on the most ordinary occasions of business: but on occasions of distress, to omit this sympathetic ceremony, even towards the most ordinary acquaintance, would be considered as an instance, rarely occurring, of pertinacious or misanthropic opposition to the common charities of nature. Ill may it befal the traveller, who has the misfortune of meeting a Welsh wedding on the road. He would be inclined to suppose, that he had fallen in with a company of lunatics, escaped from their confinement. It is the custom of the whole party who are invited, both men and women, to ride full speed to the church porch, and the person who arrives there first has some privilege or distinction at the marriage feast. To this important object all inferior considerations give way; whether the safety of his majesty's subjects, who are not going to be married, or their own, incessantly endangered by boisterous, unskilful, and contentious jockeyship. The natives, who are acquainted with the custom, and warned against the cavalcade by its vociferous approach, turn aside at respectful distance: but the stranger will be fortunate, if he escapes being overthrown by an onset, the occasion of which puts out of sight that urbanity, so generally characteristic of the people.

Benj. Heath Malkin, The Scenery, Antiquities and Biography of South Wales, from materials collected during two excursions in the year 1803, 1804

WELSH

....

"It is the language of a brave people"

....

Welsh was seen as a poetic language, as long as words were not played with for poetic effect.

As this people have made no very considerable progress

in a state of civilization, we might naturally be induced to think that their language is barbarous and uncultivated; but the contrary is true. It is not clogged with those many inharmonious monosyllables, the signs of moods, tenses, and cases, as the English language. It is much more harmonious and expressive in its numbers and formation; one word in Welsh frequently expressing as much as a sentence in the English; which a late ingenious writer has given abundant specimens.

Though this is the language of a people, who inhabit a small barren spot of earth, scarce known in the world; unimproved in the arts of life, entirely neglected and uncultivated; and not spoken, except by such who willingly forfeit every claim to politeness; yet its variety, copiousness, and even harmony, is to be equalled by few, perhaps excelled by none.

But our wonder ceases, when we consider that it is not solely the language of a people confined in a little corner of this island. It is the language of populous and even civilized nations, the antient Celts. Hence its variety and its harmony. It is the language of a brave people. Hence those sounds that roused the soul to action. Animated by these, they despised danger and death for their country.

[…]

This language seems to be more particularly adapted for poetry; which, however extraordinary it may seem to some, on account of the multiplicity of gutturals and consonants with which it abounds, has the softness and harmony of the Italian, with the majesty and expression of the Greek. In the formation of its poetical numbers, it differs from all modern languages. Every line consists of a certain regular number of feet, like other languages; but herein it differs, that it has a certain kind of rhyme, jingle, or alliteration, not that terminates the line, but runs through every part of it.

The poets, or such as pretend to be such, arrogate to themselves a most unwarrantable poetical licence of coining words, for the sake of sound; and this they will seldom scruple to do, whenever they want a word for rhyme. Hence the greatest part of their poetry, is nothing more than melodious nonsense, a perfect jargon of harmonious sounds. And when translated, scarce reducible to common sense. This unbounded poetical licence, though generally, yet, is not universally adopted. For there are not wanting many poets, who seldom claim this unwarrantable prerogative of coining words ad libitum.

Joseph Cradock, Letters from Snowdon, 1770

....

"I fear they will not soon get rid of it"

....

In Little England beyond Wales, people tried to sound English but rarely succeeded.

Being just returned from a visit, where I have left my party behind me, I am at leisure to give you some account of the dispositions and manners of the Welsh. It requires a much more discriminating pen than mine, to mark every minute difference in a people who so nearly resemble ourselves; and I often smile, when I reflect upon the number of absurd ideas that are entertained of them by ignorant persons; and indeed by some who would be highly offended, if I should rank them in that class. They look upon the Welsh as foreigners, and expect to hear them speak unintelligibly, to see them dress grotesquely, and behave uncouthly. To these one knows not what to answer; for they think you are only deceiving them, when you say they are in most respects like the rest of the world, except in such points as are not so strongly marked as to be easily described. The most striking difference betwixt the Welsh and the English is their dialect, particularly that of the females; and as they are not at all conscious of it, I fear they will not soon get rid of it. It consists in a mixture of Welsh and English, with a strong Welsh accent. To me the Welsh language itself sounds a great deal more musical than this jargon. The ladies are so little sensible of this defect, that many of them believe they are not the least tinctured with it, and have asked me very seriously, whether I should know them to be natives of Wales by their speech. It distressed me very much to make a reply to this question, because it implied that they expected I should answer in the negative. Their having so strong a dialect is rather unaccountable, because Haverfordwest is certainly a polite place, and is frequented by strangers of all countries, especially English and Irish; and throughout all that part of Pembrokeshire there is not a word of Welsh spoken, or even understood, by any genteel person none but the lower people speak it in common: it is there almost looked upon as an indication of vulgarity to know it. If you ask a lady whether she can speak Welsh, she answers in a sharp tone of voice, and with a kind of indignant look, "Not I indeed."

Mrs. Morgan, A tour to Milford Haven,
in the year 1791, 1795

"But this affected contempt is retaliated upon them"

As with Little England beyond Wales, the people of the Gower were a plantation, and disdained to speak Welsh.

The language of the Gower people is English, with the intermixture of a few Norman French words; and the dialect rather broad and coarse. So that a traveller might fancy himself in the west of England. While if you enter into a Welsh village, though not three miles distant, they will, if able, even refuse to speak to you in English. They seldom intermarry, and have an utter aversion for each other. When a man of Gower is asked the residence of one in Llangevelach, a village on the Welsh side of the line, it is a common reply, "I danna knaw, a lives somewhere in the Welshery." But this affected contempt is retaliated upon them by the Welsh, who never speak of the people of Gower without adding *lleidrai* or *yspeilwri*; thieves and robbers. The manners of the Welsh are however more engaging than those of their high-bred neighbours: the former are simple and civil, while the latter are forbidding and insolent: they seem to have inherited a considerable share of the haughty and overbearing disposition, which so strongly characterised the Norman invaders; but the reserve and frequent irritations of the Welsh are not calculated soon to subdue it.

John Evans, Letters written during a tour through South Wales, in the year 1803, and at other times, 1804

....
"None that propagate principles of infidelity"
....

The moral probity of the Welsh was believed to stem from the purity of Welsh language publications. This was linked to a high level of literacy.

It is very remarkable, that great immoralities do not prevail in any part of Wales, not even in places contiguous to large manufactories, especially if the English language happens to be but little spoken. One reason for this probably is, that though there are accounted to be about two thousand books in the Welsh language, there are none of immoral tendencies, none that propagate principles of infidelity. Indeed, so alive are the common people to the dignity of their own literature, that it is probable, no modern refinement in either branch of instruction would be tolerated, but would, on the contrary, expose its author to the indignation of his countrymen, who are not yet aware of the possibility, that the sacredness of a printed book ever was, or can be, converted to any but moral and beneficial purposes. It may perhaps in some measure be attributed to their general acquaintance with their own legendary poems and tales, composed by scholars in the literature of the age and place, such as it was, that there are few if any parts of England, where the lower classes of the people speak with so grammatical a propriety. Those of them who speak English, though but a few words, pronounced in an accent that an Englishman can scarcely recognize, still contrive to translate literally, but with an unwitting accuracy, their vernacular idioms into a phraseology, the figurative style of which produces a most whimsical effect in its foreign clothing. A countryman, who shewed me one of the lakes in Cardiganshire, with very great difficulty both to himself and me, conveyed an idea of its depth by saying, that a house might stand at the bottom of it, with his forehead under water. This is a most uncouth personification in English; but I doubt not that he translated his thought in the best manner he could, and that the expression in Welsh would have sounded neither absurd nor far-fetched. The common conversation of the country is altogether made up of metaphors and figures: a man in distress has a black cloud hanging over him; and every object in nature is mustered in regular array, to furnish a description of his joys or sorrows, his circumstances or wishes. Another reason why the people are more respectable and better informed, than might be expected in a district apparently little calculated for the progress of improvement, is, that the advantages of decent education have been longer established in Wales, than in most parts of England. I do not mean to affirm, that at the present moment the Welsh peasantry are better taught than the English, because the instruction of the poor has of late been taken up in England by persons of condition; and the benevolent institutions of this country, when once their necessity is felt and acknowledged, are seldom allowed to relax in their progress towards universal utility. But I apprehend our middle-aged and elderly poor to be much more ignorant, than the middle-aged and elderly poor of Wales, at least in that part with which I am acquainted: and a certain portion of knowledge having descended hereditarily from father to son for several succeeding generations, it is more firmly rooted and more generally spread, than where it is of very recent acquirement, though the immediate opportunities are superior. It has been urged as an objection to Sunday and other day-schools with us, that the children unlearn at home with their ignorant parents, faster than the efforts of their instructors can induce them to learn: but this objection would rarely be found to apply in the principality. There are few persons in the towns, who are unable to read; and even in the villages, and the more mountainous parts, schools are very common, and in many instances of ancient establishment. Where there is no hall, as before described, and especially in the mountains, the school is kept either in the church porch, or in the body of the church.

There are many circumstances of local manners, totally differing from the habits and character of their fellow islanders, which cannot fail to strike the most superficial observer. An uncommon vivacity, both of tone and gesture, meeting halfway the saturnine demeanour of the English and the caricatured vehemence of the French, with an uniformity and peculiarity of dress, gives in a great degree a foreign air to every concourse of the country people.

Benj. Heath Malkin, The scenery, antiquities and Biography of South Wales, from materials collected during two excursions in the year 1803, 1804

....

"This mark of ignominy has had the desired effect"

....

In Anglicised parts of North Wales, the 'Welsh Not' or Welsh lump was used in schools to force children into only using English.

During our former, as well as present progress through Flintshire, we have had occasion to observe that English

275

is very generally spoken by all classes of society; in so much, as nearly to supersede the use of the national tongue. We were unable to account for this circumstance till to-day, when our landlady's sprightly son acquainted us with the cause of it. One great object of education, it seems, in the schools (both of boys and girls) of North-Wales, is to give the children a perfect knowledge of the *English* tongue; the masters not only having the exercises performed in this language, but obliging the children to *converse* in it also. In order to effect this, some *coercion* is necessary, as the *little Britons* have a considerable aversion to the Saxon vocabulary; if, therefore, in the colloquial intercourse of the scholars, one of them be detected in speaking a Welsh word, he is immediately degraded with *the Welsh lump*, a large piece of lead fastened to a string, and suspended round the neck of the offender. This mark of ignominy has had the desired effect; all the children of Flintshire speak English very well, and were it not for a little curl, or elevation of the voice, at the conclusion of the sentence, (which has a pleasing effect) one should perceive no difference in this respect between the North-Wallians and the natives of England. The pride of the *Englishman* may, perhaps, be gratified by so great a compliment paid to his vernacular tongue; but the *philosopher* will lose much by the amalgamation that is rapidly taking place in the language and manners of Wales, and our own country.

Richard Warner, A second walk through Wales in
August and September 1798, 1799

"Is a proof of its permanency"

Over two centuries ago, debates about the future of Welsh abounded. Yet even in border regions it was universally used. Walter Davies makes the case for its survival. O bydded i'r hen iaith barhau.

There is scarce an inhabitant here, who is not able, with the greatest ease and indifference, to speak both English and Welsh; the Welsh language being still spoken on the confines of Offa's dike, is a proof of its permanency; however anxious some of the mixed, or bastard tribe, may be for its total extinction. The arguments brought by those who plead that one general language only, should be spoken by all his majesty's subjects, may be specious enough. It would be convenient to a *few travellers*, is "his majesty's good subjects in Wales were all English: but however, it can hardly be desired that a whole nation should forget their own tongue, and learn another, for them; the only reasonable method for removing this inconvenience would be for such persons, before they go into that country, to take care to learn Welsh*."

[...]

Having already hinted at the purity of the dialects spoken by the people of these parts: permit me to repeat it again. The Welsh and English, though as if it were blended together for these thousand years past, yet both when separately spoken, and uncommonly pure. The former, is equal to any in the most interior and inaccessible parts of Wales; the latter, has neither the barbarism of diction we hear in our metropolis, nor the awkwardness of expression we meet with among the peasantry of the English counties.

*A quotation from Thomas Llewelyn (?1720-1783) who gained his M.A. and LL.D. at the University of Aberdeen and spent most of his life as a Baptist minister and tutor in London. His book 'Historical and Critical Remarks on the British Tongue' was published in 1769.

'Gwinfardd Dyfed' (Walter Davies), A statistical account of the Parish of Llanymyneich in Montgomeryshire, 1796

Walter Davies (1761-1849) used the pseudonym 'Gwinfardd Dyfed' (the poet of the Gwaun in Dyfed), had the bardic name 'Gwallter Mechain' and was training to become a cooper when Owen Jones (Owain Myfyr, 1741-1814) helped him to go to St. Alban's Hall, Oxford (now part of Merton College) at the age of 28 and thereafter to All Soul's College. He was a curate at Meifod in 1795-99 and at Yspytty-Ifan from 1799 before gaining his M. A. at Trinity College Cambridge in 1803. He was appointed the Rector of Manafon in Montgomeryshire from 1807-37 (when R. S. Thomas was the vicar there in 1942-54, he wrote his first three volumes of poetry and learnt Welsh) and the Vicar of Llanrhaiadr-yn-Mochnant from 1837 until his death. He was a highly regarded poet and played a significant role in setting up and supporting various London Welsh societies as well as organising a national survey of the state of agriculture across Wales.

7

RELIGION

Between 1610 and 1831, religious attitudes in Wales were transformed from reluctantly reformed to unabashed nonconformity. For the English traveller, religion was possibly the most dismaying aspect of a visit to Wales. Anglicanism was in poor shape, a plethora of dissenting chapels were in operation, where nonconformist services did not conform to expected norms, and the Old Faith echoed in holy wells.

Following the publication of the Book of Common Prayer and Edward VI's Act of Uniformity in 1549, from 1552 all services in Wales were solely conducted in English. Under Queen Mary, Catholicism resumed in 1553, as did services in Latin. Neither did much towards the edification of largely monoglot Welsh congregations.

After Queen Elizabeth I's accession in 1558, Protestantism and services in English were restored. Her Act of 1563 required that by 1567 all churches in Wales and Herefordshire should have a Book of Common Prayer and the New Testament in Welsh alongside their English equivalents, and allowed for services to be conducted in Welsh. With the Anglican liturgy being preached in their language, the Reformation was soon embraced in Wales.

William Salesbury and Bishop Richard Davies translated the Welsh New Testament and Book of Common Prayer (Testament Newydd ein Arglwydd Jesu Christ) of 1567. Davies then worked with Bishop William Morgan in translating the whole Bible (Y Beibl Cysegr Lan), published in 1588, revised into a standard version in 1620, with a more affordable edition (Y Beibl Bach) in 1630. These books were, so to speak, a godsend. This was the only Bible published in a non-state language anywhere in the century following the Reformation.

The sea of Anglican faith of the English imagination never quite swept so far up the beach in Wales, due to its benign neglect and the emergence of Protestant dissent. In Wales, the Church of England could easily be dismissed as being administered by English Bishops, and managed by a scattering of indifferently trained Vicars and Curates whose livings were often so poor that many Parishes were barely served at all. Before St David's College was founded in Lampeter in 1822, there was nowhere in Wales for training clergy. Some went to Oxford (especially Jesus College) or Cambridge, but these were remote and costly options for any but the sons of the gentry.

Catholicism endured through the seventeenth and eighteenth centuries, but recusants were limited to a handful of noble families and few others. They had no public profile. Catholic emancipation did not take place until 1829. Even so, there are plenty of accounts of how Catholic traditions prevailed in various places, to the pious horror of several visitors.

Wales has been distinguished by religious dissent. The first Congregationalist church opened in 1639 and the first Baptist congregation was formed in 1649. The 1660 Restoration clamped down on dissent until 1689 after which nonconformity soon revived. Unlike the Anglicans, nonconformists ran their own academies in Wales from the late seventeenth century. The Methodist revival from 1738 spurred popular dissent with the Established Church and in 1811 Welsh Methodism seceded from the Anglican Church. Such was Protestantism's popularity that by the first religious census, conducted in 1851, nonconformists outnumbered Anglicans by four to one.

Six themes emerge in the following accounts; the Anglican Communion, Methodists and Nonconformists, echoes of Catholicism, sundry superstitions, weddings, and death.

THE ANGLICAN COMMUNION

....

"An inferiority of condition"

....

Being in Holy Orders did not guarantee prosperity.

Llangunnog is singularly situated, surrounded on all sides by barren and sandy hills. The place consists only of a few houses, amongst which there is a small building ycleped a church, where once a week a sermon is delivered in the Welsh language. Whilst we were at dinner in a little ale-house (which by the bye was the only one in the place), we had a glance at the clergyman, who happened to enter the house at that very time; his appearance altogether bespoke an inferiority of condition, disgraceful to that respectable body of which he was a member; upon observing us, he abruptly went out, while our landlady informed us, with an air of triumph, as if he was something superior to the rest of mankind, that "that was the parson." He was standing near the house when we went out, and wishing to enter into conversation with him, I desired him to inform me which was the direct road to Bala; he appeared somewhat confused, and waving his hand towards the way we had enquired for, answered only by the monosyllable "that," and walked hastily away. I felt much hurt, and at the same time a great degree of admiration, both at his truly laconic answer, as well as at his manner of address, in which pride seemed to be struggling with poverty; in such a situation any degree of sensibility would be to him rather a misfortune than a blessing. Fixed to a spot in which there could be no one proper for his company, or capable of his conversation, he might be driven to pass his evenings, for the sake of society, with people very far inferior to him, and by degrees lose those finer qualities of the mind, that refinement of action as well as of thought, which properly distinguish the gentleman from the honest but blunt peasant, or the industrious mechanic.

J. Hucks, A pedestrian tour in North Wales
in a series of letters, 1795

"The oblations are oftentimes very considerable"

One way of improving the rural Clergy's lot was to retain customs that might elsewhere have been considered inappropriately Catholic.

When a person dies, the friends and relations of the deceased meet in the room where the corpse lies, the evening previous to the funeral. Here the male part of the company are seen smoaking, drinking, cracking their jokes, and sometimes indulging themselves with a *Welsh air;* whilst the women are kneeling round the corpse, weeping bitterly, and bewailing, in terms of "loud lament," the loss they have experienced. When the body is committed to the ground, the sexton, after casting the earth upon it, holds out his spade to the attendant mourners, who, in turn, contribute as much money as they can conveniently afford. The sum thus collected is a compliment to the officiating minister, and intended by the donors as a bribe to extricate the soul of the deceased as quickly as possible out of *purgatory*. It is evidently a remnant of the Roman Catholic faith, and nothing more than the *mass money* which formerly was bestowed in large proportions for the same purpose. On these occasions the oblations are oftentimes very considerable; and we are informed by a clergyman in Anglesey, that he had more than once received ten pounds in that way.

From this custom, and certain other perquisites, the curacies of North-Wales afford very comfortable incomes; the character of *poverty*, therefore, which attaches to the subaltern clergy of South-Wales, does not extend to those of the northern part of the principality. The stipends, it is true, are in both cases very trifling; but the *arian-rhew*, or offering at the graves just mentioned, (so called from the money being cast into the *spade)* and some other sources of profit, make the amount of many of the North-Wales curacies above one hundred pounds a year.

**Richard Warner, A second walk through Wales in
August and September 1798, 1799**

....

"Its modern ecclesiastical establishment
is highly respectable"

....

*St. David's Cathedral gained admiration at a time when many
Bishoprics were in a state of genteel decline.*

Saint David's, said to have been a Roman station, was the seat of the primacy of Wales, transferred here from Caerleon by St. David in the sixth century. Its modern ecclesiastical establishment is highly respectable, consisting of the bishop, six canon residentiaries, four archdeacons, and several minor canons. The modern residence of the bishop, these splendid ruins being no longer habitable, has been transferred to Aberguilly near Caermarthen, a central part of his diocese, in a pleasant country. One of the canons is generally resident at St. David's in rotation, where a handsome house is appropriated for his habitation, and the rest of the institution appear to be well lodged. Much praise is due to the establishment for the excellent repair in which the cathedral and those buildings which are still in use, are preserved; and the service of the church in this remote corner of the kingdom, where there are few to witness it, is conducted with a degree of decorum and attention which would put some of our proudest choirs in England to the blush.

Henry Skrine, Two successive tours throughout the whole of Wales, 1798

....

"With a devout Aspect"

....

The Church of England's services were considered eccentric by the more fastidious.

All our Company went to *Llanbadern* Church, except Mrs. and Miss *Slip Phli*, Mrs. *Van'se*, and *Winifred*. We having breakfasted and dress'd, thought it too late and far to go and hear a *Welch* Sermon; but upon consulting our Landlord, we understood that we might be soon enough at Mr. *Jones's* Meeting-House, which he shewed us down below on the same *Rosse*; accordingly we went down, and two or three People coming at that Juncture at the Door, we followed them in.

The Building is as large as an ordinary Barn; it is new, and raised at the above Gentleman's Expence; at the East End of it is the Pulpit; under that is Mr. *Jones's* Pew, the only one there, all the Congregation besides setting on Benches; we went to the West End, and sat down; they were then singing a *Welch* Psalm, in the most doleful Tune I ever heard, the Clerk pronounced the Words in a Tone almost as disagreeable; having finished the Singing, which was very long, we all stood up, and the Preacher having delivered his Text, both in *English* and *Welch*, he continued and finished his Discourse in the latter Tongue. He was a young Man, and teaches School in this Place; as to the Sermon, I understood but little of it, though, verily I think, that provided an *English* Curate deserves Thirty Pounds *per Ann. a Welch* one does Sixty, if the Sermons were of the same Number and Length: I declare I thought sometimes he would have burst some of his inward Vessels, or make his Throat so sore that he would not be able to speak in a Fortnight. On my Right Hand were two Boys, who had the Itch abominably; one of them underwent a great Mortification, for his Fellow-Sufferer, every time I looked that Way, prevented his scratching, by saying I observed him; in about twenty Minutes the *Welchman* concluded, and came down from the Pulpit, which Place was immediately supplied by a Brother of the Justice's, at which Time came in that Gentleman and his Lady. The *Domine,* after wiping his Face, with a devout Aspect told us, in *English,* that from *Revelations, Chap.* iii. *Verse* I. he had taken his Text. He advanced, that it was the Aim and only View of a great Part of the World to live only to a Name; this he frequently repeated, that they had not that inward Feeling of the Spirit, which Christians ought to have. Some, continued he, come to hear the Word of God for Form's Sake, others for Interest, and some out of Curiosity, or, what is worse, to see and be seen, and make Games and Observations; but he desired us all, to hold fast the Faith, and not live deceivingly to a Name only. After a long Prayer, in which he particularly prayed for the Royal Family, he finished, to my great Satisfaction, considering my two neighbouring Boys. Indeed I expected to have heard a deal lower Language, and the Performance every Way worse. Most of the Flock had little Horses at the Door, which they mounted, and rode away full Speed. We walk'd home, and found ourselves ready for Dinner before the Return of our Church People; one of our Landladies inform'd us, for there was two, that the Company desired we would drink separate from them, which gave us no Uneasiness; we imagined that our talking up Stairs procured us this Mortification, as they were pleased to imagine it.

In about half an Hour our Company came Home; the young Squire carried the Ladies with his Arms round their Legs, from the Chairs into the House; Mr. *Slip Phli* and Family din'd with a Countryman of theirs, who jodg'd in the Neighbourhood; Mrs. *Lobluck* sat at the Head of the Table at which we all din'd; we had four or five Dishes of Meat indifferently dress'd, no Garden-stuff but a few Greens, which were boil'd almost black, a Couple of Fowls roasted, but the Liver and Gizard were thrown on the Dunghill, which the Cook thought useless; our Plates, Knives and Forks, were quite black with using, our Table Linnen dirty; our other Dishes of

Meat, besides the Fowls, were a Piece of Beef boil'd, a Shoulder of Mutton roasted, a Bit of Veal and Bacon, and two Sorts of Cheese; our Bread was the same as last Night: We being so blameably complaisant to sit low at Table, our good-natur'd Company favour'd us with cooling our Meat for us, and indeed our Case for some Time was like that of *Tantalus*. The Miss *Sadvies* told us they had an exceeding good Sermon delivered by a genteel young Clergyman, but the Text and Subject they had (reasonably) forgot: These Things they remembered, that a young Gentleman in a pearl'd-colour'd Coat, white Waistcoat and Stockings, and red Breeches, had ogled their Sister *Tythe*, (which was the eldest, about thirty-four) all the Time of divine Service, which pleased the old Maid to that Degree, that she almost thought her last Prayer had prevail'd. They observ'd that there was a full Congregation; but that Miss *Thomas's* Hoop was too little, Miss *Edwards's* Cap came too forward, Miss *Richards* they acknowledg'd would have been a pretty Girl, if her Hair had been curl'd like their own. A great many more Observations of this Sort were delivered by Miss *Ariam Sadvie*, who is the most affected, proud, and handsome featur'd of the Three. Mr. *Van'se* took a great deal of Trouble with this affected Creature, and made himself a great deal of satisfactory Merriment, with their ridiculous Nonsense, when his good natur'd, genteel, generous, and much more sensible Wife, sat by, without having the least Notice taken of her by the Husband, whom she had rais'd from the Ground.

'Countryman', A Journey to Llandrindod Wells in
Radnorshire, 1746

METHODISTS AND NONCONFORMISTS

....

"To excel each other in jumping, screaming, and howling"

....

In North Wales, there was a Methodist revival at Bala in 1791, based on the 'Jumpers' first seen at the Llangeitho revival in Ceredigion during 1762. The Welsh Calvinistic Methodists had their own Chapels by the time of the following account and by 1811 they had broken away from the Church of England.

Being unavoidably prevented visiting the celebrated Paris Mountain, the property of Lord Uxbridge and the Rev. Mr. Hughes, we again returned to the hotel, at Caernarvon, purporting to stay the following day, (Sunday) for the purpose of making a strict enquiry into the religious sect, settled here, and in many parts of Wales, called *Jumpers*. The account we had received from our landlord, we imagined was exaggerated, and this more strongly induced us to visit the chapel, that we might be enabled, in future, to contradict this ridiculous report.

At six in the evening the congregation assembled, and on our entrance into the chapel, we observed on the north side, from a sort of stage or pulpit, erected on the occasion, a man, in appearance, a common day-labourer, holding forth to an ignorant and deluded multitude. Our entrance at first, seemed to excite a general dissatisfaction; and our near neighbours, as if conscious of their eccentricities, muttered bitter complaints against the admittance of strangers. The chapel, which was not divided into pews, and even destitute of seats, contained near an hundred people; half way round was erected a gallery. The preacher continued raving, and, indeed, foaming at the mouth, in a manner too shocking to relate: — he allowed himself no time to breathe, but seemingly intoxicated, uttered the most dismal howls and groans imaginable, which were answered by the congregation, so loud, as occasionally to drown even the voice of the preacher. At last, being nearly exhausted by continual vociferation, and fainting from exertion, he sunk down in the pulpit: the meeting, however, did not disperse: a psalm was immediately sung by a man, who, we imagined officiated as clerk, accompanied by the whole congregation. The psalm had not continued long, before we observed part of the assembly, to our great surprise, jumping in small parties of three, four, and sometimes five in a set, lifting up their hands, beating their breasts, and making the most horrid gesticulations. Each individual separately jumped, regularly succeeding one another, while the rest generally assisted the jumper by the help of their hands. The women always appeared more vehement than the men, and infinitely surpassed them in numbers; seeming to endeavour to excel each other in jumping, screaming, and howling. We observed, indeed, that many of them lost their shoes, hats, and bonnets, with the utmost indifference, and never condescended to search after them; in this condition, it is not unusual to meet them jumping to their homes. Their meetings are twice a week, Wednesdays and Sundays. Having accidentally met with a gentleman, at the hotel, a native of Siberia, we invited him to our party, and, induced by curiosity, he readily accompanied us to the chapel. On the commencement of the *jumping*, he intreated us to quit the congregation, exclaiming, "Good God! I for a moment forgot I was in a Christian country; the dance of the Siberians, in the worship of the Lama, with their shouts and gesticulations, is not more horrid!" This observation so forcibly struck me, that I could not avoid inserting it in my note-book.

With disgust we left the chapel, and were given to understand, by our landlord, they celebrate a particular day every year, when instances have been known of women dying by too great an exertion; and fainting is frequently the consequence of their excessive jumping.

This sect is by no means confined to the town of Caernarvon, but in many villages, and in several market towns, both in North and South Wales, they have established regular chapels. "They have" (says a correspondent to the *Gentleman's Magazine*) "periodical meetings in many of the larger towns, to which they come from thirty to forty miles round. At one, held in Denbigh, about last April [1798], there were, I believe, upwards of four thousand people, from different parts. At another, held in Bala, soon afterwards, nearly double that number were supposed to be present." The last number appears rather to be exaggerated, though the latter, being dated from Denbigh, should be considered as authoritative.

Another correspondent to the *Gentleman's Magazine*, gives the following information respecting the sect: "That they are not a distinct sect, but *Methodists*, of the same persuasion as the late Mr. Whitfield; for though there are several congregations of *Wesleyan Methodists*, in this country, there is no such custom amongst them. But jumping during religious worship is no new thing amongst the other party, having (by what I can learn) been practised by them for many years past. I have seen some of their pamphlets, in the Welch language, in which this custom is justified by the example of David, who danced before the ark; and of the lame man, restored by our blessed Saviour, at the gate of the Temple, who leaped for joy." How far this gentleman's account may be accurate, I leave for others to decide; it is certainly to be lamented, in a country where the Christian Religion is preached in a stile of the greatest purity and simplicity, that those poor ignorant deluded wretches should be led to a form of worship so dissonant to the Established Church of England, and, indeed, by a poor ignorant fellow, devoid of education, and devoid of sense.

'The Author' (Allen Cliffe),
The Cambrian Directory, 1800

....

"The methodists, in all their endless diversity"

....

Nonconformity is often seen as a monolithic institution by outsiders. By 1796, it was preached in many cloths and with varying degrees of fervour.

The sectaries in this parish have been computed at one third of it; if by sectaries are only meant regular dissenters, such as anabaptists, presbyterians, &c. who totally withdraw themselves from the communion of the established church, the estimate may nearly hold good, but if those partial separatists, the methodists, in all their endless diversity of shades, be involved in it, I am certain that the computation must be erroneous; for whilst the meeting houses are always overflowing, and their congregations, though supplied with three, and sometimes four meals of piety a day, never sated, yet good old mother church, whose bell but once a week invites to a plain Sunday repast, shall want guests, and even on the few days in the year, when her altar presents its heavenly banquet, the occasion to mourn that the partakers of it are so few; wheras , let a parson of the methodistical class, a popular extempore ranter, mount the pulpit, or enter the communion rails, the scene is changed, and within those walls which were wont to echo back the mild responses of a few solitary pensioners on the ordinary service, a tempest of groans and ejaculations is heard, and the press is too immense to be contained, as is the mountebank in religion kept the keys of heaven, or the consecrated came with a greater blessing from his hand, than that of a poor curate, with pimpled face alone perhaps exposes to the unjust censure of drunkenness, or other intemperance, or who , for want of that worldly guarded discretion which passes for sanctity, and that sheep's cloathing, which too often masks the wolf, may be by accident detected, after a fatiguing walk from one remote cure to another, steeping his cares in a Lethæn cup at the alehouse, a sin, if sin it be, which many a bishop commits with much greater latitude and less excuse, but in better company, and better liquor.

'Gwinfardd Dyfed' (Walter Davies), Statistical account of the Parish of Fishguard in Pembrokeshire, 1796

ECHOES OF CATHOLICISM

....
"To foretel good or ill fortune"
....

Holy wells abounded in Wales at the time and were used for a variety of purposes, most notably for the veneration of saints, thus associating them with popishness. In the following case, they were used for divination.

At no great distance from the church there is a *well* dedicated to St. Peris, and inclosed within a square wall. In the holes of this a person of the adjoining cottage generally has a small fish, from the appearance or non-appearance of which, when a bit of bread is thrown into the water, the common Welsh people pretend to foretel good or ill fortune. The general reward of a piece of silver from such strangers as visit the place, affords a temptation for them still to keep on foot at least the appearance of this superstition.

William Bingley, North Wales, Vol. I, 1804

....
"By those of the Romish persuasion"
....

Holywell was one of the most famous wells, being noted (see Chapter 1) by four writers between 1586 and 1698.

Holy-well, or as it's called in the British language TRE-FYNNON, i.e. the town of the well; is a neat small town, situated on the side of a hill. At the bottom of which is the famous well of St. Winifred, from whence the town derives its name. The well is surrounded with very high hills on every side, to which may be attributed the amazing spring of water. It flows, according to the relation of the inhabitants, at the rate of a ton a minute. All the miraculous powers of healing attributed to these waters, are ascribed to their patroness St. Winifred. So great is the veneration in which she is held, by those of the Romish persuasion, that in honor of her, they to this day, perform pilgrimages to Holy-well. You would not excuse me, were I to relate to you all the strange stories recorded of St. Winifred, by the monkish legendary writers. These serve only to shew the superstition of those times, and create disgust in a modern reader.

Joseph Cradock, Letters from Snowdon, 1770

....
"The vengeance of St. *Ælian*"
....

Holy wells could be used to curse as well as to bless.

The well of St. *Ælian*, a parish not far from *Llandrillo* in *Caernarvonshire*, has been in great repute for the cures of all diseases, by means of the intercession of the saint; who was first invoked by earnest prayers in the neighboring church. He was also applied to on less worthy occasions, and made the instrument of discovering thieves, and of recovering stolen goods. Some repair to him to imprecate their neighbors, and to request the saint to afflict with sudden death, or with some great misfortune, any persons who may have offended them. The belief in this is still strong; for three years have not elapsed since I was threatened by a fellow (who imagined I had injured him) with the vengeance of St. *Ælian*, and a journey to his well to curse me with effect.

Thomas Pennant, A tour in Wales, Vol. II, 1781

······································
"Inquiries of the saint"
······································

Llanelian church was popular for prophesies.

St. Elian's closet, is yet left in the east wall, and is supposed to have served both the office of a communion table, and as a chest to contain the vestments and other utensils belonging to the chapel. There is a hole in the wall of the chapel, through which the priests are supposed to have received confessions: the people believe this hole to have been used in returning oracular answers to persons who made inquiries of the saint respecting future events. — Near the door is placed Cyff Elian, *Elian's chest,* or poor box. People out of health, even to this day, send their offering to the saint, which they put, through a hole, into the box. A silver groat, though not a very common coin, is said to be a present peculiarly acceptable, and has been known to procure his intercession, when all other kinds of coin have failed! The sum, thus deposited, which in the course of a year frequently amounts to several pounds, the churchwardens annually divide among the poor of the parish.

William Bingley, North Wales, Vol. I, 1804

··
"The superstition has suffered no reformation"
··

Paying a Clergyman with 'mass money' was to be frowned upon.

On our arrival at the inn at Llangollen, we found it in the possession of some mourners, who were just returned from the funeral of a friend; however some tolerable quarters remained for us.

The dismal solemnity of these weeping countenances soon evaporated, and the sorrows and senses of the company were quickly drowned in large potations of ale. Such is the general conclusion of a Welsh meeting, whether it be merry or melancholy.

I was here informed, that a burial was esteemed the most profitable function of a Welsh clergyman. The neighbours and relations of the deceased attend in large numbers at the funeral, and make considerable offerings to the officiating priest; for they are taught to believe that their respect to their friend's memory is in proportion to the oblations they give.

Though the man who was here interred was but a common tradesman, yet the collection at the church amounted to more than five pounds.

This custom is evidently derived from the ancient mass money collected for purgatory indulgences, and it is fortunate for the clergy of Wales, whose income is generally moderate, that the superstition has suffered no reformation.

H. P. Wyndham, Gentleman's Tour through Monmouthshire and Wales in the months of June and July, 1774, 1775

"Reading prayers for the success of the fishery"

This is an echo of the pre-Reformation tradition of blessing men's work, especially where it involved a degree of danger.

It must excite some little astonishment, that a situation which boasts such a variety of attractions, and so many advantages for sea bathing in comfort and security, should have remained neglected till within the last twenty years, and further still, that at a period much later the elevated spot on which the new town has partly risen, should be only occupied by the cottages of a few fishermen.

The circumstances that conspired in their outset to exalt Tenby to consideration as a bathing place, are rather extraordinary, and may be best explained by the recital of a local anecdote that came to our knowledge while we remained for a few days in the town. It appears from this relation that the ancient Welsh custom of reading prayers for the success of the fishery before the men ventured to cast their nets into the sea, was observed at this port with much religious scruple, till about five and twenty, or at most thirty years ago. There was a small chapel stationed on a rocky projection of the shore, that was appropriated solely to the performance of this singular service. Thither the parish priest repaired before the fishery began, to invoke a benediction on the draught, and there his deputy remained to receive the tythe of the capture when the fishery was over. This custom, which had prevailed in monastic times throughout the Principality, had been sensibly on the decline for the last sixty years. In most of the fishing towns it became extinct by degrees, till at length about the time before-mentioned it only remained in force at Tenby. The worthy incumbent, aware of this, conceived it might as well be laid aside in his district. To this the fishermen had no objection, provided he should wave his tythe with the ceremony. But, if the tongue of rumour reports true, he tenaciously insisted this could not be right. Although the prayers were deemed superfluous, he seems to have considered it as a matter both of conscience and of duty to demand his share of the capture as before. At last the altercation was happily terminated by mutual compromise, the clergyman consented to receive a moderate compensation in lieu of his tythe of fish, and the custom being abolished, the chapel was no longer useful to either party.

E. Donovan, Descriptive excursions through South Wales and Monmouthshire in the year 1804, and the four preceding summers, 1805

SUNDRY SUPERSTITIONS

....

"That superstition still reigns here"

....

A visitor to Anglesey found much to object to when it came to local beliefs.

In a small chapel attached to the south east end of the church (which is said to have been the original edifice founded by Saint Elian) there is a kind of semicircular chest or cabinet made of oak into which whoever can enter and turn himself round is sure in the opinion of the vulgar to live out the year but if he fails it will prove fatal to him. People from all parts come at stated periods to try their destiny in this absurd way.

There is also an old chest well secured by bolts bars and nails in another part of the church having a small slit in the lid through which the country people are said to drop a piece of money uttering their maledictions against their enemies the black gentleman is thus seed to work evil against the offender, this uncharitable and unchristian custom if true seems almost too bad eve for monkish times much worse to be continued now. Having viewed these relics of superstition we ascended by a circular tower to the roof [of] the church which is very nicely leaded. On enquiring afterwards of a Welsh clergyman why Llanelian was so much better taken care of than other parish churches I found that some lands had been appropriated by one of the Welsh princes centuries ago by way of expiation for his sins to keep it in constant repair, this accounts for its having a steeple, being leaded, &c. &c.

[...]

Approaching nearer to Amlwch we observed our quondam loquacious compation become very silent, and just as we had passed an old wall about half a mile from the town he told us with evident marks of trepidation that there was a ghost sitting there every night, on asking him if he had ever seen it he said no but that many of his friends had, it was in the shape of a woman and once had attempted to pull a farmer's wife off her horse but was prevented by the arrival of a second person when it vanished. That on Christmas Eve the inhabitants of Amlwch used to come to the spot in order to see how many lights would pass by and as many did so many persons as travelled that road would die within the twelve-month.

I just mention these ridiculous stories to show that superstition still reigns here and this superstition has perhaps been the guardian to many of the druidical remains we noticed in the island. It was past six when we returned to the inn where we were welcomed by a most excellent repast.

John Skinner, Ten Day's Tour through the Isle of
Anglesea, 1802

"The residences of subordinate intelligences"

Richard Warner considered a modicum of superstition as more desirable than an excess of disbelief.

I have before observed, that a religious spirit prevails amongst the lower orders of the Welsh, which produces a characteristic decency of manners in that description of people. It is, however, much tinged with superstition, and the belief in spirits and apparitions is very general. The names of many mountains and rocks evince, that they are considered as the residences of subordinate intelligences; and this is accounted for, not so much, perhaps, from the credulity natural to ignorant people, as from the circumstances of the *scenery* wherein they reside, the gloom and desolation of which, added to its being liable to singular and striking variations in appearance, have a strong tendency to affect the human mind (naturally timid) with superstitious fears and whimsical notions. Similar situations will produce similar manners; and hence it happens that their brethren of the Scotch Highlands entertain the same opinions, in this respect, with the inhabitants of Wales.

[…]

These notions are, probably, unfounded, but they are not uninteresting, nor do we feel ourselves inclined to reprobate the *mild superstition* in which they originate. It is a principle that arises from the feelings and affections of nature; and is, at all events, more amiable, than the cold *philosophism* of the present day, which disbelieves every thing, which contracts and petrifies the heart, deadens the affections, and destroys all the finer sensibilites of the soul.

Richard Warner, A walk through Wales in August 1797, 1798

···

"An universal spitting seized the congregation"

···

Thomas Pennant, who was one of the best informed travellers across North Wales noted a fading of superstitions.

I shall here bring into one point of view the several religious customs used among us in former times; which have been gradually dropped, in proportion as the age grew enlightened, several were local, several extended through the whole country: perhaps some, which were expressive of their hatred of vice, or which had a charitable end, might as well have been retained, notwithstanding the smack of folly that was often to be perceived in them.

In church, at the name of the Devil, an universal spitting seized the congregation, as if in contempt of that evil spirit; and whenever *Judas* was mentioned, they expressed their abhorrence of him by smiting their breasts.

If there be a *Fynnon Vair*, the well of our Lady, or any other saint, the water for baptism was always brought from thence; and after the ceremony was over, old women were very fond of washing their eyes in the water of the font.

Previous to a funeral, it was customary, when the corpse was brought out of the house and laid upon the bier, for the next of kin, be it widow, mother, sister, or daughter (for it must be a female) to give, over the coffin, a quantity of white loaves, in a great dish, and sometimes a cheese, with a piece of money stuck in it, to certain poor persons. After that they present, in the same manner, a cup of drink, and require the person to drink a little of it immediately. When that is done, all present kneel down; and the minister, if present, says the Lord's Prayer: after which, they proceed with the corpse; and at every cross-way, between the house and the church, they lay down the bier, kneel, and again repeat the Lord's Prayer; and do the same when they first enter the church-yard. It is also customary, in many places, to sing psalms on the way; by which the stillness of rural life is often broken into, in a manner finely productive of religious reflections.

To this hour, the bier is carried by the next of kin; a custom considered as the highest respect that filial piety can pay to the deceased. This was a usage frequent among the *Romans* of high rank; and it was thought a great continuance of the good fortune which had attended *Metellus Macedonicus* through his whole being, that when he had, in the fulness of years, passed out of life by a gentle decay, amidst the kisses and embraces of his nearest connections, he was carried to the funeral pile on the shoulders of his four sons; and, let me add, that each one of them had enjoyed the greatest offices of the commonwealth.

[...]

It is still usual to stick, on the eve of St. *John* the *Baptist,* over the doors, sprigs of St. *John's wort,* or in lieu of it the common Mugwort. The intent was to purify the house from evil spirits; in the same manner as the *Druids* were wont to do with *Vervaine,* which still bears with the *Welsh* the significant title of *Cas gan Gythral,* or *the Daemons aversion.*

Upon *Christmas-day,* about three o'clock in the morning, most of the parishioners assembled in church, and after prayers and a sermon, continued there singing psalms and hymns with great devotion, till broad day; and if, through age or infirmity, any were disabled from attending, they never failed having prayers at home, and carols on our Saviour's nativity. The former part of the custom is still preserved; but too often perverted into intemperance. This act of devotion is called *Plygan,* or the *Crowing of the Cock.*

Thomas Pennant, A tour in Wales, 1781

....

"None ever molest the flowers"

....

Flowers were used for many occasions in Glamorgan.

It may be observed of the Glamorganshire customs, that when a young couple are to be married, their ways to the church are strewed with sweet-scented flowers and evergreens. When a young unmarried person dies, his or her ways to the grave are also strewed with sweet flowers and evergreens; and on such occasions it is the usual phrase, that those persons are going to their nuptial beds, not to their graves. ... None ever molest the flowers that grow on graves; for it is deemed a kind of sacrilege to do so. A relation or friend will occasionally take a pink, if it can be spared, or a sprig of thyme, from the grave of a beloved or respected person, to wear it in remembrance; but they never take much, lest they should deface the growth on the grave. This custom prevails principally in the most retired villages; and I have been assured, that in such villages where the right of grazing the churchyard has been enforced, the practice has alienated the affections of very great numbers from the clergymen and their churches; so that many have become dissenters for the singularly uncommon reason, that they may bury their friends in dissenting burying-grounds, plant their graves with flowers, and keep them clean and neat, without any danger of their being cropt. This may have been the fact in some places; but I confidently believe, that few of the clergy would urge their privileges to an unfair or offensive extent.

Benj. Heath Malkin, The Scenery, Antiquities and Biography of South Wales, from materials collected during two excursions in the year 1803, 1804

WEDDINGS

....
"With a troop of his friends"
....

In North Wales, the groom may chase his bride on horseback.

In all countries custom has established some forms, previous to connubial connections. In many places, custom acts the part of an inexorable tyrant, whose rigid commands we must implicitly obey. Here she bears a milder sway. I will not offend the ear of delicacy, with a description of what had better be concealed. I may say, that in general the women discover such prognostics, before they enter into the marriage state, as denote they will not be unfruitful members of society. Nor does custom stamp the opprobious stigma of infamy upon such an appearance.

The ceremonies attending the marriages of these people, may afford you some entertainment, as they are different from anything of the kind, that may have fallen within your observation.

The bridegroom on the morning of the wedding, accompanied with a troop of his friends, as well equipped as the country will allow, comes and demands the bride. Her friends, who are likewise well mounted on their MERLINS [The Welsh word for a little mountain horse], give a positive refusal to their demands, whereupon a mock scuffle ensues between the parties. The bride is mounted on one of the best steeds, behind her next kinsman, who rides away with her in full career. The bridegroom and his friends, pursue them with loud shouts. It is not uncommon to see, on such an occasion, two or three hundred of these merlins, mounted by sturdy Cambro-Britons, riding with full speed, crossing and jostling each other, to the no small amusement of the spectators. When they have pretty well fatigued themselves and their horses, the bridegroom is permitted to overtake his bride. He leads her away in triumph, as the Romans did the Sabine nymphs. They all return in amity, and the whole is concluded with festivity and mirth.

Let us now view the women, in the very essential characters of wives and mothers. You would naturally suppose, that a young woman who had, without fear or restraint, enjoyed an almost unbounded liberty in a single state, would not be easily debarred from enjoying the same in the married. But the case is the very reverse.

Infidelity to the bed of Hymen, is scarce ever known or heard of in this country.

Joseph Cradock, Letters from Snowdon, 1770

....
"There is, undoubtedly, less refinement"
....

According to Samuel Pratt, post wedding parties could go on for a very long time indeed.

The ceremonies of the Cambrian peasants, in the unpolished parts of the country, are no less singular than those at their wooing. The friends and relations of both parties, not only testify the usual demonstrations of joy during the daytime, but keep it up the whole night, the men visitors putting to bed the bridegroom, and the females the bride, after which the whole company remain in the chamber, drinking jocund healths to the new-married couple, and their posterity, singing songs, dancing and giving into every other festivity, sometimes for two or three days together.

Preposterous enough you will say! but as this, generally speaking, happens to a man and woman but once in a life, and gives now and then an holiday, that is, a few hours or days labour to a race of harmless, hard-toiling creatures, it may be dispensed with. Their relaxations are few, and our own many. There is, undoubtedly, less refinement, perhaps, less delicacy in theirs; but are they not as innocent, as reasonable as ours?

Samuel Pratt, Gleanings through Wales, Holland and Westphalia, 1795

....
"A wedding exhibits the gayest scene imaginable"
....

In Fishguard, there is a musical walk to the Church.

Marriages here amongst the common people has its
season from Michaelmas to Christmas, in which time,
love offers frequent sacrifices to the shrine of Hymen.
And as the majority of the people are sailors, a wedding
exhibits the gayest scene imaginable, for all the vessels
in the port, out of compliment, display their colours,
whilst some old swivel or musket in repeated vollies,
proclaims the occasion. The happy pair, attended by
their friends in their holiday clothes, walk to the church,
preceded by a violin, and sometimes by a bagpipe, the
old nuptial music of this country, though now rarely
used, as being too discordant for ears attuned to joy, and
the whole ceremony is marked with a most becoming
festivity. The funerals are marked with a great want of
solemnity; no knell announces the departing spirit, as is
usual in other places; no psalm appropriate to the
mournful circumstance is sung as the corps advances
towards the church, or at its entrance into the cemetery;
and an indecent hurry seems to characterise every stage
of the awful procession.

'Gwinfardd Dyfed' (Walter Davies), Statistical account
of the Parish of Fishguard in Pembrokeshire, 1796

DEATHS

....
"The night of lamentation"
....

A wake was observed in North Wales.

I have already described to you the different ceremonies, attending the marriages of this people, they are no less singular in their funerals.

The evening preceding the burial, they have what they call WYL-NOS, i.e. the night of lamentation. All the neighbors attend at the house of the deceased, the minister, or in his absence the clerk of the parish, comes and prays over the dead, and psalms are sung agreeable to the mournful occasion. This it may not unreasonably be supposed, is the remains of the Romish superstition of requiems for the souls of the deceased. However there is nothing improper in the custom if conducted with decorum and devotion, which is not always the case. At the funeral, the relations and friends of the deceased make presents, to the officiating clergyman, and the clerk of the parish. These offerings are altogether voluntary, generally proportionable to their circumstances, and the respect they bear to the memory of their departed friend. In some populous parishes, the offerings are very considerable, and constitute a great part of the profits of a living. There is no doubt but that this is likewise a relict of the Popish custom, of giving money to their priests, for praying that the soul of the deceased may be relieved from purgatory.

Joseph Cradock, Letters from Snowdon, 1770

....
"The misguided devotees"
....

While its well spelt peril, Llanelian's Chapel was associated with good fortune.

The wakes of Llanelian were formerly held on the three first Friday evenings in August; but they are now confined to only one of those days. Young persons from all parts of the adjacent country, and even from distant counties, assemble here, most of whom have along with them some offering for the faint, to ensure their future prosperity, palliate their offences, and secure blessings on their families, their cattle and corn.

The misguided devotees assemble about the chapel, and having deposited their offerings, many of them proceed to search into their future destiny, in a very singular manner, by means of the wooden closet. Persons of both sexes, of all ages, and sizes, enter the small door-way, and if they can succeed in turning themselves round within the narrow limits of the place, (which measures only betwixt three and four feet in height, about four feet across the back, and eighteen inches wide,) they believe that they shall be fortunate till at least the ensuing wake. But if they do not succeed, in this difficult undertaking, they esteem it an omen of ill fortune, or of their death within the year. — I have been told, that it is curious enough to see a stout lusty fellow, weighing sixteen or eighteen stone, striving to creep into these narrow confines, with as much confidence as a stripling a yard high; and when he fails in the attempt, to see him, contrary to all reason, fuming and fretting because his body, which contains in solid bulk more than the place could hold, were it crammed into all corners, cannot be got in. But when we consider, that superstition and enthusiasm have generally little to do with reason, we must not wonder at this addition to the heap of incongruities that all ages have afforded us.

William Bingley, North Wales, Vol. I, 1804

....

"The virtuous feelings of this illiterate peasantry"

....

A funeral procession above Llanberis impressed William Bingley.

During my residence in Caernarvonshire I one day rode with the worthy rector of Llanberis, to attend the funeral of a girl, a child about seven years old, whose parents resided in the parish of Llanddiniolen, somewhat more than five miles distant. The coffin was tied on the bier, and covered with a sheet, tied also at the corners. It was borne on the shoulders of four men. The number of attendants at the outset was near a hundred, but this increased by the continued addition of men, women, and children, some on foot and some on horseback, till, by the time we arrived at the church, we had more than double that number. At the head of this cavalcade my friend and myself ascended the steep paths of the rocks, passed over mountains, and wound our way along some of the most rugged defiles of this dreary country. To any stranger who could have observed, at a little distance, our solemn procession, in this unfrequented tract of mountains, in one place some hundred feet above the lake of Llanberis, to the edge of which we had to descend, it would have borne much the air of romantic times. When we came to the church, we found

310

that place nearly full of people awaiting our arrival. The service was read in Welsh in a most impressive manner; and the coffin was let down into the grave by four of the female mourners. A more solemn office I had never witnessed, and the circumstance of the body being committed to the bosom of the earth by the hands of relatives or friends was altogether new to me. A few rushes were strewed upon the coffin; and I shall never forget the stifled shriek that was uttered, when, in Welsh, the solemn words, "we commit her body to the ground," &c. were read. How enviable were the virtuous feelings of this illiterate peasantry, while thus attending a sister to the verge of peace. — The ceremony being over, the grave was filled up and planted with slips of box and some other evergreens. — The offerings in the church amounted to near two pounds, of which more than thirty shillings were in silver.

William Bingley, North Wales, Vol. I, 1804

....

"The innocence of primaeval manners"

....

In Glamorgan, graves were dug on the south side of the Church and marked with flowers.

Too much praise cannot be due to the becoming attention the inhabitants of this part of the country [Bonvilston village, near Cowbridge] bestow upon the very soil that covers the remains of their deceased friends and relatives. According to the superstitious notions tenaciously retained in almost every district in the Principality, the custom of never interring the dead on the north, or *wrong side* of the church, is here most scrupulously observed. The graves lie invariably on the south side, or at the east and west extremity of the church, where the burial ground displays all the neatness and simplicity of a rustic flower garden. Some of the graves are surrounded with a bordering of box, others with basket work, and the enclosed spaces bedecked with a pleasing variety of plants. With the exception of the various kinds of evergreens employed on this mournful occasion, those plants whose flowers exhibit the greatest diversity of colours, seem to be preferred. The deep purple of the aconite are artlesly contrasted with the livelier hues of the expanded rose, the pink, and variegated pansy: daisies are profusely intermingled. The corn bottle and the wall flower, with many others that are distinguished for the gaiety of their blossoms, appeared among the humble tributes of grateful memory concentrated within the verge of this embellished little spot. — There is something sweetly expressive of the innocence of primaeval manners in the observance of this ancient custom. The practice of thus adorning the graves of the departed with flowers, prevailed in the earliest days, to which the poetical compositions of the Cambrian bards advert. The fugitive remains of their ancient poesy affords some very beautiful allusions to it.

[...]

We were much inclined to regret, that a custom so innocent in its origin, so conducive to the moral happiness of the people, and congenial with the sympathetic feelings of human nature, should have become in a material degree, if not entirely, neglected in many parts of the Principality; for contrary to the commonly received opinion in England, founded on the erroneous assertions of English tourists, the practice of planting the graves with flowers is rather local, and prevails only in a partial measure in certain parishes. This neglect is attributable to the impolitic, I had almost said the unbecoming conduct of the clergy in enforcing their claims to the right of pasturage for their horses within the precincts of the burying ground. Wherever this privilege has been assumed, as it must naturally be imagined, this ancient custom has been unavoidably ably laid aside. When a person is buried in such grounds, the ceremony of bestrewing the grave with flowers is oftentimes observed, more particularly when the deceased happens to be of an early age, whether male or female; but these, not being planted, very soon decay, and are seldom replaced by others after the expiration of a month from the time of burial.

E. Donovan, Descriptive Excursions through South Wales and Monmouthshire in the year 1804, and the four preceding summers, Vol. I, 1805

....

"It is perhaps a prettier custom"

....

The practice might not have declined as much as Mr Donovan feared.

Their customs in case of death are not less remarkable. The bed on which the corpse lies is always strewed with flowers, and the same custom is observed after it is laid in the coffin. They bury much earlier than we do in England; seldom later than the third day, and very frequently on the second. This haste would be considered here as less respectful and affectionate: yet, take their customs in the aggregate, and they will be found to be more so. Indeed, respect or the reverse on such occasions is altogether determined by opinion. The custom or ceremony is in itself nothing, any further than as it is supposed to indicate the mind. It appears to me that the custom of burying early is in every respect the most proper, where the evidence of actual mortality is decisive. In this part of the country especially it is for the interest of the living; for the habit of filling the bed, the coffin, and the room, with sweet-scented flowers, though originating probably in delicacy as well as affection, must of course have a strong tendency to expedite the progress of decay. The attentions which immemorial prescription demands from a family, are such as could not be continued long without serious inconvenience.

It is an invariable practice, both by day and night, to watch a corpse; and so firm a hold has this supposed duty gained on their imaginations, that probably there is no instance on record of a family so unfeeling and abandoned, as to leave a dead body in the room by itself for a single minute, in the interval between the death and burial. Such a violation of decency would be remembered for generations. The hospitality of the country is not less remarkable on melancholy than on joyful occasions. The invitations to a funeral are very general and extensive; and the refreshments are not light, and taken standing, but substantial and prolonged. Any deficiency in the supply of ale would be as severely censured on this occasion, as at a festival. With respect to these peculiarities, it is to be understood that they apply rather to the farmers and peasantry, than to persons of condition, who are apt to lose their nationality, and contract the manners and opinions of the polite world: but strewing flowers and watching the corpse are universal among all ranks and degrees, because the observance or neglect of such ceremonies depends on servants and nurses, whose minds are always peculiarly susceptible of local and superstitious prejudices. The grave of the deceased is constantly overspread with plucked flowers for a week or two after the funeral: the planting of graves with flowers is confined to the villages, and the poorer people. It is perhaps a prettier custom. It is very common to dress the graves on Whitsunday, and other festivals, when flowers are to be procured: and the frequency of this observance is a good deal affected by the respect in which the deceased was held. My father-in-law's grave in Cowbridge church has been strewed by his surviving servants, every Sunday morning for these twenty years. It is usual for a family not to appear at church till what is called the month's end, when they go in a body, and then are considered as having returned to the common offices of life.

> Benj. Heath Malkin, The Scenery, Antiquities and
> Biography of South Wales, from materials collected
> during two excursions in the year 1803, 1804

"A much more simple and harmless nature"

And indeed, it was to be seen throughout South Wales.

The other custom to which I allude, is of very ancient date likewise, but of a much more simple and harmless nature; I mean, strewing the graves with flowers. Upon going into the church-yard, your senses are on a sudden surprized and regaled with the scent of the most delicious new-blown flowers and aromatic herbs. When you look around you to discover from; whence this profusion of sweets proceeds, you see several fresh graves strewn all over with these primitive and rural tokens of respect and regard. This tribute is always paid by some near and dear relation of the deceased, who rises very early on a Sunday morning, and, unobserved, distributes these frail, yet certain, marks of an unfeigned affection. A twelvemonth after their relation or friend is dead, they continue this *pious* office.

[...]

The church-yard is never without fresh strewn graves, owing to their continuing their attentions for so long a time. The paths too are thus primitively and profusely adorned. The contemplation of this custom gave me the most agreeable ideas, and reminded me of many a poetical description of times, when to compliment a friend or a mistress with a wreath of flowers or a nosegay, was esteemed as great a mark of attachment, as it would be, in these vain and degenerate days, to present them with a set of jewels, or a birth-day suit.

I was walking one day in the environs of Carmarthen, and happening to cast my eyes in at a window that stood open, I saw a pretty young woman, very neatly dressed, leaning over the edge of a small coffin, with her head resting upon her arm. The coffin stood upon a table under the window, and in it was a beautiful female infant, that looked as if it was not dead, but asleep. The mother was indulging her placid grief by admiring it as it lay, and decorating the corpse with the fairest flowers she could select. She was not a little soothed and gratified at my stopping to take notice of the little angel.

Mrs. Morgan, A tour to Milford Haven,
in the year 1791, 1795

8

MAKING A LIVING; FARMING, FISHING, MINING AND THE INDUSTRIAL REVOLUTION

Malkin's account of visiting 'Rontha Vawr' and 'Rontha Vach' in 1803 (The Scenery, Antiquities and Biography of South Wales, Chapter 9, Glamorganshire) depicts a landscape with a 'pure transparent stream', where meadow contrasts with mountain in Arcadian settings. He also notes that 'the people are indeed thinly scattered, as well as miserably poor'. Agriculture, even when 'improved', offered little comfort to most. A brief look at Tithe Maps made in Wales from 1838 to 1850 reveals a landscape speckled by minute dwellings where barely a bump in the soil remains today. As soon as people had an alternative to rural poverty, many left. For the Welsh, the early stages of the Industrial Revolution offered another future, within your own borders and only a short journey away, where your language and culture carried on unchanged.

FARMING

From the grain of Anglesey to the cattle of Montgomery, each county had its characteristic harvest, as noted by Brome in 1694 and Crouch in 1695, and elaborated upon by others ever since. Little appears to have changed over the eighteenth and nineteenth centuries, hence the various accounts of rural poverty in the previous chapter.

Throughout the following accounts we encounter descriptions of climates, growing conditions and the need for agriculture to be improved. Sometimes, there are hints that landowners might consider this. The impression given is of a caste of owners, content to get what they could from their land, with little concern for those who paid their rents. Fishing rarely appears in these accounts, although one chronicler despairs about people in Fishguard not being in 'manufactories', presumably because they earned enough from catching fish. Two accounts here cover coracle fishers.

"A certain stupinenese in the greatest part of country gentlemen"

Joseph Cradock was unimpressed with the attitude of landowners in North Wales.

A considerable part of Carnarvonshire and the island of Anglesea, is naturally a very good soil, but very much unimproved. What they principally want, are good fences and shelter for their cattle. The only inclosures that that they have, are small banks of earth or turf-mounds thrown up. These continue but a very little time, as the cattle destroy them in the winter, and the farmer is at a considerable expence in repairing them every spring. In such places as are exposed to the sea winds, the trees will not grow to any height; and all kinds of quicksets are long in their growth. So that the gentlemen and farmers seldom judge it worth the trouble and expence to plant. But satisfied I am that in a few years it would answer; and nothing would contribute more to the improvement of the country, than if such a practice was generally adopted.

There are extensive fens undrained, and the greatest part of the country consists of nothing but furze. The best land lets in general from three to five shillings an acre; the price of labor about six-pence a day. There is great plenty of manure easily to be had, and notwithstanding these advantages, the country is unimproved. How shall we account for this? There is a certain stupinenese in the greatest part of country gentlemen, which renders them inattentive even to their own good. They live upon their estates, unsolicitous of what passes in life, and provided they enjoy the dull comforts of an animal existence, they are satisfied. Undisturbed with the spirit of enterprise and ambition, they follow the dull track of their ancestors, without thought, and without remorse, and live and die unknown.

Joseph Cradock, Letters from Snowdon, 1770

....
"And let the morrow provide for itself"
....

Concerning farmers, Cradock noted that the system of tenancy and rental discouraged any investment or improvement.

Several counties of Wales have made but a very slow progress in agriculture. In many places bordering upon England, they have in a great degree adopted the English manner of tillage. In some parts of the counties of Montgomery, Denbigh and Flint, the lands are well improved. I have made this observation, that the remoter they are from the English counties, the less is there of the spirit of industry and improvement among the inhabitants.

[...]

The farmers and laborers are most of them miserably poor, they hold the lands generally from year to year at rack rent. If one more industrious than the rest, should make any improvement, the landlord advances his rent, or turns him out. Thus it is the interest of the farmer to let them lie waste, as he has no certainty of a return, when he is liable to be turned out at the landlord's pleasure. Thus they only take care to get just sufficient by their industry to supply present want, and let the morrow provide for itself.

Nothing would contribute more to the cultivation of the country, than the granting of leases for life to the farmers, even at advanced rents. Then they would have a certain prospect of profit for their labor and expence; which would ultimately turn out to the benefit of the landlord, the tenant, and the public.

Joseph Cradock, Letters from Snowdon, 1770

....

"Glamorgan is a *rearing*, rather than a grazing county"

....

Good quality butter was made in Glamorganshire at the expense of its cheese.

The excellency of Glamorgan butter is too well known to need any eulogy; it is as highly celebrated as that of Epping forest with the London epicures. Great quantities arc annually salted and exported to Bristol and other places. This article of luxury seems to have been invented by the natives. It is certain that they very early arrived at perfection, and the country still preserves both the art and the fame.

[...]

Where butter, is a staple commodity, you must not expect the cheese should be of *prime* quality. The greater part of that made here, and through South Wales, is very inferior indeed. Deprived of the most nutritious part of the milk, and made strong by a superabundant quantity of rennet, it is highly disgusting to the palate of an Englishman. It is however eagerly sought after, and much eaten by the Welsh, who prefer it when *new*; for if long kept, it becomes prodigiously hard, very similar to what in Hampshire is called *Isle of Wight rock*. Though the generality of cheese is of this inferior quality, yet it must not be inferred, that the country is unfit for cheese making, or that the people are entirely ignorant of the art. A kind of cheese is made in some parts of the country of all sheeps' milk, or a mixture of sheep and cows' milk, exceedingly rich and high flavoured; and when of a proper age, little if at all inferior to the boasted *Parmesan*. That made at Ewenny sells for one shilling per pound; while that of the dairies about St. Fagans *brings sixteen pence*. Whether the art of manufacturing this useful article was known to the early Britons, might be a subject for antiquarian research.

[...]

The custom of *milking the ewes,* which is general here, will excite from you a smile; and you will perhaps ask, where is the profit, and what becomes of the lambs? The quantity of milk given, from one to two quarts per day, would by the English farmer be scarcely thought an equivalent for the trouble of milking; and every quart of milk so obtained, he would consider as lost in the proof of the mother and her offspring. But so rivetted are these people to this custom, that they suppose both are better in consequence of the practice; and allege as a proof, the generally prevailing and analogous custom of milking the cow. It should at the same be remembered, that Glamorgan is a *rearing,* rather than a grazing county; and the highest ambition of the farmer is to be considered *a good breeder.* There may be some solidity in this reasoning, and a long established practice should not be condemned, without being thoroughly canvassed; and the injurious consequences clearly proved.

John Evans, Letters written during a tour through South Wales, in the year 1803, and at other times, 1804

"The ignorance, prejudice, indolence, and poverty of the tenants"

John Evans was scathing about the state of agriculture in South Wales. Much of this was due to the same problems seen in North Wales.

The prejudices against a rational course of husbandry are numerous and strong; nor is there a probability of their eradication, but by the introduction of a new race, or the reformation of the junior part of the present by a better education.

In this country thistles and saneworts are considered as signs of good land; and a multiplicity of weeds serviceable to the future ley. Loose stones are looked upon as beneficial to arable crops, and accordingly they are carefully preserved while the land is under grass, being laid up in small heaps to give room for the grass to grow; and again regularly spread when the land is subjected to the plough. Wales is said to be so mountainous and rocky, that it is not calculated for corn; and so subject to rain and vapours, that wheat must on the average be planted with certain loss: and this unphilosophical idea we are sorry to see taken up by a respectable agriculturist, in his communications to the board of agriculture.

The first of these prejudices prevents the farmer from attempting the destruction of his worst enemy, lays him under the necessity of sowing a double quantity of seed, and leaves him the *satisfaction* to see more than half the crop stifled before it arrives at maturity, and the future herbage an ill-conditioned ley.

As to the second, how far land more than half covered with stones, and the surface beneath prevented the benefits of air and sun, can be equally or more productive than land wholly exposed to these vivifying influences, is a paradox I cannot solve: perhaps stones thrown on a seed bed of onions would be a solution little favourable to such a theory.

The third is in a great measure unfounded: Wales abounds with plains, vales, and slopes accessible to the plough; and it is proved by experience that a rocky bottom is not a bar to vegetation, but often favourable to it, particularly to farinaceous crops; nay madder, hops, saffron, &c. that have been supposed to require *deep*, have been successfully tried on *shallow soils*; and experience teaches us that fruit trees, with the top roots cut off while young, flourish better in soils with an indurated substratum, their horizontal roots spreading more; and being nearer the surface, are consequently more subject to the two powerful causes of fructification, heat and moisture.

[...]

Many of the errors so visible in the agriculture of this country, certainly arise from the ignorance, prejudice, indolence, and poverty of the tenants; but there are others, which attach to the proprietors of estates. The letting of farms on rack rent, or from year to year, is highly injudicious, as it throws a certain obstacle in the way of improvement: for who would be forward to expend his money in improvements which may not be likely to benefit himself or family. The letting lands by *auction*, a practice frequently adopted here, is still more injurious; for he who has been unwise enough to be the highest bidder, will not fail attempting to repair the loss his folly has occasioned, by draining the land of its extractable nourishment, during the short term he may be in possession.

The want of proper outhouses is an essential deficiency in the encouragement justly due to the tenant; for without these, it is in vain for him to attempt improvement — the *barton,* with its accompanying barn, stables, and stalls, is the source whence must be derived the principal substances to enrich the farm. The putting the repairs of buildings as an onus upon the tenant, is another instance of mistaken economy: few are disposed to repair the houses of others, and none less so, perhaps, than rude uneducated farmers. The maxim "obsta principiis" [resist the beginnings] is peculiarly urgent here.

The general inattention to proper fencing, is too obvious to require an observation; for land badly fenced reverts to the state of common, and thus it is added to the numerous *wastes* (here called mountains), which are of no advantage to the farmer, and highly injurious, in their present unproductive state, to the public. It has been stated that they are friendly to breeding cattle, affording the breeder a cheap run for his young stock: but are not these a stunted race of little comparative value? and do not many of them die for want of shelter and food? which, had they been on inclosed land, would have lived and thriven; and has it not been ascertained, that four times as many sheep and cattle could be bred and reared upon a given extent of land, fenced and in an improved state?

The observation, that cottagers would be greatly injured by a general inclosure of the waste lands, is made for want of attending to the state of the case: the supposed advantage is, that of keeping a cow, or a few sheep; but it has been clearly proved, if a cottager would place his cow to some neighbouring farm to tack, even at three shillings per week, the extra profit would amount to more than the whole of such a cow kept upon the starving waste.

John Evans, Letters written during a tour through South Wales, in the year 1803, and at other times,1804

....

"As powerful motives to decency and integrity"

....

In Pembrokeshire, farm workers were paid in both cash and kind.

Our object was Eglwyswrw, a small village in Pembrokeshire, about six miles from Kilgarran, where we had already bespoken accommodations for the night. The road to this place carried us through a rich country, which, unlike any thing we had hitherto seen in Wales, (excepting in the vale of Clwyd) exhibited a general system of good husbandry. We observed with much satisfaction the admirable effects of this system in the appearance of the lands, and the heaviness of the crops; but were still more gratified by the comfort and decency visible amongst the little farmers and labouring poor.

Perhaps throughout the whole British empire, there is no spot where the peasantry exhibit more happiness than in the northern parts of Pembrokeshire. Their families, on an average, consist of five people, provided for in the following manner: —

The father is generally employed through the whole year by the same farmer, who allows him during the eight summer-months fourpence per day, and for the remaining four months three-pence per day. He eats however his meals, breakfast, dinner, and supper, at the farmer's, and is usually allowed beside a jug of skimmed milk. The mother employs all the time not dedicated to domestic labours in knitting, or more commonly in making pieces of flannel, to be disposed of at some of the neighbouring fairs, of which there are several annual ones in every Welsh town; out of the profits of this, the rent of the cottage is usually paid. No increase of wages to the labourer takes place in general, *at harvest*, as he experts to be recompensed in another way. But this is optional on his part; and if he choose money, the farmer gives him eightpence per day during that season. If not, he is paid by what the people in this country call *an huggling*, a practice of the following singular nature: — At Christmas, the farmer pays off any little debt which his labourer may have contracted at the miller's, and presents him with three large coarse loaves, and two large wheaten loaves, (each about two gallons) together with a quarter of good mutton. Thus assisted, the Pembrokeshire peasant partakes, in some little degree, of those gifts of a bountiful Providence, which the higher classes of society in other countries monopolize entirely to themselves. He sees himself brought to something like a rational level with his fellow-creatures, perceives that he has a stake in society, and feels that the practice of certain duties results from this situation; all which convictions operate upon him as powerful motives to decency and integrity, to cheerfulness and content.

Richard Warner, A second walk through Wales in August and September 1798, 1799

FISHING

....

"What these frightful creatures were"

....

Mrs Morgan was most alarmed when she saw coracle fishers for the first time.

My wrapt imagination dwelt upon these scenes, combining the faint shadow of what I saw by the dim light of declining day, with the stories I recollected, till we had nearly reached the village of Aberguilly; when I was awakened from my delightful reverie by an object that startled me exceedingly. I had never in my life seen any thing that wore such an appearance; nor could I at all conceive or guess what it was. Four very gigantic figures, perfectly black, occupied the whole road, and moved with an even but quick pace towards us. I thought I could discern feet and legs like men's;

but the upper parts were spread out three or four feet wide into a shapeless trunk, without arms or head. I did not long remain silent, but earnestly enquired what these frightful creatures were. Mr. M—, well acquainted with such appearances, told me, they were men with their boats upon their backs, which is the Welsh manner of carrying them, after they have been fishing in the Towy for salmon. By this time we were nearly come up to them; and I then became apprehensive, lest the horse should be as foolish as his mistress had been. But he, not having filled his imagination with legendary tales, let them pass close by him, without even laying his ears close to his head. This certainly shewed a wonderful degree of either philosophy or dulness in the animal, but I could not discover which.

[...]

As the manner of catching salmon is remarkably entertaining, I must not omit to describe it to you. When the tide is retiring, several men in pairs walk down to the river, with each a coracle upon his back. This is a small boat, in shape exactly like a walnut-shell, made originally of hides, but at present with canvas, strained over slight ribs of wood. There is a seat across, on which the fisher sits, with a paddle in one hand and the line of his net in the other. Thus equipt, he follows the tide, coasting one side of the river, whilst his partner does the fame on the opposite side, holding the other line of the net. They thus sweep the Towy, as they go down the stream. When they feel a salmon in the net, they approach each other, and uniting the lines, completely inclose the fish, which they draw into one of the coracles, and then dispatch it with their paddles. They sometimes take fish of a very large size; and the dexterity which they display in getting them into so light and so small a boat without over- setting it, is wonderful. Having deposited the fish in the bottom of one of the coracles, they again separate, and proceed as before; and when they think proper, they come on shore and walk home, in the same manner as they set out, with their boats slung upon their backs, by means of a leathern strap crossing their breasts. When the tide is not favourable in the day, they pursue their fortune by moon-light, which has a very picturesque effect in the eye of the beholders.

Mrs. Morgan, A tour to Milford Haven, in the year 1791, 1795

"Like the shells of so many enormous turtles"

Mr Wyndham took a more sanguine view.

The fishermen, in this part of Caermarthenshire, use a singular kind of boats, called Coracles.

They are generally five feet and a half long, and four broad; their bottom is a little rounded and their shape is exactly oval. These boats are ribbed with light laths, or split twigs, in the manner of basket-work, and are covered with a raw hide, or strong canvas, pitched in such a manner as to prevent leaking. A seat crosses just above the center, towards the broad end. The men paddle them with one hand and fish with the other, and when their work is finished, bring their boats home with them on their backs.

In riding through Abergwilly, we saw several of these phænomena in the street, with their bottoms upwards, which at first sight appeared like the shells of so many enormous turtles.

H. P. Wyndham, Gentleman's Tour through
Monmouthshire and Wales in the months of June and
July, 1774, 1775

....

"No manufactory has been set on foot"

....

'Gwinfardd Dyfed' lamented the lack of industry in Fishguard. He did not perhaps enquire too deeply about how the people made their living through fishing.

In a place so well situated in every respect, and so well circumstanced as Fishguard, it is much to be lamented that no manufactory has ever been set on foot, were it only for the tendency it would unavoidable to idleness and its inseparable evils, and disseminate a spirit of industry, to say nothing of the gain that would otherwise result from it, especially when there is so striking an instance of its good effects on one of the most steril districts in the whole principality, a country labouring under every disadvantage that this is free from, namely Merionethshire.

...and a person there, may have a bill on London for one hundred pounds, or a much greater sum, at the shortest notice, whereas at Fishguard (I will not go so far as a certain tour writer, who in a wanton defiance of truth and common sense, asserted that at Haverfordwest they knew not what a bank-bill was) it is with the greatest difficulty one can get a bank-note for ten pounds, or a bill amount, on London or Bristol, for cash or *vice versa*, cash for a note or bill of that value...

'Gwinfardd Dyfed' (Walter Davies) Statistical account
of the Parish of Fishguard in Pembrokeshire, 1796

MINING

Industry in Wales revolved around two themes; extracting minerals, metals and coal, and turning these into goods fit for use at home and export abroad. Mining in Wales extends back to the Bronze Age. While the quarries at Parys Mountain in Mon were substantial operations by 1800, most other mines were relatively small. Swansea's docks had begun exporting coal well before 1720, and were fast growing in size. Smelting copper started in earnest in Swansea in 1730 and by 1760, iron was being forged in Merthyr Tydfil. From that point on, the rate of change across the whole of South Wales would be dramatic. During this period, accounts about coal mining depict a number of small scale shallow mines. A visit to the Rhondda when it was a remote farming valley in 1803 (see Chapter 10) gives an idea of the scale of the changes.

....
"Even the mosses and lichens of the rocks have perished"
....

Thomas Pennant describes the revival of mining in Parys Mountain, Anglesey. He also outlines its effect on the local environment.

From hence I visited *Trysclwyn* mountain; on part of which, called *Parys mountain* (probably from a *Robert Parys,* who was chamberlain of *North Wales* in the reign of *Henry* IV.) is the most considerable body of copper ore perhaps ever known. The external aspect of the hill is extremely rude, and rises into enormous rocks of coarse white quartz. The ore is lodged in a bason, or hollow, and has on one side a small lake, on whose waters, distasteful as those of *Avernus,* no bird is known to alight. The whole aspect of this tract has, by the mineral operations, assumed a most savage appearance. Suffocating fumes of the burning heaps of copper arise in all parts, and extend their baneful influence for miles around. In the adjacent parts vegetation is nearly destroyed; even the mosses and lichens of the rocks have perished: and nothing seems capable of resisting the fumes but the purple *Melic* grass, which flourishes in abundance.

[...]

In the year 1762, one *Alexander Frazier* came into *Anglesey* in search of mines. He visited *Parys mountain;* called on Sir *Nicholas Bayley,* and gave him so flattering an account of the prospect, as induced him to make a trial, and sink shafts. Ore was discovered; but before any quantity could be gotten, the mines were overpowered with water. In about two years after, Messrs. *Roe* and Co. of *Macclesfield* applied to Sir *Nicholas* for a lease of *Penrhyn ddu* mine in *Caernarvonshire;* with which they were, much against their wills, compelled to take a lease of part of this mountain, and to carry on a level, and make a fair trial. The trial was accordingly made: ore was discovered; but the expences overbalanced the profits. They continued working to great loss: and at length determined to give the affair up. They gave their agent orders for that purpose, but he, as a final attempt, divided his men into ten several companies, of three or four in a partnership, and let them sink shafts in various places, about eight hundred yards eastward of a place called the *Golden Venture,* on a presumption that a spring, which issued from near the place, must come from a body of mineral. His conjecture was right; for in less than two days they met with, at the depth of seven feet from the surface, the solid mineral, which proved to be that vast body which has since been worked to such advantage. The day that this discovery was made was *March 2d* 1768; which has ever since been observed as a festival by the miners. Soon after this discovery, another adventure was begun by the reverend Mr. *Edward Hughes,* owner of part of the mountain, in right of his wife *Mary Lewis* of *Llys Dulas* so that the whole of the treasure is the property of Sir *Nicholas Bayley* and himself.

[…]

These works have added greatly to the population of the island; for about fifteen hundred persons are employed, who, with their families, are supposed to make near eight thousand persons, getting their bread from these mines. The little village of *Amwlch,* the port of the place, is encreasing fast, and the market grows considerable. At the season of the greatest work, *Mr. Hughes's* men alone receive, for many weeks, two hundred pounds in one week, and a hundred and fifty in another, merely for subsistence. The port is no more than a great chasm between two rocks, running far into land, and dry at low-water; into which sloops run, and lie secure to receive their lading.

Thomas Pennant, A tour in Wales, Vol. II, 1778

THE INDUSTRIAL REVOLUTION

While Parys Mountain was served by two substantial towns for the time (Amlwch and Penysam), similarly important towns were emerging in South Wales. Swansea grew steadily throughout the eighteenth century, although the growth of Merthyr Tydfil was much faster and greater.

....
"The greatly increased bustle of commercial thoroughfare"
....

Swansea was noted for the variety of industries based there as well as being the first major port in South Wales.

About the year 1730, or not much sooner, the first copper work was established, on the eastern side of the river; and I have been informed that it was not till about the year 1760, or thereabouts, that any thing additional of this nature took place. Since that time, the copper works and collieries have increased in so great a degree, that it is not at all improbable it may at some distant period rival Bristol or Liverpool. This supposition will scarcely appear extravagant to those who have witnessed the rapid change in this county within the last thirty years. At present, it is nearly doubled in population by Merthyr Tydvil.

[…]

From a little Welsh account of the principality, first printed about the year 1720, it appears that Swansea was then noted for the manufacture of straw hats; that it had a considerable trade in coal; and that it was the best built and most cleanly town in all Wales. It was, till of very late years, remarkable for its cleanliness and neatness.

The streets were every where swept very clean early in the morning, and strewed with sand. This usage is, as much as possible, still continued; but the greatly increased bustle of commercial thoroughfare, the great influx of occasional visitors, and its occupations, dirty in many of their departments, do not admit of the former nicety. Still it is a very cleanly place, and the most so of any large town in. Wales. In this respect it is unlike Caermarthen, which, though esteemed a good town where the towns are so bad, is filthy to an unpardonable excess. There is a very flourishing pottery carried on here, on Mr. Wedgwood's plan.

[...]

The increase of trade at Swansea will appear from the number of vessels employed in different years, which were six hundred and ninety-four in 1768, sixteen hundred and ninety-seven in 1790 and two thousand five hundred and ninety in 1800. The church is neat, with some good monuments. It is a very favourite bathing place, and would be delightful, if the smoke of the works in the vale did not in some measure affect the atmosphere, as well as impair the beauty of the scenery.

> **Benj. Heath Malkin, The Scenery, Antiquities and Biography of South Wales, from materials collected during two excursions in the year 1803, 1804**

"These liberal exhibitions of Cambrian beauty"

When investigating the development of mining and industry in Swansea and Neath, it was not always a good idea to examine naked bathers too closely.

A large tract of country northward of Swansea is
covered with coal, copper, and iron-works, the
operations of which are much facilitated by a canal
passing among them. The dismal gloom of the
manufactories, hanging over the river Tawe, is
pleasingly contrasted by the whitened walls of their
appendant villages, springing from the dark sides of the
hills that rise above the river. Conspicuous above the
other resorts of the manufacturers is MORRISTOWN, a neat
newly created village; and on the summit of a steep hill
Morristown castle, a quadrangular building, which is
the habitation of upwards of thirty families; these
buildings owe their origin to Mr. Morris, a gentleman,
who, in partnership with Mr. Lockwood, conducts one
of the leading works. The introduction of Major Jones
obtained me a view of Messrs. Freeman's copper
manufactory: we took care to be there at noon, when the
furnaces are tapped and all the interesting processes
gone through. The effect in passing through these
dismal buildings, contrasted by the vivid glare of the
furnaces, and the liquid fire of the pouring metal, is to a
stranger very striking. I was much surprized at the
quantity of condensed sulphureous vapour that
yellowed the roof of the building. Sulphur often forms
the greatest bulk of the ore; yet no means are employed
to collect the vapour, which might easily be managed,
and could not fail of turning to a source of profit: at the
same time, it would save the health of the workmen, and
spare the vegetation, which appears stinted for a
considerable distance by the noxious effluvia.

We left these sulphureous chambers to enjoy a purer air
on the sea-shore, where another curiosity awaited us. As

we were strolling oil the sands, about a mile above the town, we remarked a group of figures, in birth-day attire, gamboling in the water: not suspecting that they were women, we passed carelessly on; but how great was our surprize, on approaching them, to find that the fact did not admit of a doubt. We had not paused a minute, before they all came running toward us, with a menacing tone and countenance, that would seem to order us away. Though we did not understand their British sentences, we obeyed, and very hastily too, on finding a volley of stones rattling about ear ears. This hostile demonstration, we afterwards found, arose from a suspicion that we were going to remove their clothes, a piece of waggery often practised by the visitants of Swansea, to enjoy their running *nudiores ovo*. The girls knew that we were not their countrymen, or we should have passed unconcerned; unless, indeed, acquaintances, who would have made their usual salutation, and perhaps joined in the party's amusement. In our subsequent rambles on the beach these liberal exhibitions of Cambrian beauty afforded us many pleasing studies of unsophisticated nature.

J. T. Barber, A tour throughout South Wales and Monmouthshire, 1803

WORKS AT NEATH

"The inexhaustible collieries"

The abundant supplies of high quality coal and good access to the coast made South Wales an ideal place for refining metal. The following account considers the development of the Neath copper works.

Last summer they seemed to labour under a temporary
check from the continuance of the war, but the shock
was much more severely felt at the commencement of
hostilities. The works are now by degrees reviving, with
the exception of one or two that has ceased entirely; and
a principal copper work that was lately removed from
hence to Lanelly, fifteen miles west of Swansea. After all,
however, the inexhaustible collieries by which the town
of Neath is surrounded, in addition to its commodious
situation on the banks of a navigable river, must ever
render it a place of extensive business in the coal and
foundery line. Some conception may be formed of the
local advantages of this spot, from one particular of
information we received here. Notwithstanding the
immense quantity of this valuable article consumed
daily in the works, and the demand for exportation, coal
of the best quality is sold to the inhabitants at the pits in
strikes, a measure peculiar to those parts, at about the
average price of three half-pence or two-pence per
bushel.

Stone coal abound, and may be obtained in any
quantity along this part of the country, Hitherto the
value of this commodity has been too much
disregarded. As a fuel it burns with a slow yet gradual
heat, emitting very little smoke, and if blown like other
coal, the fire immediately expires. Towards the close of
the last century, this stubborn material has been
employed by several persons in lieu of coaked coal for
drying malt, with every degree of success; it has been
found to answer equally well for the purpose, at the
same time that it is far more oeconomical in point of
expence. We are inclined to think, that other important

advantages are still to be derived from the use of this kind of coal. Mr. Edward Martin, of Morristown, near Swansea, is so far convinced that pig and cast iron may be drawn from the ore with this raw material, that he obtained a patent for carrying his scheme into practise the beginning of this summer.

The copper manufactured at Neath is imported in a crude state from the same mine as that at Taybach, as nearly as we could learn. Close to the bridge we noticed a party of labourers lading their dram waggons with masses of grey, and reddish argillaceous iron ore, that lay in heaps along the shores, in order to convey it from the landing place along the rail road to the works near the abbey. — This ore is the product of most part of the southern coast of Wales.

E. Donovan, Descriptive excursions through South
Wales and Monmouthshire, in the year 1804, and the
four preceding summers, 1805

....

"The gaunt figures of the workmen"

....

The rapid development of Merthyr Tydfil and the nature of the ironworks meant that it was not a healthy place.

MYTHER TIDVIL, is a most miserable dirty place; the soil and the inhabitants both partook of a dark dingy colour: the women destitute of shoes and stockings, the men and boys the slaves of Vulcan. The Iron-works, under the direction of Mr. Cramshaw, are the largest in the kingdom; not less than one thousand hands are employed by this gentleman, who allows the person who inspects the machinery one-eighth of the profits, to keep them in repair.

[...]

The gaunt figures of the workmen excite both pity and terror, and the fallow countenances and miserable air of the people, prove it is a labour very prejudicial to their health.

'The Author' (Allen Cliffe),
The Cambrian Directory, 1800

"His house is surrounded with fire, flame, smoke, and ashes"

Malkin's description of Merthyr Tydfil deserves to be quoted at some length. It paints a picture of a complex, fast growing society. Great wealth was enjoyed by some, next door to those living 'in scattered confusion' bereft of water or sanitation.

The road from Aberdare across the mountain, that divides it from the vale of Merthyr Tydvil, is of rugged and toilsome ascent, and passes by the works of Mr. Scales. The communication between the two places is constant, and renders the scene widely different from the unfrequented wilds of Aberdare. From the summit, the town of Merthyr Tydvil, with its populous vale, stretches itself under the eye. The first perception of singularity that it occasions in the mind, is the extreme disproportion between the population and the visible means of sustenance. A mountain valley, overspread, as far as the eye can reach, with the comparatively commodious habitations of masters, agents, engineers, and workmen, seems to have been peopled in the teeth of every obstacle, and to assert the triumph of fact over probability. The vale is of considerable width, and inaccessible to all but the equestrian traveller, except at the very narrow passes of the extremities. The

341

mountains are bleak, barren, and devoid of wood: the bottom has its sprinkling of successful cultivation; but the inhabitants live on the contributions of distant parts, and enhance the prices far beyond their natural level, at the same time that they drain the surrounding country of its labourers. It is seldom that so populous a district and so bare a soil are found to coalesce. It is, however, owing to the difficulty of mountain tillage, which strong inducements will always overcome, and not to a defect of vegetative powers when called into action, that this tract exhibits these peculiarities, in a fair train for being diminished and effaced by time. Since the establishment of the iron-works, the great increase of the population, and the proportionately imperious demand for articles of consumption, the farmers have been excited to improve their lands; so that all sorts of corn, in very good and plentiful crops, are now raised upon lands, where it was once taken for granted that no corn could possibly be produced. Agriculture is perhaps improving here more rapidly, than in parts of the county more favourable to its efforts; and the energies thus awakened seem likely to be crowned with a success, not predicted by the most sanguine hopes of the projectors.

[…]

Merthyr Tydvil…continued a very inconsiderable village till about the year 1755, when the late Mr. Bacon took more notice of the iron and coal mines, with which this tract of country abounds, than they had before excited. For the very low rent of two hundred pounds per annum, he obtained a lease of a district, at least eight miles long and four wide, for ninety-nine years. It is to be understood, however, that his right extended only to the iron and coal mines found on the estate, and that he had comparatively a very small portion of the soil on the surface, on which he erected his works for smelting and forging the iron. He possessed in addition some fields for the keep of his horses, and other necessary conveniencies. He at first constructed one furnace; and little besides this was done, probably for at least ten years. The next advance was the erection of a forge for working pig into bar iron. About the beginning of the American war, Mr. Bacon contracted with government for casting cannon. Proper founderies were erected for this purpose; and a good turnpike road was made down to the port of Cardiff, along an extent of twenty-six miles. At Cardiff likewise a proper wharf was formed, still called the cannon wharf, whence the cannon were shipped off to Plymouth, Portsmouth, and wherever the service required. These were carried in waggons down to Cardiff, at a prodigious expence of carriages, horses, and roads. There are those who do not hesitate to assert, but I know not with what truth, that sixteen horses were sometimes employed to draw the waggon that contained only one cannon.

[...]

Soon afterwards, about the year 1783, he [Mr. Bacon] granted leases, I believe for thirty years.

[...]

I conclude them [the rents from these leases] to amount in the whole to three thousand pounds, because it is very generally asserted and believed, that the heirs of Mr. Bacon have from all those works a clear annual income of ten thousand pounds. Mr. Crawshay's iron works of

Cyfarthfa are now by far the largest in this kingdom; probably, indeed, the largest in Europe; and in that case, as far as we know, the largest in the world. He employs constantly upwards of two thousand men; and pays weekly in wages and other expences of the works, twenty-five thousand pounds. He makes upon an average between sixty and seventy tons of iron every week; and has lately erected two new additional furnaces, which will soon begin to work; when he will be able to make, one week with the other, one hundred tons of bar iron. Mr. Homfray makes weekly, on a moderate average, fifty tons of bar iron and upwards, and is now extending Penderyn and its buildings, which will soon be completed. He will then make at least eighty tons per week. Dowlas Iron Works, belonging to Messrs. Lewis and Tate, are on as large a scale as those of Penderyn, and about to be augmented in an equal proportion.

[…]

This town, as it may properly be termed, is now by far the largest in the whole principality. Its population, in the year 1802, was found to be upwards of ten thousand; and it is supposed that it amounts at this time, December 1803, though at the interval of only one year from the date of the numeration, to considerably more than eleven thousand.

[..]

It is true, the external appearance of Merthyr Tydvil is not to be compared with that of Swansea. The house of Mr. Homfray at Penderyn is large and elegant, with fine and well-planted gardens, green-houses, hot-houses, and all the accommodations befitting the residence of a wealthy family: but the splendours of

Merthyr Tydvil begin and end with this mansion. When the first furnaces and forges were erected, there could not exist the slightest glimmering of prescience, that this little obscure Welsh village would, in less than forty years, grow up to such a magnitude, as to be far more populous than any other town in Wales. The first houses that were built were only very small and simple cottages for furnace-men, forge-men, miners, and such tradesmen as were necessary to construct the required buildings, with the common labourers who were employed to assist them. These cottages were most of them built in scattered confusion, without any order or plan. As the works increased, more cottages were wanted, and erected in the spaces between those that had been previously built, till they became so connected with each other, as to form a certain description of irregular streets, very much on the plan of Crooked Lane in the city of London. These streets are now many in number, close and confined, having no proper outlets behind the houses. They are consequently very filthy for the most part, and doubtless very unhealthy.

Some streets, it is to be observed, have within these few years been built, and more are building, on a better plan; in straighter lines, and wider, having decent houses, with commodious outlets, and other necessary attentions to cleanliness and health. In some of the early, and rudely-connected streets, we frequently see the small, miserable houses taken down, and larger and very seemly ones built in their stead. Such improvements are increasing with some degree of rapidity. Shopkeepers, innkeepers, forge-men, some of them at least, and in no inconsiderable numbers, are making comfortable fortunes, and consequently improving their dwellings. Mr. Crawshay, however, is more conspicuously qualified to set them an example of industry than elegance. His house is surrounded with fire, flame, smoke, and ashes. The noise of hammers, rolling mills, forges, and bellows, incessantly din and crash upon the ear. Bars and pigs of iron are continually thrown to the hugely accumulating heaps that threaten to choke up every avenue of access. It is more humorously than truly said in the neighbourhood, that such scenery is most congenial to the taste, such sounds most lulling to the repose of the owner. The fact, however, is, that the situation of the master's dwelling was fixed long before Mr. Crawshay came to it: and when it is considered how conveniently it lies for the superintendence of the business, few men, brought up in the habits of commercial prudence, would consult agreeable prospects and domestic elegance, at the expence of that best security, the everlasting eye of a principal. The machinery of this establishment is gigantic; and that part of it, worked by water, among the most scientifically curious and mechanically powerful to which modern improvement has given birth.

[...]

The workmen of all descriptions at these immense iron works are Welshmen. The language is almost entirely Welsh. The number of Englishmen among them is very inconsiderable. But the ill effects, which large collections of the lower classes produce upon the state of manners, are here very observable, though by no means to so great an extent, as in the manufacturing towns of England. The simplicity, sincerity, and disinterestedness, of the peasant is lost in the mercenary cunning or extortion of the mechanic. But a few miles off, you can scarcely prevail with the rustic to accept your gratuity, though he has lost half his day's work by directing you over the mountains:

[...]

The men employed at these works are too much addicted to drinking; but in other respects no great immoralities are to be found among them; far less indeed than might have been expected, from the tide of dissoluteness which is usually found to flow in upon a place, from the rapid increase of vulgar population. The principal check to immorality arises from the iron-masters, as the proprietors are called, being magistrates of the county.

[...]

There are several book societies at Merthyr Tydvil, and a philosophical society is in its infancy. The parish church is well attended, and it has been furnished with an organ of late years. It is rather large, but not sufficiently so for the place; in consequence of which a spacious and elegant chapel of ease is now erecting, and nearly finished. This is an octagon building, to be furnished also with its organ. There are about ten dissenting and methodist meeting-houses; and their denominations are thus divided: three baptists, two presbyterians, two independents, two in the connection of Wesley, and one, if not two, in that of Whitfield. A theatre has lately been erected at Merthyr Tydvil, where an itinerant company of actors, by no means of the lowest description, perform at stated times.

Benj. Heath Malkin, The Scenery, Antiquities and Biography of South Wales, from materials collected during two excursions in the year 1803, 1804

9

NORTH WALES

*North Wales covers the old counties of Caernarfon (Carnarvonshire),
Merionnydd (Merionethshire), Yns Mon (Anglesey), Sir Y Fflint
(Flintshire) and Sir Dinbych (Denbighshire). Camden included Sir
Drefaldwyn (Montgomeryshire) as these six counties were the areas
ruled by the Ordovicians in Roman times, but Sir Drefaldwyn is
most often regarded as being part of South (or more correctly Mid)
Wales. English and Welsh names, where possible, are both included.*

ANGLESEY ~ YNS MON

Anglesea (though it is called the granary of Wales)
appeared to us as one continued picture of desolation;
and for twenty miles of our road through it, we could
not discover more than five or six corn fields, and the
grass land so miserably poor, that it starved rather than
fed its hungry inhabitants. We undoubtedly did not see
the country to the best advantage, because the excessive
heat of the summer had parched up the ground, and
occasioned a general appearance of dearth.

> **J Hucks, A pedestrian tour in North Wales
> in a series of letters, 1795**

AMLWCH

Amlwch is a small sea port, from whence the copper
(that is found in the Paris and Mona mines, which are

not more than a mile from the town), is shipped to London, Liverpool, &c. The Mona mine produces the finest ore; they also make quantities of copper from old iron...

These mines have an appearance uncommonly grand and striking — a vast yawning chasm, displaying full to the view of the astonished stranger its sulphurous contents; hundreds of workmen employed in a variety of different occupations; some boring shafts, others selecting the ore, which is slung up to the top, or, if I may use such an expression, ushered into the world in little baskets. In some places the chisel and the pickaxe find room for employment; in others the men are sedulously engaged in blowing up large pieces of the rock by means of gunpowder, the report of which reverberating from side to side, in this immense cavity, occasions such a tremendous explosion, that all nature seems to tremble to its center. — Upon the whole these mines bear an apt resemblance to the infernal regions, and, like the pestilence from the pit of Acheron, the sulphur which issues from them, spreads desolation around, so that not the slightest vestiges of verdure are to be traced in the neighbouring fields.

**J Hucks, A pedestrian tour in
North Wales in a series of letters, 1795**

Amlwch is a long straggling place and may contain from four to five thousand inhabitants though before the working of the Parys mines there were not an hundred tenements in the parish. Besides two or three good houses a church has been lately erected by the copper company on a neat substantial plan and a quay formed near the smelting houses where ships of two or three hundred tons burthen may take in their lading. These we passed in our way to Llanelian church this morning which we had been directed to examine as one of the most curious structures in the island. This church differs from most others in North Wales in having a kind of spire rising from a square tower. I cannot say that this edition is very elegant it being coated all the way up with small slate. The body of the church is ornamented with battlements, pinnacles, and buttresses in the style of our parish churches built about the time of Henry the seventh. Having procured the key we found the interior still retaining its catholic collection of saints and apostles, and the seats, chancel, and communion table, were decorated with a profusion of carving in oak. On the latter on a kind of scroll we read non nobis Domine non nobis sed nomine tuo. Beneath the arches which supported the roof of the building were six grotesque little figures, playing on the bagpipe, pibcorn, and other instruments, their appearance is rendered still more ridiculous by their being painted in black coats, yellow waistcoats, and white wigs.

John Skinner, Ten Day's Tour through
the Isle of Anglesea, 1802

BEAUMARIS – BIWMARES

The entrance into the town was pretty: the bay and castle, with Penmaen Mawr, and the Ormes Head at a distance, are seen in a direct line in front; and the road, which lies down a steep hill, is shaded on each side with trees. The town itself is finely situated on the western bank of the Menai, just where it opens into an extensive bay. The houses are in general neat, and well built, and one of the streets is very good. — On examining the church and church-yard, I found nothing worth notice.

[...]

Beaumaris Castle ... Is situated close to the town, within the grounds of Baron Hill, the seat of lord Bulkeley. It covers a considerable space of ground, but its walls are at present so low, that it does not excite much attention.

William Bingley, North Wales, 1804

HOLYHEAD – CAERGYBI

Holyhead is situated on an island, at the extreme west point of Anglesea, but, except at high water, the dividing channel is passable without boats. The island is seven or eight miles long, and, in most parts towards the sea, so rocky, as to be inhabited only by the various species of sea-fowl, which breed among the cliffs. — From being the nearest point of this kingdom that lies towards Dublin, it has always been much resorted to by company passing to and from Ireland. In itself, however, it possesses but few attractions for the tourist on pleasure.

[...]

The name that the Welsh have given to this place is Caer Cybi, *The Fort of Cybi*...Its name of Holyhead is supposed to have been acquired from its having been, at different times, the place of interment of a great number of holy men.

The church-yard is on a rock directly above the sea: it forms a quadrangle of about ninety yards, by forty. Three sides are inclosed by strong walls, and the fourth is nearly open to the sea, having only a parapet defended by steep rocks.

[...]

The church is a handsome embattled edifice, built in the form of a cross.

William Bingley, North Wales, 1804

CARNARVONSHIRE ~ SIR GAERNARFON

ABEREFRAW

Curiosity induced me to view the seat of the ancient British princes, Aberfraw; but how much were my expectations disappointed! It is a little country village, without any remains of grandeur, or monuments of antiquity, that I could discern.I was told that part of the wall of the king's palace, was converted into a barn. It is astonishing how the princes of North Wales could have chosen such a situation for their residence; eligible for no reason that can now be conceived.

Joseph Cradock, Letters from Snowdon, 1770

BANGOR – MANGOR

I arrived at Bangor, *The chief Choir*. This, although at present only a very small place, had formerly so much importance, as to be denominated from its size Bangor Vawr, *The Great Bangor,* to distinguish it probably from Bangor is-coed in Flintshire. It is seated in a vale, from the back of which arise the vast mountains of Caernarvonshire. The streets are narrow, and the houses bad and irregular: a spirit of improvement would, however, render it one of the most beautiful places in Great Britain. From the entrance either way it is seen to advantage, the square tower of its cathedral, and some of the best houses which are near it, presenting themselves from among the trees. The cathedral is small, but every thing around it is now kept exceedingly neat. From near the churchyard there is a fine prospect of part of Anglesea, and the town and bay of Beaumaris.

William Bingley, North Wales, 1804

BARDSEY – YNS ENLLI

From this port I once took boat for *Bardseye* island, which lies about three leagues to the west. The mariners seemed tinctured with the piety of the place; for they had not rowed far, but they made a full stop, pulled off their hats, and offered up a short prayer. After doubling a headland, the island appears full in view: we passed under the lofty mountain which forms one side. After doubling the farther end, we put into a little sandy creek, bounded by low rocks, as is the whole level part. On landing, I found all this tract a very fertile plain, and well cultivated, and productive of every thing which the main land affords. The abbot's house is a large stone building, inhabited by several of the natives: not far from it is a singular chapel, or oratory, being a long arched edifice, with an insulated stone altar near the east end. In this place one of the inhabitants reads prayers: all other offices are performed at *Aber-daron*.

[…]

The *British* name of the island is *Ynys Enlli*, or the

Island in the Current, from the fierce current which rages particulary between it and the main land. The *Saxons* named it *Bardseye,* probably from the bards who retire here, preferring solitude to the company of invading foreigners.

[...]

We re-embarked from the rocks on the opposite side of the island to that on which we landed. Rowed through the rapid current called the *Race of Bardsey,* between the island and the great promontory *Braich y Pwll,* the *Canganum Promontorium* of *Ptolemy:* part of it is called, from certain yellow stones, *Maen Melyn;* the rest is a vast precipice, black and tremendous. After landing at *Aber-daron,* I rid to its summit, and found the ruins of a small church, called *Capel Fair,* the Chapel of our Lady; and I was informed, that at the foot of the promontory, below high-water mark, was a fountain of fresh water, to which devotees were wont to descend by a circuitous and most hazardous path, to get, at low-water, a mouthful of the spring; which, if they carried up safe to the summit, their wish, whatsoever it was, was to be surely fulfilled. This was under the protection of our Lady, and called *Ffynnon Fair.* The chapel was placed here to give the seamen opportunity of invoking the tutelar saint for protection through this dangerous sound, and I dare say, in old times, the walls were covered with votive tables. Not far from hence I passed by the ruins of *Capel Anhelog,* or, the Chapel without Endowment.

Thomas Pennant, A tour in Wales, 1778

CARNARVON – CAERNARFON

This town is justly the boast of *North Wales*, for the beauty of its situation, the goodness of its buildings, the regularity of the plan, and, above all, the grandeur of the castle, the most magnificent badge of our subjection.

Thomas Pennant, A tour in Wales, 1778

LLANBERIS

The village of Llanberis is romantic in the extreme. It is situated in a narrow grassy dell, surrounded by immense rocks, whose summits cloud-capped, are seldom visible to the inhabitants from below.

[…]

All the parts immediately surrounding the village were formerly covered with wood; but, except some saplings from the old roots, there are at present very few trees left. In the memory of persons now living there were great woods of oak in several different parts about these mountains.

Except two tolerable houses in the vale, the one occupied by Mr. Jones the agent to the copper mine, and the other, which is on the side of the lake opposite to Dolbadarn castle, occupied by the agent to the slate quarries, the whole village consists but of a few scattered cottages, and these apparently the most miserable. They are in general constructed of the shaly stone with which the country abounds, and have but just so much cement as to keep out the keenest of the mountain blasts. The windows are invariably small, and many of them that have been broken, are so blocked up with boards, that the light down the chimney is even greater than that from the window.

There are two cottages in this village where the wearied traveller may take such poor refreshments ... The other is kept by the parish clerk, who may be employed as a guide over any part of the adjacent country. I found him well acquainted with the mountains, and a much more intelligent man than guides in general are. He does not speak English well, but his civility and attention are a sufficient compensation for this defect. — Neither of these places affords a bed, nor any thing eatable better than bread and butter, or cheese, and, perhaps, eggs and bacon.

The first time that I came to Llanberis, being somewhat fatigued with traversing the adjacent mountains, I went to the former of these houses to rest myself and obtain some refreshment. It was just at the dinner hour, and a scene was exhibited altogether novel to me. At one table were seated the family of the house, consisting of the old host, his wife, and their son and daughter, eating their bread and milk, the common food of the labouring people here: a large overgrown old sow was devouring her dinner, with considerable dissatisfaction on account of the short allowance, from a pail placed for her by the daughter in one corner; whilst I was eating my bread and butter, with with an appetite steeled against niceties by the keenness of the mountain air, at a table covered with a dirty napkin, in the other corner.

William Bingley, North Wales, 1804

LLYN

Llyn or *Lleyn* is a very extensive hundred: in general flat, but interspersed with most characteristic hills or rocks, rising insulated in several parts: none makes so conspicuous a figure as *Carn Madryn* and *Carn Boduon*. The houses of the common people are very mean; made with clay, thatched, and destitute of chimnies. Notwithstanding the laudable example of the gentry, the country is in an unimproved state, neglected for the sake of the herring-fishery. The chief produce is oats, and black cattle. I was informed that above three thousand are annually sold out of these parts. Much oats, barley, butter, and cheese, are exported. The land is excellent for grazing, being watered by a thousand little rills. It is destitute of trees, except about the houses of the gentry.

Thomas Pennant, A tour in Wales, 1778

DENBIGHSHIRE ~ SIR DDINBYCH

The fertile vale of Clwyd, extends from Rhyddlan-marsh to the town of Rhythin, which is about fifteen miles. It is one of the most pleasant and fertile vales in the whole kingdom. It has three considerable towns, St. Asaph, Denbigh and Rhythin. The former is not remarked for beauty or situation. It is the see of a bishop, and has a good cathedral.

Joseph Cradock, Letters from Snowdon, 1770

DENBIGH – DINBYCH

Denbigh is situated upon a fine eminence, on which arise the turrets of a majestic castle. It is in ruins, but the

357

very ruins are venerable. Great part of the hall is still standing, which the rude inhabitants mistake for the ruins of a church. The remains of the hall, give the traveller an idea of the grandeur of the place.

Joseph Cradock, Letters from Snowdon, 1770

LLANGOLLEN

A few miles from Chirk-castle, is the village of Llangollen, in a bottom, surrounded on every side with high hills. The village is remarkable for nothing but a fine bridge, esteemed one of the curiosities of Wales. The castle of Dinas-bran, is on the summit of one of the hills, above the village. This castle belonged formerly to the princes of Powisland. Dinas-bran, is I apprehend a corruption of DINAS-BRENING, i.e. the residence of the king. The hill upon which the castle stands, is very high and steep, and must have been an almost inaccessible place. It has the appearance of great antiquity, being probably built by some of the first British princes.

Joseph Cradock, Letters from Snowdon, 1770

RUTHIN – RHUTHUN

Rhythin is a more populous and opulent town than Denbigh, and consists of better houses; but in point of situation, is far inferior. There are here the ruins of a castle but so much defaced by the hand of time, that nothing can be discerned, which attracts the notice of a traveller.

Joseph Cradock, Letters from Snowdon, 1770

The town of Ruthin is large and populous, situated on the river Clwyd, at the south-eastern extremity of its celebrated vale. Like most other Welsh towns of any conseque it was formerly defended by a strong castle; of which some small remains appear at the southern end of the town, but are now converted to much more pleasing purposes than hostile ones, sheltering a neat bowling-green, formed within them by the inhabitants for their occasional relaxation. The church is a handsome modern edifice; and if the *pavement* of the streets were but smooth and regular, Ruthin would be upon a par with some of our English towns. But the general practice throughout Wales, of paving the streets with oblate oval pebbles, their sharp extremities standing outwards, is extremely unpleasant to those unaccustomed to such treadings; and a walk of twenty-eight miles had not prepared us for being less sensible of the inconvenience. On reaching our inn, we learned that the assizes, or great sessions for the county, had been closed that morning, and, as was generally the case, had been a *maiden assize,* without the trial of a single felon.

**Richard Warner, A second walk through Wales in
August and September 1798, 1799**

WREXHAM – WRECSAM

The last place that we visited in North-Wales was Wrexham, which is the richest and most populous town in the whole country. The only curiosity that travellers remark in it is a fine steeple, which is esteemed one of the wonders of Wales.

The inhabitants of this place are so perfectly

Englished, if I may use such an expression, in their language, manners, and customs, that it bears no resemblance to the generality of Welsh towns.

Joseph Cradock, Letters from Snowdon, 1770

From thence we visited Wrexham, having heard much of a fine church there, but we were greatly disappointed: There is indeed a very large tower steeple, if a tower may be call'd a steeple, and 'tis finely adorn'd with imagery; but far from fine: the work is mean, the statues seem all mean and in dejected postures, without any fancy or spirit in the workmanship, and as the stone is of a reddish crumbling kind, like the cathedral at Chester, Time has made it look gross and rough.

There are a great many antient monuments in this church, and in the church-yard also; but none of note, and almost all the inscriptions are in Welch. The church is large; but they must be much mistaken, who tell us 'tis the finest in England, no not among those which are as old as itself.

This town is large, well built and populous, and besides the church there are two large meeting-houses, in one of which we were told they preach in Welch one part of the day, and in English the other. Here is a great market for Welch flannel which the factors buy up of the poor Welch people, who manufacture it; and thence it is sent to London; and it is a very considerable manufacture indeed thro' all this part of the country, by which the poor are very profitably employ'd.

Daniel Defoe A tour thro' the whole island of Great Britain, divided into circuits or journies, 1724

FLINTSHIRE ~ SIR Y FFLINT

FLINT ~ Y FFLINT

Flint is a market town, small, irregularly built, and by no means pleasant. It has once been surrounded by a ditch and ramparts, but these are now nearly destroyed. Being situated near the sea, it is resorted to by a few from the neighbouring country, as a bathing-place; but the marshy coast which extends from the edge of the water almost to the town, must render it, in this respect, extremely disagreeable. The *church,* or rather chapel, for it is but a chapel of ease to Northop, is a dirty ill-looking building, with a boarded turret. — From this place there are packets which fail every tide, when the wind permits, for Chester and Park-Gate. This is from hence a charming, and, as far as relates to Park-Gate, certainly an expeditious mode of travelling.

Though the great sessions for the county are held at Mold, the *county gaol* is at Flint, situated in the castleyard, in a fine healthy situation. It is a good building, and constructed on a plan similar to the gaol of Ruthin.

William Bingley, North Wales, 1804

HOLYWELL ~ TREFYNNON

Holywell is ten miles from St. Asaph, now a considerable market-town in North Wales, and very populous. On the side of the hill stands the famous well of *Saint Winifrede,* whose spring almost exceeds credibility, as it is calculated to throw up *twenty-one tons of water every minute,* and is certainly the finest in these kingdoms. In times of Romish superstition, history acquaints us that this was the resort of pious and noble pilgrims, who had great faith in its miraculous healing powers; and if we cast our eyes up to the arched roof above the well, ample testimony now remains, that some, even in our own days, have experienced the efficacy of its virtues; one instance of which comes within present memory. I well remember, when a school-boy, wantonly teasing a poor man, who had, by a severe cold, lost the use of his *limbs,* and had two *crutches.* The expense of his maintenance many years on the parish, at last induced the overseers to send him to Holywell, to try the effects of that surprising *Well*; and, however singular it may appear, before two months had elapsed, he returned, leaving one crutch behind. The next season he renewed his visit, and came home with a stick, leaving his other crutch; since which period he has provided for himself, without the alms of the parish. Bishop Fleetwood has written a volume on the legend of St. Winifrede, whose head being cut off by Prince Cradocus, we are told was miraculously reunited by the holy prayers of St. Bruno. It is said the spring of water instantly flowed from the spot to which the head rolled.

During the reign of pilgrimages, nothing but a corn mill or two, the property of monks, found employ for this beneficial stream — How great the contrast now? Here are several manufactories of considerable importance, belonging to the cotton twist company, which, while they render the stream less tranquil, afford employment to hundreds of poor people, in both the town and neighbourhood. There is little doubt but that this town will, in a few years, be by far the greatest in Wales; the inhabitants are now calculated to be 5396 souls.

Upon the stream of the said well is the copper and brass work which supplies the principle of motion to the great variety of mechanical force here employed. The works belonging to the Anglesea companies are, in fact, a continuation of the same processes that are carried on at the Paris mountain. The works occupy a large extent of ground. The refined copper is received from Swansea, &c. in solid blocks or pigs, then passes between large iron rollers, which reduce it to a thickness to be applied to a variety of purposes. Here are likewise corn mills worked by this stream, and the banks are likely to be covered with works partaking of its benefits down to the level of the sea, which is a mile in length. Here is likewise a small coin of halfpenny and penny pieces in circulation, with the Druid's head stamped upon them, and made current by the company. Above the well stands the church, dedicated to St. Winifrede; a little beyond which is a hill called Bryn castle, which is narrow and rather steep on the sides, projecting at the end over the little valley. It is rather singular that in Doomsday-book no mention is made of either the chapel, church, or well, though townships of less note are named, such as Brunford, &c. The town of Holywell, at the beginning of the present century, was very inconsiderable; the houses, in most part, thatched, the streets unpaved, and even destitute of a market.

Anon., A Collection of Welsh Tours; or, a Display of the Beauties of Wales, selected principally from Celebrated Histories and Popular Tours, with Occasional Remarks, 1797

ST. ASAPH – LLANELWY

I descended into the vale, crossed the bridge over the little river Clwyd, and soon after arrived at St. Asaph, or, as it is called by the Welsh, Llan Elwy, *the Church of Elwy*, a name obtained from its situation oh the bank of the river Elwy, which runs along the west side of the place. It consists of little more than a single street, the houses pretty uniformly built, up the side of a hill. It has a cathedral and parish church; and, as a city, is, except one or two, the most insignificant in the kingdom. The cathedral, though small, is plain and neat. The episcopal palace is a large and convenient building, under the grounds of which the Elwy runs. The deanery is on the opposite side of the river, and stands due west of the cathedral.

William Bingley, North Wales, 1804

MERIONETHSHIRE ~ MEIRIONNYDD

THE inhabitants of this county are more purely British, than those of any other part of Wales. Like the clans of Scotland, or Hebrew tribes, they scarce ever intermarry, except with those of their own lineage. Through the whole county, they are all cousins, all of the same Welsh blood, and most of them of the same names.

If you would ask them, how they spend their lives in this part of the world; they have it in their power to answer you in a few words; We drink, dance, and are merry. Indeed, I do not know a people so much addicted to mirth. The complexion of their country, one would imagine, could not inspire such sentiments of festivity and joy. They sing, dance, and drink, not by hours, but by days and weeks; and measure time only by the continuance of their mirth and pleasure.

The men estimate their strength not by feats of activity, as in other places, but by the quantities of ale they can drink; and, I am told, it is no uncommon thing for a lover to boast to his mistress, what feats he has performed in this way. Such is the mark of prowess, by which the women judge of their paramour's vigor and strength of constitution.

[...]

Unembarrassed with the pedantry of learning, and the disgusting forms of politeness, the good people of Merionydd are free, hospitable, and chearful. Let them enjoy their mirth unrivalled, undisturbed by foreigners, in security, arid ease. They always will remain unenvied in the participation of that happiness, which none but a native of that country can feel.

The Welsh language is here spoken with the greatest classical purity. Here they boast of their Welsh bards, who are poets by nature. These bards are idle fellows, who subsist on the bounty of the Welsh gentry. They, and their alliesmen the harpers, who form a very numerous corps are generally invited to entertain the company at their feasts, which is done by buffoonery and illiberal abusive extempore rhyme. Sometimes a bard comes to the door, and demands admittance in rhyme; he is answered by the bard within, in rhyme likewise; if the stranger, in the opinion of the company, gains the victory in this poetical contest; he is admitted to partake of the feast, while the vanquished bard is turned out to the former's uncomfortable situation.

Joseph Cradock, Letters from Snowdon, 1770

BALA – Y BALA

We proceeded to Bala, situated upon the borders of a large lake. The country round is grand and sublime, but not interesting; stupendous mountains seem "to mix their heads with dropping clouds" but with respect to cultivation, or even verdure, they are entirely destitute. It is a small town in the parish of Llanckil, noted for its vast trade in woollen stockings, and its great markets every Saturday morning. Much of the wool is bought at the great fairs at Llanrwst in Denbighshire. Close to the south-east end of the town is a great artificial mount, called Tommen y Bala, in the summer time usually covered in a picturesque manner with knitters of both sexes and all ages. This mount appears to have been Roman, and placed here with a castelet on its summit, to secure the pass towards the sea, and keep the mountaineers in subjection. The town is of a very regular form; the principal street very spacious, and the lesser fall into it at right angles. Bala takes its name from its vicinity to the place where a river discharges itself from a lake which lies at a small distance from the town, and is a fine expanse of water, near four miles long, and twelve hundred yards broad in the widest place; the deepest part is opposite Bryn Golen, where it is forty-six yards deep, with three yards of mud; the shores gravelly; the boundaries are easy slopes, well cultivated and varied with wood: in stormy weather its billows run very high. It rises sometimes nine feet and has overflowed the fair vale of Edeirnion. The waters are discharged under Pont Mwnwgl y Llyn, a bridge of three arches. They seem inconsiderable in respect to the size of the streams which feed the lake; for the Dee does not make in dry seasons the figure we expected. Report says that the Dee passes through the lake from end to end, without deigning to mix its waters, as the Rhone was fabled to serve the lake of Geneva; but, in fact, the Dee does not assume its name till it quits its parent.

Anon. A Collection of Welsh Tours; or, a Display of the Beauties of Wales, selected principally from Celebrated Histories and Popular Tours, with Occasional Remarks, 1797

DOLGELLAU

Dolegelly is a large and dirty town: we took up our quarters at the Golden Lion, a good hospitable inn; and next morning, after breakfast, procured a guide to conduct us to the top of Caer Idris. We armed him with stores, and warlike preparations of all kinds (to wit): ham, fowl, bread, and cheese, and brandy, and began the ascent at nine in the morning, and continued to toil for three hours and a half before we reached the top. But, alas! expectation had again flattered us; for, though it was a most lovely day in the valleys, yet here we could not see fifty yards before us; the summit of the mountain is not of greater extent than the base of a common sized room; and, on one side, falls almost perpendicularly many hundred yards in depth.

J. Hucks, A pedestrian tour in North Wales in a series of letters, 1795

HARLECH

Harlech stands on the north-west side of the county of Merioneth; its houses are mean. There is a good harbour for ships, but few ships for the harbour. It is remarkable only for its old decayed castle, which was defended by a British nobleman against Edward the Fourth, till an Earl of Pembroke, after almost incredible difficulties, compelled it to surrender. It has been confidently asserted, that this castle was built before Edward the First's time, and that all he did was the making some additions, especially to the fortifications; but I should be rather inclined to think that it was planned at least by Edward. A tradition goes, that the workmen, after they had got to a considerable height, were all taken off to build the castles of Aberystwith and Caernarvon; and, indeed, there are evident marks of a separation.

An unpolished people, it is observed, have little or no curiosity; I had seated myself by the fire-side in one of the houses at Harlech, without the inhabitants expressing the least surprise at it; the guide and attendants began to be rather clamorous for some refreshment, and the people at length brought them some oatmeal bread, &c.

> Anon. A Collection of Welsh Tours; or, a Display of the Beauties of Wales, selected principally from Celebrated Histories and Popular Tours, with Occasional Remarks, 1797

MONTGOMERYSHIRE ~ SIR DREFALDWYN

The town of Welsh-pool is the most considerable in the whole country. It is regular, well built, and superior to most Welsh towns. About a mile from Pool is Powis-castle, the seat of lord Powis, it is situated on a fine hill, which commands a prospect of an extensive, variegated, and fertile country. The vale of Montgomery, which we see from the castle, is not equalled by any in point of fertility and beauty in Wales, nor perhaps in England. The Severn winds its serpentine course thro' this vale, and heightens the beauties of the prospect. On each side the vale, the hills tower in majesty and grandeur. I do not hesitate to prefer this situation and prospect, to that of the vale of Clwyd. Some even venture to affirm that it is not equalled by any in Great-Britain.

Joseph Cradock, Letters from Snowdon, 1770

MACHYNLLETH

From hence a good turnpike-road soon conducted us to the romantic town of
MACHYNLLETH,
considered as the centre of the woollen manufactory in this part of the country, principally of the *strong cloth* or *high country cloth*. The situation of Machynlleth, (or as it is pronounced by the Welch, *Mahunthleth*) is extremely romantic ; stupendous mountains forming a natural rampart round the town. We here visited the neglected Mansion, where Owen Glendwr assembled the States of the Principality, in 1402, and accepted from their hands the crown of Wales. Part of the house is now allotted for the purpose of a stable, the remainder is turned into a butcher's shop. ...In fine, the only evident remains of its ever having been celebrated in the annals of history, is a spacious door way. The town itself, in many parts, bears the appearance of antiquity; the streets are considerably wider than Welch towns in general, and the market-place is well built.

Allen Cliffe, The Cambrian Directory, 1800

MONTGOMERY – TREFALDWYN

Montgomery is but a very small town, thinly inhabited. There are to be seen the remains of a castle, which was built in the time of William Rufus; in order most probably to secure the colony of Normans, who were sent here to subdue the Welsh, under the command of Sir Roger de Montgomery. The castle is guarded by a craggy precipice on one side, and a deep fosse on the other.

Joseph Cradock, Letters from Snowdon, 1770

WELSH POOL – Y TRALLWNG

Welsh Poole is a place of some note — it is one of the five boroughs in Montgomeryshire, which jointly send a member to Parliament. It takes its name from a contemptible black pool, which is said to be unfathomable.

[...]

About a mile from hence stands Powis Castle, or *Red* Castle, from the colour of the stones of which it is built. The situation of it is certainly very noble; but I cannot agree with Lord Lyttleton, that three thousand pounds would make it the most august place in the kingdom: there is much to be done in the mere approach, and at present you are obliged to ask where the Severn runs. The ground is laid out in that formal style of gardening that was brought in at the Revolution, and there will be much difficulty in altering it with propriety.

On my return to Poole, I ordered a carriage to convey me to Llanvair; this was to be my last stage on known ground — the road was perfectly good, the people in general spoke English, and their civility was so remarkable, that the very turnpike man was grateful for the toll.

Joseph Cradock, An Account of some of the most
Romantic Parts of North Wales, 1777

10

SOUTH WALES

South Wales consists of the old counties of Mid Wales, (Sir Faesyfed – Radnorshire, Sir Frycheiniog – Brecknockshire & Sir Drefaldwyn – Montgomeryshire now called Powys), South West Wales, (Ceredigion / Sir Aberteifi – Cardiganshire, Sir Gâr – Carmarthenshire and Sir Benfro – Pembrokeshire, which from 1974-96 were grouped together as Dyfed), and South East Wales, (Morgannwg – Glamorganshire and Sir Fynwy – Monmouthshire). Camden classified them by their tribes as described by the Romans: Radnor, Monmouth, Brecknock, and Glamorgan as Silures and Carmarthen, Pembroke, and Ceredigion as Demetae. Under this system, Montgomery was grouped with the Ordovices in North Wales.

BRECKNOCKSHIRE ~ SIR FRYCHEINIOG

Brecknockshire is a meer inland county, as Radnor is; the English jestingly (and I think not very improperly) call it Breakneckshire: 'Tis mountainous to an extremity, except on the side of Radnor, where it is something more low and level. It is well watered by the Wye, and the Uske, two rivers mentioned before; upon the latter stands the town of Brecknock, the capital of the county: The most to be said of this town, is what indeed I have said of many places in Wales, (viz.) that it is very antient, and indeed to mention it here for all the rest, there are more tokens of antiquity to be seen every where in Wales, than in any particular part of England, except the counties of Cumberland, and Northumberland. Here we saw Brecknock-Mere, a large or long lake of water, two or three miles over; of which, they have a great many Welch fables, not worth relating: The best of them is, that a certain river call'd the Lheweni runs thro' it, and keeps its colour in mid-chanel distinguish'd from the water of the lake, and as they say, never mingles with it.

[...]

Tho' this county be so mountainous, provisions are exceeding plentiful, and also very good all over the county; nor are these mountains useless, even to the city of London, as I have noted of other counties; for from hence they send yearly, great herds of black cattle to England, and which are known to fill our fairs and markets, even that of Smithfield it self.

Daniel Defoe, A tour thro' the whole island of Great Britain, divided into circuits or journies, 1724

As soon as we emerged from the hollow of the pass, every thing before us bore a different appearance; a dreary valley lay extended on the right beneath the extremity of the Black-mountain, closed by the hill of Talgarth, and floated by the naked pool of Llangors; while in front the vale of Brecknock expanded itself, disclosing beauties of a wilder nature than those we had lately admired in the animated scenes about Abergavenny and Crickhowell. The Uske still flowed pleasantly through a chain of meadows, but the villages were less frequent, and the woods less abundant; yet the outline of the country was grandly imposing, and the semicircle of mountains, from the Alt to the pointed summits of the Van of Brecknock, inexpressibly striking. As we descended, nature assumed a more smiling aspect; the large seat of Buckland, with its extensive plantations, decorated the western side of the Bwlch, and the charming territory of Peterstone, surrounding its handsome mansion, covered a beautiful eminence above the manifold windings of the Uske, on whose banks we followed an admirable road to Brecknock, the capital of its county.

Henry Skrine, Two successive tours throughout the whole of Wales, 1798

BRECON – ABERHONDDU

Greatly superior to Abergavenny in its buildings and decoration, Brecknock is not unlike it in some points of its situation, being placed in a plain which may be called a miniature of the former, at the head of two fine vales, and near the conflux of two rivers. From the north, the rapid Honddy, descending in a torrent from the hills, forms a romantic valley decorated with the hanging groves of the priory, and meets the Uske just before it passes under the stately arches of the bridge of Brecknock. Towards the south, the hill of Canthriff, clothed from its summit to its base with wood, opposes a barrier finely impending over the river, and fronting the bold and bare eminence of the Craig. Thus are the two vales formed, each of which, divided by the Uske, displays its characteristic beauties, while the Van, the mighty monarch of the Breconian mountains, exalts its two majestic summits, and stretches out its furrowed sides with ineffable dignity.

[...]

The present town consists principally of three handsome streets; in the most spacious of which stand the county hall and market-place. Its compact form and its eminence above the Uske, give it an advantage over most of the towns in Wales when viewed from without; while its superior neatness within is not less striking. It is in general well-built, and some of its modern houses may even be called magnificent, but a little clearing of old irregular buildings about the centre of the town is still wanting to render it perfect, and the pavement is capable of further improvement. Its bridge and its two old churches add much to its appearance, and few towns can boast of two such public walks as those on the Uske, and in the groves of the priory.

Henry Skrine, Two successive tours throughout the
whole of Wales, 1798

CARMATHENSHIRE ~ SIR GÂR

CARMARTHEN – CAERFYRDDIN

THE situation of Caermarthen, one of the most wealthy and polite towns in Wales, can scarcely be enough admired; rising above a noble river, and commanding a full view of one of the most beautiful vales in the kingdom. Internally, there is less to commend; as most of the streets are very steep, and irregularly built; yet there are many good private houses, belonging to the neighbouring gentry that resort here in the winter months; and a handsome town-hall and some other buildings do credit to the public spirit of the town, though a solitary church may reflect but little on its sanctity. Very small remains of the castle, now built up into a gaol, appear; or of the walls that formerly encompassed passed the town. The trade of the place is much facilitated by its fine river, which conveys ships of a good size up to the bridge.

J. T. Barber, A tour throughout South Wales and Monmouthshire, 1803

The streets of the town are infested with beggars; indeed mendicity seems systematically pursued, both here and in many parts of South Wales. The police is badly attended to, and the morals of the people appear peculiarly depraved. A general ambition prevails to imitate and be thought like the English, since the intercourse is become so frequent and easy; and it is too obvious to pass unobserved, that they copy the worst points of the original, and generally adopt the worst examples for imitation.

John Evans, Letters written during a tour through South Wales, in the year 1803, and at other times, 1804

Travellers in general are too fastiduous in their comments upon the buildings of Caermarthen. They regret so many good houses are promiscuously huddled together with the meanest buildings in every street, without more attention to the respectability of appearance. This remark is not more applicable in my mind to Caermarthen than any other town in Wales, where the symmetry of whole streets are not quite so frequently consulted as the convenience of the builders. In the metropolis, or opulent towns, and cities, wealthy speculators may indulge their vanity in such arrangements, but in a place like Caermarthen this ought not to be expected. Neither are its streets so remarkable for uncleanliness as report represents; if there are towns in Wales kept in better order in this respect, there are also others far more filthy.

A complaint more just than the foregoing, is the want of internal manufactories for the employment of the lower orders of society, whose condition is far from comfortable, at the same time that the heavy pressure of the poor rates for their support are severely felt by the middling classes. Formerly the lead and iron works of lord Cawdor, at the old priory, engaged a number of hands, but these ceased early in the last war, and have not been resumed since. A tin work at a small distance further down the river is the only manufactory of the place worth mentioning.

E. Donovan, Descriptive Excursions through South
Wales and Monmouthshire in the year 1804, and the
four preceding summers, Vol. II, 1805

LLANDEILO

The inn at Llandovery is a bad one, but the people are very civil. The road from thence hither is good, and very beautiful. I begin now to be somewhat familiarized to the sight of mountains. I thought the town of Llandovery a miserable one, but this of Llandilo is much worse. I never saw any place that had a more deplorable appearance. The streets, if so they may be called, are narrow, dirty, and half paved with stones the sharp ends upwards. The houses are built with a kind of stone; but it is of so crumbling a nature, that they appear to be all falling to decay. The inhabitants are very decent in their manners, and in their outward semblance; they do not seem fit tenants for such wretched dwellings.

Mrs. Morgan, A tour to Milford Haven,
in the year 1791, 1795

LLANDOVERY – LLANYMDDYFRI

Here the sublime and the beautiful alternately share your attention, and so equally display their charms, that you know not which to admire the most. Look up to the immense height of the impending rock, and behold the silver waters pouring down its rugged sides, sometimes bounding from stone to stone, and sometimes tumbling headlong down the smooth way which itself has worn, and at others softly trickling through the hollow grottos; but at all times hastening to refresh the valley beneath. Turn your eyes on the other side, down the steep below, there you see rural beauty in all its native simplicity. White cottages spot the "thinly – peopled vale;" clean and healthy peasants, with their wives and lovely children, tending their flocks, their gardens, and pastures, where eternal spring seems to reign. The rivulet keeps them so constantly watered, that every thing appears as if it sprang up spontaneously.

[…]

Added to this, before you, as far as the eye can stretch, is a long ridge of mountains, many of them partly cultivated, some barren, and some covered with woods of such a length and thickness as in England we have no idea of.

In short, this must undoubtedly be one of the most beautiful and finest roads in the kingdom.

It was made by a society of gentlemen, to prevent the necessity of going over Trecastle mountain, one of the highest and most dreary in South Wales. Not the least curious and admirable part of this road is their having thrown arches over the gullies, made in the sides of the mountain by the winter torrents; and wherever the natural surface of the ground rises or falls abruptly, the ascent or descent is in this manner diminished.

I must now quit these charming scenes, to give you an idea of Llandovery; though an account of it may be comprized in very few words. It is the meanest and dirtiest town I have yet seen in Wales. We are at breakfast in a room, that looks into the market-place; and, there being a fair held to-day, my surprize is very great, instead of seeing peasants walking barefoot, dirty, and poorly clad, to find a hundred or two of women all on horseback, and most of them in an uniform dress, which is a blue cloth jacket and petticoat, and black beaver hat. The neatness and decency of this is a striking contrast to the gay and tawdry cottons worn by English women of this order; for these, I understand, are little farmers wives, who are come to Llandovery fair to sell their corn.

Mrs. Morgan, A tour to Milford Haven, in the year 1791, 1795

LLANELLI

Lanelly is a small dirty looking town, supported chiefly by the productive collieries that lie contiguous: there is a smelting work for iron established lately here by Messrs. Raby and Co. of Swansea, and another of copper, in its vicinity. The Lanelly coal is of a good quality. Probably those pits were the first worked in the lordship of Kidwelly: Leland speaks of them in Henry the eighth's time, and the mines still appear to be inexhaustible. A large steam engine has been recently erected on the spot, for the purpose of carrying off the water with which some of the pits are overflowed. — Petrifactions, or impressions of fossil plants in coal slate, it should be observed, are occasionally discovered in the veins that overlay the coal in this neighbourhood. I have also some in sand stone from this place, one in particular, a large fragment of the gigantic stem of some unknown kind of vegetable, eleven inches in circumference, and bearing a singular reticulated surface, with a deep longitudinal sulcus on one side. This spot affords, likewise, a peculiar kind of *Anthropomorphi,* impressed on dark slate.

E. Donovan, Descriptive Excursions through South Wales and Monmouthshire in the year 1804, and the four preceding summers, 1805

CARDIGANSHIRE – CEREDIGION

Cardiganshire affords perhaps a stronger contrast to the general condition of things, than almost any other part of the island. To understand this difference, it will be necessary to turn our attention towards its local circumstances. It is not that it abounds with rugged inequalities; for the modern facility of communicating between place and place softens down, where it exists, the peculiarities which an unusual conformation of nature is apt to engender. North Wales is becoming English. The northern counties of England are relinquishing their cheapness and simplicity, from the influx of strangers, who make a fashionable tour. But the case is altogether otherwise in Cardiganshire. Its beauties are only beginning to be the subject of panegyric; consequently the appearance of strangers, except in the neighbourhood of Aberistwid, is still an occurrence of some wonder. I know of no district so confined within itself. I have already mentioned that the only postchaises in the county are at Aberistwid and the Havod Arms. I believe, however, that a vehicle of that kind is meditated at Lanbeder, and will probably be carried into execution in the course of the present year, unless the war, and the hazardous state of public affairs, would interfere to prevent it. The travelling, therefore, is little and difficult. The nearest point at which a mail-coach touches is Llandovery in Caermarthenshire. A letter is two complete days in going from Havod to Cardigan, a distance of only forty miles, within the county. This tardiness and paucity of intercourse has a strong tendency to fix the manners of the people, to suppress the very idea of wandering or innovation, and rivet the connexion between the resident landlord and his tenants. To this it may in a great measure be attributed, that, without in the slightest degree countenancing the principle of political levelling, there appears a remarkable fellow-feeling; if I may so express it, a speaking acquaintance, between the higher and lower ranks of society. The happy result of this speaking acquaintance is affability on one fide, and attachment on the other. I do not mean, by particularizing this circumstance, covertly to satirize the more distant demeanour of leading persons, living in populous and mixed districts. The manners of men necessarily take their colour as much from their situations as from their tempers.

Benj. Heath Malkin, The Scenery, Antiquities and
Biography of South Wales, from materials collected
during two excursions in the year 1803, 1804

ABERYSTWYTH

Going N. from the Tyvy about 25 miles, we came to Abrystwyth, that is to say, the town at the mouth of the River Ystwyth. This town is enrich'd by the coals and lead which is found in its neighbourhood, and is a populous, but a very dirty, black, smoaky place, and we fancy'd the people look'd as if they liv'd continually in the coal or lead mines. However, they are rich, and the place is very populous.

Daniel Defoe, A tour thro' the whole island of Great
Britain, divided into circuits or journies, 1724

ABERISTWYTH is a less agreeable town on entering it, than as a distant object. Most of the streets are narrow and ill-paved; and the stone used being of a black colour, gives the whole rather a dirty appearance; but this remark is not applicable to some houses that have lately sprung up for the genteel company which resorts to it in the bathing-season. Nor must I mention the bathing at Aberistwyth, without observing, that it is conducted with more propriety than at any other watering-place that I have seen in England or Wales. The ladies' and gentlemen's machines are placed nearly a quarter of a mile asunder; and the indecency of promiscuous dipping, so disgusting at more fashionable resorts, is in consequence avoided: the bathing too is excellent, with a good sandy bottom at all hours of the tide.

J. T. Barber, A tour throughout South Wales and Monmouthshire, 1803

Aberistwith is a very respectable bathing place. There are some fine remains of a castle, that formerly commanded the approach from the sea on one side; and that to the town, from the land on the other.

The trade of Aberistwith is not by any means contemptible; great quantities of coal, and lead, are found in the neighbourhood, and shipped from this port to different parts of England.

J. Hucks, A pedestrian tour in North Wales in a series of letters, 1795

This town is neither good nor bad. The streets are beyond comparison the dirtiest I ever saw, a proof of which is their being at this moment indicted by the inhabitants. No wonder, therefore, if strangers complain. Indeed, they must be rugged and unpleasant at all times, for the country here is flat, stony, and rugged. The environs are neither barren nor fertile, and the only walks, or in truth *walkable* places, are those at the end of the town, round the ruined castle, another, round the church-yard, and another, very short one, by the side of the harbour. The beach is impassable, and the bathing places difficult and unchearful. In fine, it is in almost all respects the reverse of Barmouth, except that it has the advantage in the number of houses, and, of course in the company. I should not have thought any thing here worth mentioning, had it not been to give you a few hints by way of directory, not to let the greater popularity of this place draw you from other (Barmouth), where your bath will be more comfortable and your *agrémens*, from the surrounding objects, out of all comparison whatever.

Samuel Pratt, Gleanings through Wales, Holland and
Westphalia, Vol. I, 1795

CARDIGAN – ABERTEIFI

The appearance of Cardigan is handsome from a distance; but on a closer acquaintance, it does not fulfil its promise. With the exception of a few good houses, it has nothing to recommend it. I have already observed, that this can never be a great commercial place, owing to a dangerous bar at the mouth of the Tivy; but at present it seems scarcely qualified to answer the limited demands of the internal trade. The shops are mean, and apparently ill supplied. I have so far personal experience on which to found my judgment, that this county town could not furnish me with a pair of ready-made shoes, of which I stood in need. It evidently, therefore, has nothing to spare for strangers, though it may contain enough for its own scanty wants. But though the interior of the town is indifferently built, and wears an air of poverty, considering its rank as a capital, its environs, about the edge of the water, are highly interesting. The ancient bridge, the ruins of the castle, the priory church, with its venerable tower, and shady precincts, are objects of the most engaging contemplation.

Benj. Heath Malkin, The Scenery, Antiquities and
Biography of South Wales, from materials collected
during two excursions in the year 1803, 1804

HAFOD – HAFOD UCHTRYD

Descriptions of country houses have, in general, been avoided in this collection. It is worth making an exception here though for Hafod. On inheriting Hafod, Thomas Johnes transformed the house and estate into one of the finest in Wales, instructing the estate workers to plant three million trees in over a thousand acres of landscaped woodlands. Having built a mansion there in 1788, it housed his press, library of manuscripts, and paintings by Caravaggio, Rembrandt and Vandyck amongst others. It was one of the most desirable destinations for the well-connected traveller.

This delicious retreat has not yet arrived at its perfection. It is intended to enlarge it, by making the river the boundary; and it is still further to be ornamented by a Doric temple, from a design in Stuart's Athens. There is another flower garden, of very different character, and still more singularly situated, to which strangers are never admitted. Almost behind the wall of the lower garden, there is a very grand rock, lofty and naked, standing alone in the midst of woods, too extensive for the eye to measure. This rock is an object from almost every part of the opposite hills. Its top is a natural platform, as if placed there for the purpose, on which is to be erected a column to the memory of the late Duke of Bedford. Behind this rock the mountain rises higher, and is covered with the dwarfish growth, to which alone the ridges of these hills give birth. In the centre of the thicket is planted a flower garden, so carefully sheltered and judiciously disposed, as to realise a paradise in the wilderness. The taste in which it is laid out is not so studiously ornamental as that of the garden below: it aims at a coincidence with the peculiarities of its situation, and exhibits in a nursed state many of the most curious plants, which are the natural growth of high exposures in foreign climates. The moss-house gives a hermit-like air to the retirement; and the vase, which I left my friend Mr. Banks in the act of placing there, inscribed with a few lines from the muse of Mr. Rogers, to commemorate a domestic circumstance, will finish most happily the contemplative character of the scene.

The cold-bath is the only object, to detain the attention, in the sequestered path from the lower flower garden to the lawn: but there are many other walks of large compass and extensive variety, about the grounds, not to be explored in a single day.

[...]

The house was built by Mr. Baldwyn of Bath, in the Gothic, with pointed windows and pinnacles. It does much credit to the taste and talents of the architect. It is light and airy, though capacious, and avoids that appearance of over-building, which is so generally the fault of mansions that are shown. Originally the offices were differently placed, but, being thought to press too forward into notice, were afterwards thrown into their present form. The arrangements have, indeed, undergone various changes; and the library has been added, under Mr. Johnes's own direction. But the house itself, as Mr. Baldwyn planned it, has never been altered, nor could it be, for the better. I have indeed heard it objected, that the rooms are not large enough; but that depends entirely on the object of the owner, which I take to have been rather elegance and comfort, than ostentatious magnificence.

The rooms, which are submitted to the curiosity of strangers, consist of a hall, a music room, summer and winter dining rooms, a library, and a drawing room, each rich and appropriate in their ornaments, and furnished with specimens of art, not numerous, but tastefully selected.

[...]

The library is an octagon, with the light admitted from the dome. It is surrounded by a gallery, supported on pillars of variegated marble. These pillars are very magnificent, of the Doric order. The symmetry of this room would be perfect, if the pillars were not somewhat too large for their height. This circumstance arose from some error of measurement among the workmen, when the room was building. As it is, however, it reflects high credit on the owner of Havod, who was in this instance his own architect; and this library is the triumph of the place. It opens into a conservatory, one hundred and sixty feet in length, filled with rare and curious exotics, with a walk down the centre. The doors are all pannelled with plate glass; so that when the entrance-door of the library is shut, and the communication open, the view from the end of the conservatory, through the library, into a seeming second conservatory, almost realizes the fictitious descriptions of enchantment. Nor is the first entrance into the library, with the paradise of rarities beyond, less striking.

Benj. Heath Malkin, The Scenery, Antiquities and Biography of South Wales, from materials collected during two excursions in the year 1803, 1804

TREGARON

Tregarron is a miserable hole, in the which however we were constrained to sleep, and to break the windows in our bed rooms to let in the fresh air. We took a guide from thence to Llanindovrey, over the lonely and trackless mountains of Cardiganshire; it rained hard the whole way, and we had not even the gloomy consolation of seeing a partner of our misfortunes: for, to speak within compass, we neither beheld a single habitation, nor even a human creature, for more than twenty miles. From Llanindovrey I journeyed on alone, for the rest of the party not being pressed for time, could make their observations at pleasure, having no necessity for hurrying over the country as I was obliged to do.

J. Hucks, A pedestrian tour in North Wales in a series of letters, 1795

GLAMORGANSHIRE ~ MORGANNWG

ABERAVON

As we approached the river Abravon, our views degenerated still more. Margam sand-bank, which was now only the boundary of marshes, became offensive to the eye; and tho, on the left the woody hills continued still shooting after us, yet they had lost their pleasing shapes. No variety of breaks, like the members of architecture, gave a lightness, and elegance to their forms, No mantling furniture invested their sides; nor tufted fringe adorned their promontories; nor clumps of scattered oak discovered the sky, through interstices along their towering summits. Instead of this, they had degenerated into mere uniform lumps of matter, and were every where overspread with one heavy uninterrupted bush.

Of this kind were Lord Mansell's woods which covered a promontory. Time, with its lenient hand, may hereafter hang new beauties upon these hills, when it has corrected their heaviness, by improving the luxuriance of youthful foliage into the lighter forms of aged trees.

William Gilpin, Observations on the River Wye, and several parts of South Wales, &. Relative chiefly to picturesque beauty: made in the summer of the year 1770, 1782

CARDIFF – CAERDYDD

Caerdiff is a populous but ill-built town, nor is there any thing very pleasing in its environs; its situation is on a low flat, near the mouth of the Taafe.

The old walls of Caerdiff are very extensive, and the ruins of them are still considerable. They were probably built, as well as the large octagon tower, on the keep of the castle, by the first Norman invaders.

[…]

The remains of the old cathedral are very beautiful; the door cases are all of Norman work, and well executed;

[…]

The abbey church is a Norman edifice, in the best taste: the circular arches of the nave are finely proportioned, and the capitals of the small pillars at the west-door, are more pleasing in their variations than any

I have seen: it is still used as the parish church, though many parts have greatly suffered from the injuries of time and violence.

H. P. Wyndham, Gentleman's Tour through Monmouthshire and Wales in the Months of June and July, 1774, 1775

On entering CARDIFF, the capital of Glamorganshire, between the ivy-mantled walls of its castle, and the mouldering ruin of a house of White Friars, we were much pleased with the aspect of the town: nor were we less so on a closer examination of its neat and well-paved streets; it appearing to us one of the cleanest and most agreeable towns in Wales. The high, tower of its church, crowned with four transparent Gothic pinnacles, had long engaged our interest; but on a near view we did not find the body of the church to correspond with it; it being of an older date, a plain Norman structure. This, I believe, was the conventual church of the Franciscan Friars that are described as having occupied the eastern suburb of the town. The other parish church, for Cardiff is divided into two parishes, was undermined by the action of the river, about a century and a half since, and fell down. The house of the White Friars has been already noticed; and without the west gate stood a monastery of Black Friars. This town was formerly encompassed by a wall, and vestiges of its four gates yet remain. Cardiff, having the benefit of a good harbour, carries on a brisk trade with Bristol, and other places, and has of late considerably increased its commercial importance: but perhaps its chief interest with tourists will be derived from its castle.

CARDIFF CASTLE, a seat of the Marquis of Bute, (Baron

Cardiff and Earl of Windsor), was until lately a Gothic structure of considerable elegance; but having undergone a repair, without attention to the antique style of architecture, it presents a motley combination, in which the remaining Gothic but serves to excite our regret for the greater portion destroyed. The misguided direction of this work is prominently conspicuous in the enlargement of the building, wherein fashionable square windows appear throughout the lower apartments, while the original character of the edifice is imitated in the Gothic lines of the upper windows: a strange violation of common propriety, to raise an antique superstructure upon a modern foundation! The part of the castle which is kept up is a single range of building; and an elegant machicolated tower, overlooking the whole, still frowns defiance on the petty innovations beneath. The internal has been entirely new planned, and a number of portraits of the present lord's progenitors are ranged in the apartments, with the principal events of their lives, emblazoned in letters of gold; but they are for the most part indifferently executed. In front of the building is a spacious lawn, from the trim surface of which rises an artificial mound, bearing the mouldering ruin of the ancient keep, carefully shorn of shrub and briar.

J. T. Barber, **A tour throughout South Wales and Monmouthshire, 1803**

LLANDAFF

Landaff is the seat of the episcopal see, and a city; but Cardiff which is lower on the river, is the port and town of trade; and has a very good harbour opening into the Severn Sea, about 4 miles below the town. The cathedral is a neat building, but very antient; they boast that this church was a house of religious worship many years before any church was founded in England, and that the Christian religion flourish'd here in its primitive purity, from the year 186, till the Pelagian heresy overspread this country; which being afterwards rooted out by the care of the orthodox bishop, they plac'd St. Dobricius as the first bishop in this town of Landaff, then call'd Launton: Tis observable, that though the Bishop of Landaff was call'd an arch-bishop, yet the cathedral church was but 28 foot long, and 10 foot broad, and without any steeple or bells.

Daniel Defoe, A tour thro' the whole island of Great
Britain, divided into circuits or journies, 1724

NEATH – CASTELL-NEDD

Neath is another port, where the coal trade is also considerable, tho' it stands farther within the land. Kynfig Castle, is now the seat and estate of the Lord Mansel, who has here also a very royal income from the collieries; I say royal, because equal to the revenues of some sovereign princes, and which formerly denominated Sir Edward Mansel, one of the richest commoners in Wales; the family was enobled by Her late Majesty Queen Anne.

Daniel Defoe, A tour thro' the whole island of Great
Britain, divided into circuits or journies, 1724

RHONDDA VALLEY – CWM RHONDDA

For about a mile and a half above the first water-fall, the Rontha Vawr for a space becomes broad and shallow, over a bed of large, loose stones, and the road on the right bank only leading to some coal-pits close by, the traveller, who wishes to pursue this way towards Ystradyvodwg, is obliged to ford at this place. The almost impassable road then continues on the left side of the river, overhanging it at a considerable height, with opposite scenery precisely of the fame description, as what engages the attention in the way to the ford. Yet it is curious to observe, that the mere circumstance of changing sides, without any heightened features, gives it all the effect of novelty, and creates for it an increasing interest. At the distance of about a mile, there is a second fall, the height, force, and concomitant appearances of which are so nearly alike, that it would be difficult to distinguish it from the first, were it not for one point of difference. The bed of the river above the salmon-leap is narrower; here it widens above the fall, while large oaks on each side spread their luxuriant branches to a great extent over the water. To delight in pairs, is generally considered as unnatural, and consequently tasteless refinement. The practice of our ancestors, who disposed their ornamental grounds in pairs of clumps, and correspondencies of all kinds, is now considered as the excess of injudicious vulgarity. Yet, in the present instance, nature seems to have varied from her unbounded variety, and to have amused herself with uniformity where we should least have expected it, in a pair of water-falls. The traveller has scarcely turned his back on this, before his ears are saluted with the sound of a third fall, at the distance of not more than a quarter of a mile. It altogether differs in character from the other two. It is less beautiful, but larger and more grand. Immediately below it, massy rocks thrust themselves almost across the river, leaving it a very narrow, but deep and clear passage; and the depth of course gives a darkness to the hue of the water, that communicates a degree of sublimity to the general tone. The ascent from this fall is steep and lofty, and after a short space presents a new scene, at the junction of the two rivers, Rontha Vawr and Rontha Vach, which by their confluence form that more important stream, whose banks we have hitherto skirted.

There is a bridge of a single arch over the Rontha Vawr, highly ornamental to the distant prospect, which is here of considerable extent. The Rontha Vawr rises in the parish of Ystradyvodwg, and we shall, with occasional deviations, trace it to its source, through a country of uncommon wildness. The Rontha Vach takes its source in Aberdare, and flows through a district of less romantic character, but very considerable beauty.

[...]

The descent down a long hill brings the traveller to a little brook, abounding with fish, which joins the Rontha Vawr a little way to the eastward; and at a very short distance from the brook, after descending another hill, you cross a bridge over that river, which has disappeared since its junction with the Rontha Vach: but from this place the sound of it is never lost, though frequently the sight, till you arrive close by its source at the top of the parish, distant about ten miles. Here, however, it ceases to be the leading feature of the prospect. It fertilizes the valley with its pure, transparent stream, rolling over loose stones, but is no longer encumbered, yet ennobled, by massy projections, or stately and aspiring cliffs. Hereabouts, and for some miles to come, there is a degree of luxuriance in the valley, infinitely beyond what my entrance on this district led me to expect. The contrast of the meadows, rich and verdant, with mountains the most wild and romantic, surrounding them on every side, is in the highest degree picturesque. The next object of interest, for such it is in a proportion equal to that of a palace in a better inhabited country, is a substantial farm-house, placed in a most pleasing solitude, as beautifully situated as any thing in the parish. ...A second bridge over the Rontha, on the other side of which the road winds to the left, furnishes a most interesting point of view, embracing the country just traversed on the one part, and on the other the wilder grandeur of what remains to be explored. I had met with but one person of whom I could ask a question since my entrance into the parish; and then only through the medium of my attendant, whose services as an interpreter were not to be disregarded. My ears, therefore, were not unpleasingly assailed with a shout, which I found to have proceeded from a few people, with most powerful lungs, who were exulting over the lifeless remains of three or four snakes they had just killed. Soon afterwards I heard another clamour, seeming to resent the imputation of solitude, from some labourers at work in the woods. Such sudden salutations almost startle the wanderer, who can scarcely suppose that so much voice could be collected in the district, deserted as it appears to be by human habitations. The people are, indeed, thinly scattered, as well as miserably poor.

Benj. Heath Malkin, The Scenery, Antiquities and Biography of South Wales, from materials collected during two excursions in the year 1803, 1804

SWANSEA – ABERTAWE

The chief sea port is Swanzey, a very considerable town for trade, and has a very good harbour: Here is also a very great trade for coals, and culmn, which they export to all the ports of Sommerset, Devon, and Cornwal, and also to Ireland itself; so that one sometimes sees a hundred sail of ships at a time loading coals here; which greatly enriches the country, and particularly this town of Swanzey, which is really a very thriving place; it stands on the River Tawye, or Taw: 'Tis very remarkable, that most of the rivers in this county chime upon the letters *T*, and *Y*, as Taaf, Tawy, Tuy, Towy, Tyevy.

Daniel Defoe, A tour thro' the whole island of Great Britain, divided into circuits or journies, 1724

Swansea offers many attractions to arrest the progress of the passing tourist for a day or two or least. This place is the residence of a number of Welsh families; and since the custom of sea bathing has become fashionable, the influx of strangers in the summer time is considerable; a circumstance that has occasioned much improvement in the town of late years. Lodging houses have been fitted up in the most eligible situations, and baths of different kinds established for their accommodation by speculative individuals. Those in ill health have also the advantage of medical advice, two physicians of eminence, Dr.Turton and another, residing constantly in the town.

There is a commodious bathing house in particular, built at the express desire of the corporation upon the beach, where machines are kept at the distance of an easy walk, or ride across the sands below the town, for the benefit of those who prefer bathing in the open sea, to the private baths in the town.

E. Donovan, Descriptive Excursions through South Wales and Monmouthshire in the year 1804, and the four preceding summers, 1805

MONMOUTHSHIRE – SIR FYNWY

This county furnishes great quantities of corn for exportation, and the Bristol merchants frequently load ships here, to go to Portugal, and other foreign countries with wheat; considering the mountainous part of the west of this county, 'tis much they should have such good corn, and so much of it to spare; but the eastern side of the county, and the neighbourhood of Herefordshire, supplies them.

Daniel Defoe, A tour thro' the whole island of Great Britain, divided into circuits or journies, 1724

CHEPSTOW – CAS-GWENT

UPON meeting our horses at the village of St. Pierre, we proceeded towards Chepstow, and in a few minutes were surprized with a range of naked cliffs, rising in appearance from the tract of verdure before us; a venerable wood shadowed the brow of the rocks, in front of which rose a forest of masts with waving pennants. This singular combination resulted from the position of CHEPSTOW and its port, in an abrupt hollow, inclosed by considerable heights in every direction. The whole unfolded itself like a map beneath us, as we descended to the town; an irregular-built trading place, but where the well-furnished houses and opulent establishments of many of the inhabitants engaged in business prove the success of their commercial enterprize: yet the town, having no manufactories, depends altogether on the carrying trade.

[...]

As we advanced toward the massive battlements and lofty turrets of Chepstow's ancient castle, the grand entrance, a Norman arch flanked by circular towers, figured all the repulsive gloom of feudal reserve and violence; even the very knocker was emblematical of hostility; for we thundered at the portal for admission with a cannon-ball suspended by a chain; The warder of the castle did not wind his horn in reply, nor, raising, himself on the ramparts, did he demand our quality and business; but a pretty smiling damsel, conjuring up all her rosy dimples, bade the gate, or rather made it, revolve on its creaking hinges, and welcomed us into the castle.

Upon entering the court, our attention was somewhat divided, between the remains of the baronial hall, numerous apartments, and the kitchen, which surrounded the area; and the well-turned arm that pointed to the several objects. A number of rooms in this court are kept in repair, and form a commodious residence, which is tenanted by Mr. Williams under a lease from the Duke of Beaufort. From this we passed to the second court, now laid out as a kitchen-garden. The third court contained the chapel, a fine remnant of antiquity, possessing a greater degree of decoration than any other part of the castle: a range of niches appear within the walls of this structure, at some distance from the floor, which is said to have been filled with statues; and the mortices of beams seem to indicate, that a gallery was conducted round the room. The style of the windows and enrichments is Gothic; but the original part of the building is Norman. Indeed, a unity of design and architecture appears throughout the fundamental parts of the castle; although, as may be expected, the continual alterations and additions of successive proprietors have left us several specimens of the intermediate modes of building between the Norman foundation and the present age. Among the undecorative additions of the latter period, are the deserted works of a glass-house, and a dog-kennel. Beyond the chapel we ascended a flight of steps to the battlements, shadowed by wide branching trees of various descriptions, issuing from the moat beneath. Opposite to us, beyond the moat, appeared the low embowered ruins of the fourth and last court, separated from the principal mass of building by a drawbridge.

Returning, our fair guide conducted us to a subterraneous chamber with an engroined roof, excavated in the rock, beneath the ruin, and opening to the overhanging brow of the cliff. Here several old ivys darted from stony fissures that seemed to forbid vegetation, binding the mouldering summit of the cliff in their sinewy embrace; and, shedding their light tendrils round the cavern, embowered its aperture as they aspired in frequent volutions to the loftiest turrets of the pile. Here, and from several points in our perambulation of the ruin, we timidly looked down on the rapid Wye, rolling its swelling tide at an immense depth perpendicularly beneath us; and at other times the green waving hills of Piercefield rose in all their peculiar grandeur to our view, darkening the river with their widely projected shadows.

J. T. Barber, A tour throughout South Wales and
Monmouthshire, 1803

Lower down upon the Wye stands Chepstow, the sea port for all the towns seated on the Wye and Lug, and where their commerce seems to center. Here is a noble bridge over the Wye: To this town ships of good burthen may come up, and the tide runs here with the same impetuous current as at Bristol; the flood rising from six fathom, to six and a half at Chepstow Bridge. This is a place of very good trade, as is also Newport, a town of the like import upon the River Uske, a great river, tho' not so big as Wye, which runs thro' the center of the county, and falls also into the Severn Sea.

Daniel Defoe, A tour thro' the whole island of Great
Britain, divided into circuits or journies, 1724

MONMOUTH – TREFYNWY

From hence we came at about 8 miles more into Monmouthshire, and to the town of Monmouth. It is an old town situate at the conflux of the Wye and of Munnow, whence the town has its name; it stands in the angle where the rivers joyn, and has a bridge over each river, and a third over the River Trothy, which comes in just below the other.

This town shews by its reverend face, that it is a place of great antiquity, and by the remains of walls, lines, curtains, and bastions, that it has been very strong, and by its situation that it may be made so again: This place is made famous, by being the native place of one of our most antient historians Jeoffry of Monmouth. At present 'tis rather a decay'd than a flourishing town, yet, it drives a considerable trade with the city of Bristol, by the navigation of the Wye.

This river having as I said, just received two large streams, the Mynevly or Munno, and the Trother, is grown a very noble river, and with a deep chanel, and a full current hurries away towards the sea, carrying also vessels of a considerable burthen hereabouts.

Daniel Defoe, A tour thro' the whole island of Great Britain, divided into circuits or journies, 1724

PEMBROKESHIRE – SIR BENFRO

LITTLE ENGLAND BEYOND WALES

Camden calls this district, "LITTLE ENGLAND beyond Wales;" and the difference of appearance, customs, and language, between the inhabitants of southern Pembrokeshire and their neighbours, is strikingly obvious at the present day. The tourist in Caermarthenshire will scarcely meet a peasant who speaks, a word of English; but in an hour's ride, towards Pembroke, he will find it universally spoken. I remarked this to mine host at Carew; who exultingly assured me, that Pembrokeshire was out of Wales; that he (a native of the place) was an Englishman; and that for his part he did not understand any thing of the Welch gibberish.

The men, tall and well made, evidently incline more to the English character than the Welch; yet they possess some personal traits; distinct from either: I imagined, indeed, in many of the peasantry a resemblance to the present inhabitants of Flanders. Although this corner of the principality is the most remote from England, it is the most civilized. This may be accounted for, from the commercial habits brought over by the Flemings (which still continue) introducing the manners of other nations; an advantage denied to the generality of the Welch, whose ancient (perhaps wholesome) prejudices disinclined them, to extensive commerce.

J. T. Barber, A tour throughout South Wales and
Monmouthshire, 1803

HAVERFORDWEST – HWLFFORDD

The town of Haverfordwest is one of the most singular and pretty places you can conceive. It exhibits something very uncommon in its appearance to the eye of one accustomed to a flat country, who is used to see the houses in every large town discoloured with smoke, and all the streets upon a level. This is built upon the side of a hill, on which the streets stand in rows, with the houses peeping over each other, as regularly as a regiment of soldiers, when the front rank put their knee to the ground, the center rank sink a little, and the rear rank stand upright. The houses are entirely white, even the roofs; for the coals of this country are of such a nature as to emit no smoke, and therefore they whitewash them all over. When the sun shines, the lustre which it gives to their appearance makes them resemble houses made of cards, or a town built by fairies; for there being no smoke issuing from the chimnies must imply, that the food of the inhabitants is either fruits or sallads, or produced by some kind of enchantment, without the use of fire. I have heard of people who were afraid of being starved on entering Haverfordwest about dinner-time, observing this phenomenon.

Though its being built upon the side of a hill gives it so pretty an appearance, yet to strangers it is attended with very unpleasant sensations, and sometimes an awkward fall. The streets are badly paved; and the side hill gives you a slippery kind of motion, something betwixt sliding and walking. You are like a machine, that is wound up to go a certain length; for when you are once set off from the top of a hilly street, you go with impelled velocity to the bottom, and then stop with a jerk. From this circumstance the women here have acquired a very remarkable trip in their gait, and an elasticity in their walk, that is not perhaps as graceful as the smooth languid step of an English woman of fashion; but it has a sprightliness in it that well accords with the lively and healthy vivacity of a Welsh female: and though this quick motion might go near to discompose the spirits, or dislocate the bones of a modern fine lady, it has no effect upon the nerves, or the firm-knit joints, of a Cambrian beauty. I, who think myself a very agile walker upon plain ground, am obliged to be content to stop myself from sliding down to the bottom of a street, by taking hold of the sides of the walls of the houses. I was much afraid of venturing into a sedan chair; but I see the chairmen can spring from pebble to pebble, as easily as the torrent bounds from stone to stone down the rocks, and almost as swiftly. I never was carried so nimbly in my life.

Mrs. Morgan, A tour to Milford Haven,
in the year 1791, 1795

NARBERTH – ARBERTH

The small town of Narberth is constantly in sight, as we ascend the mountain. It is most sweetly situated upon the brow of the hill. It extends itself upon the utmost ridge, so that it appears as if it was built on purpose to ornament the summit of the mountain. On a very steep rock, at the entrance of the town, stands the finest ruin of a castle that a painter could imagine. One of its broken towers has assumed a very singular shape: it resembles some fabulous beast: I think it is nearer a lama than any other. For some miles on the road this gigantic figure seems to frown upon you, and forbid your approach, standing in a very menacing posture. It appears to have the head of a woman, with the face turned towards you, and her arms akimbo.

Before we arrived at Narberth, the ascent; was extremely steep. It was noon, and the sun bore an amazing power; yet, as soon as we alighted from the chaise, our feet involuntarily carried us towards the castle. We climbed the rock, and explored every part of these romantic ruins. I could willingly have secluded myself in them till the sun declined; but we were obliged to proceed on our journey. There is nothing that fills the mind with more agreeable ideas than the remains of ancient grandeur; and there being so many things of that kind in Wales, adds infinitely to the pleasures of all the views in it.

Mrs. Morgan, A tour to Milford Haven,
in the year 1791, 1795

NEVERN - NANHYFER

The church at Nevern has no pavement in it, and the frequent burials, in the manner of St. David's, have raised the ground within, seven or eight feet higher than it is without.

This parish is pleasantly situated, on the banks of the river Nevern, and backed by some fine shady hills: we ascended one of them, and, by a bad and intricate road, arrived at Cardigan, having passed through the dirty village of St. Dogmael, formerly famous for its abbey, some ruins of which still remain, and which the river Tyvy divides from Cardiganshire.

Most of the ancient monuments in these parts, have lately been destroyed, and converted to private uses; for, though the whole country is a quarry, it is generally of slate, and therefore of no advantage in building.

H. P. Wyndham, Gentleman's Tour through Monmouthshire and Wales In the Months of June and July, 1774, 1775

NEWPORT - TREDRAETH

Within two miles of Newport, a beggarly town, situated under the ruins of a small castle, the road passes close to the remains of four or five Druid sepulchres, or altars; the stones are large, and were originally supported with four upright pillars, like the legs of a table: they are all within the circumference of about sixty yards, and one of them is nearly perfect.

H. P. Wyndham Gentleman's Tour through Monmouthshire and Wales In the Months of June and July, 1774, 1775

Several Druidical monuments engaged our attention, as we drew near NEWPORT. ...The country beyond Newport presented a more pleasing countenance: wood, water, hill, and vale, all unite, even to induce the plodding citizen to pause, and wish to spend the evening of his days in the vicinity of its enchantment. In this interesting situation, we found the Village of Velindre: — we here particularly observed the slaty quality of the hills, and could not avoid condemning the folly of the inhabitants of Velindre, in building their cottages of mud, and sparingly covering them with straw, when Nature herself seemed to place comforts, if not luxuries, before their view. But, perhaps, these reproaches were ill-grounded: for, thus veiled in obscurity, they were happy, as they knew not enough of the world seriously to regret the want of these conveniences: ... For though they suffer the extremes of filth and penury, yet they enjoy the two inestimable blessings, health and felicity.

Allen Cliffe, The Cambrian Directory, or, cursory sketches of the Welsh Territories, 1800

PEMBROKE – PENFRO

From hence, the land bearing far into the sea, makes a promontory, call'd St. Govens Head or Point. But as we found nothing of moment was to be seen there, we cross'd over the isthmus to Pembroke, which stands on the E. shore of the great haven of Milford Haven.

This is the largest and richest, and at this time, the most flourishing town of all S. Wales: Here are a great many English merchants, and some of them men of good business; and they told us, there were near 200 sail of ships belong'd to the town, small and great; in a word, all this part of Wales is a rich and flourishing country, but especially this part is so very pleasant, and fertile, and is so well cultivated, that 'tis call'd by distinction, Little England, beyond Wales.

Daniel Defoe, A tour thro' the whole island of Great Britain, divided into circuits or journies, 1724

TENBY – DINBYCH-Y-PYSGOD

Before we quitted the coast, we saw Tenbigh, the most agreeable town on all the sea coast of South Wales, except Pembroke, being a very good road for shipping, and well frequented: Here is a great fishery for herring in its season, a great colliery, or rather export of coals, and they also drive a very considerable trade to Ireland.

Daniel Defoe, A tour thro' the whole island of Great Britain, divided into circuits or journies, 1724

ST. DAVID'S – TYDDEWI

A street of wretched cottages, one of which is the inn, composes the city of St. David's. I had so little notion of its being the bishoprick, that I enquired in the street, how far it was to St. David's. The reader will easily give me credit, when he hears that the palace and cathedral stand below the town, and cannot be seen from it.

The bishop's palace, which was founded in the reign of Edward the Third, is now an immense ruin; several of the apartments are uncommonly large, the walls of which are still entire. The whole parapet is Gothic, and open in arches like that at Swansea, a circumstance peculiar to these two remains of antiquity.

[...]

This melancholy description is a just picture of the whole face of the country, with a few exceptions only, for more than eighty miles.

H. P. Wyndham, Gentleman's Tour through
Monmouthshire and Wales In the Months of June and
July, 1774, 1775

From hence to St. Davids, the country begins to look like Wales again, dry, barren, and mountainous; St. Davids is not a bishop's see only, but was formerly an arch-bishop's, which they tell us, was by the Pope transferr'd to Dole in Britany, where it still remains.

The venerable aspect of this cathedral church, shews that it has been a beautiful building, but that it is much decay'd. The west end or body of the church is tolerably well; the choir is kept neat, and in tollerable repair, the S. isle without the choir, and the Virgin Mary's Chappel, which makes the E. end of the church, are in a manner demolish'd, and the roofs of both fallen in.

Daniel Defoe, A tour thro' the whole island of Great
Britain, divided into circuits or journies, 1724

A second expedition led us by the ruins of Roche castle, over a bleak and unpleasant country, on the edge of the dangerous bay of St. Bride, and across the deep hollow of the creek of Solfay, to the deserted city of St David's.- Hardly a single tree decorated this wild extremity of the coast of Pembrokeshire; a scanty shew of habitations, more like huts than cottages, were thinly interspersed; and the city itself, when we approached it, bore the aspect of an insignificant village, situated on a small eminence near that projecting head-land which terminates in the pile of rocks called St. David's head. In a deep hollow beneath the town, sheltered from those winds which ravage this stormy coast, we found a few good houses appropriated to the ecclesiastical establishment, in the midst of which the cathedral appeared rising in renovated magnificence, like a phoenix amidst the splendid ashes of the ruined grandeur of St. David's. This church is far superior to that of Llandaffe in its preservation, and has received ample justice from the attention and expence bestowed on it by its modern proprietors, the whole being in good repair, and the west front having lately been rebuilt in a taste perfectly corresponding with the rest of the structure. Its tower is finely carved in fret-work, and, like many of our English cathedrals, the Gothic ornaments of the choir contrast the Saxon pillars and arches of the great aisle, which are themselves curiously worked in wreaths. A ceiling of Irish oak also is much to be admired, together with a very perfect Mosaic pavement. Bishop Vaughan's chapel lies behind the choir, where we were much struck with a highly wrought stone ceiling, similar to the finest specimens of Henry VII's reign, with which all the surrounding ornaments of the building correspond. St. Mary's chapel must have been still more elegant, from the curious remains of pillars and arches with which its space is strewed; various also and extraordinary are the devices in sculpture to be found there, including the heads of the seven sisters who were said to have contributed to the building. The chapter-house also has a fine coved ceiling, and St. Mary's hall, now in ruins, exhibits the remains of much ancient grandeur. From the cathedral and these adjacent buildings, we visited the ruins of the bishop's palace, which must formerly have been a magnificent, and even a princely structure. Two parts of its quadrangle are yet nearly entire, and these are crowned with a light Gothic parapet, similar to those at Swansea castle and Llamphey court. The arch by which we entered the king's hall is singularly fine, with the statues of king John and his queen over it; the hall itself is a grand room, 88 feet in length by 30, and at its eastern end is a curious circular window, like a wheel, with a rim, spokes, and centre, wrought in the finest Gothic, and still quite entire. This room was built after the rest of the palace, for the reception of king John and queen Mary on their return from Ireland, being much larger than the bishop's hall, which is notwithstanding a fine building. The chapel contains the remains of a font, with some pieces of sculpture, and the kitchen is nearly entire, with four chimneys and four arches, supported by a solid pillar in the middle.-After devoting several hours to these fine remnants of antiquity, we ascended to the poor street which bears the title of a city, and found very moderate accommodation at the house dignified with the name of an inn.

Henry Skrine, Two successive tours throughout the whole of Wales, 1798

The saunter from hence to the city of ST. DAVIDS, now properly deserving the name of a village, was rather more captivating than our walk before breakfast: it was occasionally enlivened by the prospect of the wide ocean, boundless to our view on one side, whilst before us the fantastic shapes of the rocks off St. David's Head, exhibited Nature, in her most awful and striking attitudes. Above the rest, Caern Thydy lifted its bold promontory, as if to give effect to the rude landscape. About half way between Newgin and St. Davids, the beautiful little village of Solva unexpectedly burst upon our view; studded with neat white-washed cottages, and enclosed on each side with lofty rocks, which here form a picturesque and interesting chasm. These rocks, indeed, I could almost imagine, were torn asunder by some convulsive rent of the earth. The Cathedral, and dilapidated ruins of the episcopal Palace, are situated at the bottom of a steep hill, and scarcely visible in the town: these, and the prebendal houses, were formerly enclosed by a strong stone wall, with four gates, computed at eleven hundred yards in circuit.

[…]

It is much to be regretted, that so little regard has been paid to the internal appearance of this noble pile; the whole of it has lately been white-washed, which gives it too much the air of a modern building: the external part, I am sorry to add, has been equally neglected; and the chapels and monuments exposed to the wanton mischief of boys and idle people. The west front of the cathedral has very lately been repaired by a Mr. Nash, who has endeavoured, with bad success, to imitate the beautiful circular window remaining in the ruins of the Bishop's Palace. The stone, likewise, with which it is built, is of so soft a substance, that it even moulders with the touch of the finger; but possibly it may, by being exposed to the air, like the Bath stone, become more solid; and, when by time it shall have acquired a darker hue, may then better correspond with the original building.

The Bishop's Palace now stands a monument of desolation; —and as we walked over the loose fragments of stone, which are scattered through the immense area of the fabric, the images of former times rose to reflection.

Allen Cliffe, The Cambrian Directory, 1800

RADNORSHIRE ~ SIR FAESYFED

BUILTH WELLS – LLANFAIR YM MUALLT

BUALT is a small market-town comprised in two streets rising one over the other, upon the high shelving bank of the river. Although anciently and irregularly built, it is much resorted to by the neighbouring gentry, not less for the beauty of its position, than for the famed salubrity of its air.

[...]

On leaving Bualt, and crossing its bridge, the tourist enters RADNORSHIRE, where the road, traced upon heights impendent over the Wye, commands one of the most beautifully romantic vallies in the principality. The river, which we have before seen majestically flowing, rapid but unopposed, among flowery lawns, here, approaching its native source in the bosom of Plinlimmon, appears eddying, foaming, and roaring in a narrow channel, amid shelving rocks and disjointed craigs, a mere mountain torrent. With the accompaniments of towering precipices, naked rocks, and impendent cliffs, finely softened by overhanging branchy trees, or partially concealed by deep shadowy woods, and frequently enlivened by a stripe of verdant meadow, the river presents a succession of picturesque *morçeaus,* the most striking imaginable; and fully compensates the bad state of the road in this part. A considerable range of prospect also presents itself on the right, from some favoured eminences, where a long series of moorish lumpy hills extend over the greater part of Radnorshire, which shews but an indifferent mixture of cultivation with numerous heaths and forests.

J. T. Barber, A tour throughout South Wales and Monmouthshire, 1803

RHAYADER – RHAEADR GWY

RHAYDER-GOWY, wildly situated at the foot of the mountainous barrier between South and North Wales, consists of two streets of neatly whitened houses, and is graced with the vicinity of two churches. A castle also added to, the consequence of the town in the time of the Welch princes; but none of its remains now appear, except a deep trench cut in the rock of the town, and three or four barrows, which are, no doubt, connected with its history. The market-house is a neat little building, though of rough stones; and the Red Lion inn is no less remarkable for its neatness and accommodation, useful though unimposing, than for the obliging assiduities of its landlord.

The scenery of the Wye, close to this town, acquires an uncommon degree of grandeur. Raging in its rocky bed, the river is seen through the light foliage of impendent trees, and almost beneath a bold arch which bestrides the river, bounding over a ledge of rock in a

413

fall of some depth; whence it tears its way among protruding craigs in a sheet of glistening foam, but is almost immediately concealed by the embowering ornaments of its banks.

Above the town of Rhayder, a bold hilly region, overspread with treacherous bogs, or broken into precipices of fearful depth, mixes with the magnificent forms of the North Wales mountains. Here nature wears her wildest garb; no stripe of cultivation controls the dreary majesty of the scene; the mountain sheep browse on the dizzy heights unmindful of danger; the hardy ponies here sport away their early years, unconscious of restraint; and, no less free, the bold mountaineer looks round his stormy world, nor hapless mourns the gayer spheres below.

J. T. Barber, A tour throughout South Wales and
Monmouthshire, 1803

LLANDRINDOD

My Cousin not being up, Mr. *Jacome* and myself walked to the Fountain, which is about three hundred Yards from the House, though both are on the same *Rosse* or Common; which Land is of a black, soft, oozy Substance, for near a Foot deep, under which is a mixt Gravel; the Surface makes good Peat, which is a Commodity cut in the Summer, and serves almost the whole County for Fewel in the Winter; some is cut in large Squares to lay behind the Fire, others in narrow Lengths to burn in the Middle. The Ground is very even from the House to the Spring, which issues out of a Rock about seven Feet from the Ground; on the other Side a small Valley or Channel, through which runs a Brook, which falls into

414

the River *Ithon* below. The Spring is not enclosed with Building, but conveyed out of the Rock, by a piece of Bark; the Side of which Rock is covered with those Colours that generally arise from Mineral Waters. Adjoining to the Spring is a small Hut, for the Conveniency of the People that draw the Water; on the Left Hand is a great many Letters and Figures, almost unintelligible. The Place where the Water issues out is at the Top of the Rock, whose Substance is partly of the Slate Kind; the Spring runs about one Pint and a half in a Minute; and is better in proportion as the Weather is dry.

The earliest Account I could get of these Waters (which are partly of the *Scarborough* and *Cheltenham* Kind, though much preferable to either) was this: About Forty Years ago, a Gentleman in *England* being afflicted with the Scurvy, or some other dangerous Distemper, and having spent all his Fortune on Physicians to no Purpose, he came one Day to the Person he had employ'd most: Doctor, says he, I came to tell you that I have but one Guinea left, which I have brought with me, and as you have had a good deal of my Money, I beg you'd not fail telling me of something that may be of Service to me, if you can. Well, quoth the Doctor, and is it the last; the very last; are you sure 'tis the last Guinea? The other answered in the Affirmative. Then, says the Doctor, sit down, give me the Guinea, and I'll do what I can for you. He sat down, when the Doctor told him, that some Years ago, in some Person's Library, he had read the following Story, which, continued he, I shall tell you; and if you could be so fortunate to find the Well, I am satisfied it will cure you, provided the Story is true;

take the Guinea again, continued he, and God bless you with it. There was, says he, some Years ago, a Gentleman hunting in *Radnor* County on Foot, which is the Custom of the Country, and Running hard made himself hot and dry, and happening to find this Spring, he drank very plentifully of it, and set out again; but being very warm, it soon operated, and obliged him to unbutton so oft, that he put off his Breeches and carried them in his Hand, and so let it discharge itself without Trouble or Interruption. This, continued the Doctor, was in a Manuscript, with a Discourse on the Virtues of the Water, which, if true, I'm satisfied will be of infinite Service to you; for my Part I own I can do nothing more for you. I'm obliged to you, replied the Patient, but should be glad to know where this famous Spring is. I only know, return'd the Doctor, that it's somewhere in *Radnorshire*, and not many Miles from *Built* in *Brecknockshire*. The Gentleman attempted the Thing, had the good Fortune to find it, which made of him a perfect Care.

However, from some Accident happening to the Gentleman, or thro' the Ignorance of the Natives, who know very little of any Art or Science more than those that are common to the *Indians*, it was scarcely known in *England* 'till within these few Years, and Accommodation being so exceeding bad, it almost discouraged the first Company's coming again; but the Waters being of so powerful and salutary a Nature, was the chief Motive of their Returning. This induced others, and last Year, 1743. not only the Inn, but every House round it, that had a spare Bed, had Company, and might have had much more; but more of this in its Place. The

Water, as I said before, is partly of the *Cheltenham* Kind, tho' much preferable to it.

[...]

My Method was generally this; about seven o'Clock I drank a Pint of Water, and in a Quarter of an Hour it began to operate; I then drank two more, and in a Quarter of an Hour after two Pints more, which I immediately discharged, about the fame Quantity by Urine as by Stool; I never had the least Nausea, Gripes, or Lowness of Spirits, that I have frequently had in other purgative Cases; the Discharge is so easy, that it often went off insensibly. It is necessary to keep warm during the Operation; and therefore in this expos'd cold Part of the World, the Heat of Summer is the best, when the Water is more pure and unmix'd, the Beginning and whole Month of *July* consequently proper. Some of our Family (if I may so call them) drank it warm'd, and in the House, which may provoke the Operation something, but makes it more nauseous; it empties the Bowels, gives a good Appetite, easy Digestion; and notwithstanding so noisy and unseasonable a Place, (as will be seen in the following Sheets) and other Inconveniencies, I never slept better in my Life.

[...]

These Accounts of the Cures of the Water, I have had from good Hands, who have had nothing in View but declaring the Truth. I shall now continue my Journal. Above the Spring is a Hedge, behind which we walk'd, and work'd, off our Physick, (if I may so call it) which was not so agreeable, or operated so well, as the following Days. At the upper End of this Hedge we found ourselves on a steep Bank, at the Bottom of which runs the Brook already mentioned; on the other Side were three *Welch* Girls, who had no Hedge, or any Retreat when a Motion offered; we had only the Valley between us, and were looking round the Country; at this Juncture one of the Girl's Water began to operate, and I own we were so rude to stay and observe her Confusion, and Means of extricating herself: Immediately the two others stepp'd before her, and up she turn'd, when having scarce done, one of the other, was in the same Condition; and so continu'd alternately 'till we were oblig'd by Modesty and Compassion, to walk back, perfectly pleas'd at the humorous Event.

'A Countryman', A Journey to Llandrindod Wells in
Radnorshire, 1746

The wells of Llandrindod are situated in a wild extensive heath, some spots of which are rarely enlivened with a few trees, and small cultivated inclosures. The mountains bound the dreary prospect at a distance.

The lodging house is tolerably contrived for the reception of company, and in a fine summer, is frequently full. Notwithstanding the badness of the weather, and of all the roads in the environs, we found a decent society at Llandrindod, both of gentlemen and ladies, but they were chiefly invalids. Our party at dinner and supper, for we all ate together, was from fifteen to twenty.

H. P. Wyndham, Gentleman's Tour through
Monmouthshire and Wales in the months of
June and July, 1774, 1775

11

A RIPOSTE

Theophilus Jones (1758-1812) was a Brecon-based solicitor who was appointed the deputy registrar of the Archdeaconry of Brecon in 1807. As 'Cymro' he contributed to the 'Cambrian Register' for 1795 and 1796. He also wrote the 'History of the County of Brecknock' which was published between 1805 and 1809. After the death of his father in 1799, he devoted much of his time to writing.

In this review, written for the Cambrian Register for 1796, printed in 1799, he takes several visitors to task over their accounts. Messrs. Pratt, Skrine and Warner along with Mrs. Morgan come in for particular attention. The original review ran to 33 pages. This is a mildly abridged version.

THE narratives of travellers, and their delineations of foreign climes and customs, have, for a long time, offered to the public much rational instruction as well as amusement. But it was not till within the present century, (with, perhaps, a few exceptions) that English men seem to have discovered, that their own country possesses many variegated scenes and beauties, which are well worthy the attention of the admirer of nature, and of the pencil of the landscape painter: and that the important study of mankind may be essentially promoted by an observation of the characters and genius of the inhabitants of the different parts of our own island.

[...]

But it is not so in the description of men and manners. The customs and peculiarities of mankind, when the traveller has sufficient penetration to discern, and sufficient accuracy to delineate them, are subjects highly attractive of the contemplation of the philosopher, and highly worthy the observation of the gentleman. In this study, however, as far as the result is before the world, I fear that, in most of those who have honoured Wales with a visit, will be found a lamentable deficiency. Whether it be from the want of knowledge of the language, or from too transient an acquaintance with the inhabitants, it is remarkable, that, among all the tours into this country, which have met the public eye, (Mr. Pennant's only excepted, distinguished no less by local than by general knowledge) we have nothing like a resemblance of the men and manners of Wales: a circumstance the more singular, as there are several traits in both, which are equally striking; and which, one would conceive, could not have escaped the notice of any attentive observer. It is, probably, to this defect that we are to ascribe the errors of travellers, when they impute to this country vices and foibles, by which it is not generally disgraced; and virtues, by which it is not peculiarly distinguished. Thus, for instance, a rustic bashfulness, timidity, or a respectful reserve, has been sometimes mistaken for sullenness, or even brutishness: and more particularly, a rapidity of expression, or a tone of voice to which a stranger is not accustomed, in a *language not understood,* has been construed into passion. I am not now contending against the common idea of the irascibility of Welshmen: an idea; so long and so generally received, it would appear hardy to affect to doubt: at the same time, if any person were sceptic enough to deny the position, in the extent generally admitted, or as peculiarly applicable to Wales, he might very properly protest against the evidence of such travellers, bringing with them all this previous prejudice, and extremely liable, for reasons just specified, to be deceived in what they might deem appearances of passion, as very fallacious, and very incompetent to decide upon the question.

[…]

Having premised thus much, I proceed, without further preface, to accompany one of the most respectable of the Welsh travellers: a gentleman who has assumed the singular, not to say the unmeaning and affected appellation of the *Gleaner;* [this is Samuel Jackson Pratt, Gleanings through Wales, 1st edition published 1795], a name of which he seems so fond, and with which he is so pleased and delighted, that, while we travel with him, he is continually in the straw. What the produce of his sheaves will be, when bound, and threshed, remains to be examined.

[…]

Through South Wales this writer darts with the rapidity of lightning. A compliment, indeed, (envolant) is paid to its beauties; but its description, if such it may be called, is comprised in the table of contents. "Beautiful landscapes for the pencil and the pen." "Abergavenny" — "Brecknock" — "Carmarthen" — "Sea-pieces" "Rock-work" — "New and old Passage" (the dash retrograde) "Laugharne" — "Kidwelly — Llanelly — Swansea." Now, from this prospectus, the reader might

be led to expect to hear something about these places: —
Not a word. Even their names are never introduced or
mentioned through the whole chapter. As to the
remaining towns in South Wales, we must rest satisfied
with being told, that they are *sweet* places. Then, hark
for Machynlleth, (or, as the Welsh people in the
neighbourhood call it, Machyntllaith) — in North Wales!
By all the Jack o' lanthorns — if he takes such rapid
strides, there is no following this fellow! The man in the
seven league boots was a snail to him. Fat, however, as
I am, and though I puff and blow in the pursuit, I must
endeavour to overtake him. And if he should chance to
amplify, or bounce, or embellish, (synonyms of the
present day) and I should abruptly or unwarily pull him
by the coat, or tread upon his toe, he may be assured
that I have no intention whatever to hurt or offend him;
and I have that opinion of his benevolence and good
humour, that I would confidently rely on his
forgiveness.

In the first place, then, loth as I am to rob the
principality of any merit which this traveller is inclined
to ascribe to it, a more intimate knowledge of it, and a
love of accuracy, oblige me to deny the *universality* of
that hospitality which he asserts to belong to it. There
are farmers, and I am inclined to allow they are a large
majority, who will welcome the stranger to their humble
roof and homely fare: but let him not be too confident
of meeting this cordiality every where, or his occasional
disappointment will be the more disagreeable.

That any of the nobility or gentry of Wales retain
either their hawker, or their domestic bard, is another
gleaning of error here carefully collected. Some of the

nobility and gentry of North Wales have their harpers; but I do not believe that any of them has a hawker.

[...]

Find me such a family at Barmouth, as the Gleaner has gathered together, and such an author to describe them, and I will thank the collector, or traveller, without insinuating a doubt of the verity of the tale, or questioning any of the facts which he shall assert with so much pleasantry. But when the gaping, and admiring reader, who is well acquainted with the spot, which is the scene of action, has given a good natured currency to the well-told history of the breeches and the petticoat— the net makers—and the barber (not that I mean to deny the existence of female barbers) he is to be provided with still larger powers of deglutition for the tale at Aberaeron— (by mistake written Aberavon— though several places occur of this name in the principality.) To understand a part, at least, of this tale, it is necessary to state that the author talks of going into a cabin in Cardiganshire, where a fisherman, the master of it, upon taking a good haul of herrings, cries, "look, what a size they are of!—how they shine—they seemed plaguily afraid of the hurricane; and came in shoals to the nets, as if they took shelter in them. I am deuced hungry—what say you, my heart of oak," clapping me upon the shoulder, "take a drop of this dear creature; which will make a dead fish speak like an orator." Then follows a love tale—about a shipwreck or something like it—and the escape of a newly married couple, which is so well related, that if we were not taught to expect real, and not imaginary adventures, it would be wrong to scepticize.

[...]

To be obliged continually to contradict the too precipitate assertions of travellers, is truly a painful task: but when the truth of their assertions is stated to have been confirmed by the attestation of their own eyes, it becomes a more delicate business to controvert them. But I must, notwithstanding, aver, that "courtship in bed," does not form one of the general usages or customs of the lower classes of people in Wales. Among folks of this description clandestine visits, under the shade of night, is a general practice; but their assignations of this kind are, I believe, much the same as what takes place in England. Indeed, the wit of Miss's stealing out by moonlight to Pappa's garden, may apply equally well to the mountains of Wales, as to the purlieus of London: with this difference, that a barn, or an outhouse, generally shelters the Cambrian wooers, instead of the gay arbour, or a gingerbread alcove, in the neighbour-hood of the metropolis. That a favoured Welsh lover has not occasionally — or even frequently — had access to the bed-side of his mistress; — that he has frequently said soft things to her *upon* that bed, and that nothing improper has followed that permission, cannot be denied: but that it is a general custom to settle the preliminaries of a more lasting connection *in* bed, is so distant from the fact, that it scarcely requires a serious refutation; and I must, therefore, presume that the author, notwithstanding the conviction of his own eyes, in one instance, could have but very slender authority to vouch for the universality of the custom. I am happy, however, in confirming the account of the strewing flowers upon the grave; a practice frequently observed in some of the country church-yards:

and has truly the becoming appearance of veneration for the dead, at the same time that it produces a sentiment of pleasing melancholy in the living. Yet, in this, our pleasant traveller cannot help embellishing and adorning his tale, when he informs us, that the woman with whom he was in conversation, told him, "that if a nettle or a weed was to be seen to-morrow, (meaning on a Sunday) in the church-yard, the living party to whom *it* (the grave, I presume, on which it grew) belonged, *would be hooted after divine service by the whole congregation!*" Sad jade—to impose thus upon a stranger. " Hooting !"—hoot awa mon, it's nae sic a thing.

The Welsh weddings are pretty much as described by this author; noisy, riotous, and dedicated by the guests to drinking and singing. He might have added, that they are frequently preceded, on the evening before the marriage, by presents of provisions, and articles of household furniture, to the bride and bridegroom: on the wedding day, as many as can be collected together, accompany them to the church, and from thence home; where a collection is made in money from each of the guests, according to their inclination or ability; which sometimes supplies a considerable aid in establishing the newly married couple, and in enabling them to "begin the world," as they call it, with more comfort: but it is, at the same time, considered as a debt to be repaid hereafter, if called upon, at any future wedding of the contributors, or of their friends, or their children, in similar circumstances. — Some time previous to these weddings, where they mean to receive contributions, a herald with a crook or wand, adorned with ribbons, makes the circuit of the neighbourhood, and makes his "bidding," or invitation, in a prescribed form. The knight errant cavalcade on horseback— the carrying off the bride—the rescue—the wordy war in rhythm between the parties, &c. which formerly formed a singular spectacle of mock contest at the celebration of nuptials, I believe to be now almost, if not altogether, laid aside every where through the principality.

It cannot be denied that the Welsh have much superstition amongst them, though it is wearing off very fast. But the instance adduced here, that of their predicting a storm by the roaring of the sea, is a curious kind of proof of their superstition. Their predictions, if they may be so called, are commonly justified by the event; and may, I apprehend, be accounted for from causes as natural as the forebodings of shepherds; for which they have rules and data, as well known to themselves, and, perhaps, as little liable to error, as any of those established by the more enlightened philosophers of the present day. That, among the lower class of people, there is a general belief in the existence of apparitions, is unquestionable: but as to the lighted candle, springing up upon the errand of love, I believe that no person in Wales has ever before heard of it. The traveller has probably confounded it with a very commonly received opinion, that, *within the diocese of St. David's,* a short space before death, a light is seen proceeding from the house, and sometimes, as has been asserted, from the very bed, where the sick person lies; and pursues its way to the church, where he or she is to be interred, precisely in the same track in which the funeral is afterwards to follow. This light is called *canwyll corph,* or the corpse-candle.

The extravagant ravings of methodism, which the author very truly and very properly represents as exceeding every thing which can be seen or heard in any civilized country, are certainly a reproach to the good sense and understanding of the inhabitants. Between 30 and 40 years ago, a branch of the sect of Mr. Whitfield's persuasion, began to exhibit certain enthusiastic extravagancies, from which they are sometimes denominated *Jumpers*. Persuading themselves that they are involuntarily actuated by a divine impulse, they become intoxicated with this imagined inspiration, and utter their rapture and their triumph with such wildness and incoherence—with such gesticulation and vociferation, as set all reason and decorum at defiance. This presumption, seizing chiefly the young and sanguine, and, as it seems, like hysteric affections, partly spreading through the crowd by sympathy; its operation and effects extremely varying according to the different degrees of constitutional temperament, mock all description. Among their preachers, who are also very various in their character, (illiterate and conceited—or well meaning and sensible—or, too frequently, I fear, crafty and hypocritical,) some are more distinguished by their success in exciting these *stravaganzas*. One of these, after beginning, perhaps, in a lower voice, in more broken and detached sentences, rises by degrees to a greater vehemence of tone and gesture, which often swells into a bellowing, as grating to the ear—as the attendant distortions are disgusting to the sight—of a rational man. In the early part he is accompanied only by sighs, and occasional moans, with here and there a note of approbation; which, a while after, are succeeded by whinings and exclamations: till, at length, one among the crowd, wrought up to a pitch of ecstacy, which it is supposed will permit no longer to be suppressed, starts and commences the jumping; using, at intervals, some expressions of praise, or of triumph. The word most generally adopted is *"gogoniant!"* (glory!) Between these exclamations, while labouring with the subject, is emitted from the throat a harsh, undulating sound, which by the profane, has been compared to a stone cutter's saw. The conclusion, which I am almost ashamed to describe, has more the appearance of heathen orgies, than of the rational fervour of christian devotion. — The phrensy spreads among the multitude; — for, in fact, a kind of religious phrensy appears to seize them. To any observations made to them they seem insensible. Men and women, indiscriminately, cry and laugh, jump and sing, with the wildest extravagance. That their dress becomes deranged, or the hair dishevelled, is no longer an object of attention. — And their raptures continue, till, spent with fatigue of mind and body, the women are frequently carried out in a state of apparent insensibility. In these scenes, indeed, the youthful part of the congregation are principally concerned; the more elderly generally contenting themselves with admiring, with devout gratitude, what they deem the operations of the spirit. This phenomenon, from these few leading traits, suggest many important reflections, which, however, come not properly within the province of these cursory remarks.

The Gleaner next presents us with what he very properly calls his *bonne bouche.* Whether, to the raciness of its flavour, it added the recommendation of easiness of digestion, those who swallow it must determine. He tells us (and he tells it with the appearance of gravity) that, in Wales, the *belief of Fairies* is *general!* In Glamorganshire, in particular, we have an extraordinary tale of a parson who had written a book upon them, and was their intimate friend; and of a gentleman, who accompanied him to this fame fairy-loving parson, the said gentleman also firmly believing in their existence. Now, whether the traveller himself experienced, on this occasion, a little pleasant humbug of this fairy land, or is only disposed to amuse himself a little at the expence of his reader, I know not; but if there had been such a clergyman as he describes, either in Glamorganshire, or in the neighbourhood of Pontypool, he certainly would have done right to have consulted his credit in concealing his name; and, at present, it is as compleatly unknown as his book; which one may venture to say the little folks have never yet permitted him to publish. That there are silly, weak people in all countries, every man who has travelled must be convinced: and that there may be many of the lower kind of people in Wales, as well as in England, who believe in ghosts, goblins, and fairies, I know full well: but that there is a greater proportion of the credulous in the former than in the latter, (though I have seen a great deal of the manners of all ranks in both,) I have found no reason to affirm.

[...]

I wish we could admit, as a fact, that there is a harper in every village, and a bard to every mountain in Wales. The truth is, some of the villages of North Wales have their harpers: in South Wales there are very few. As to the bards, alas! they may be said to be no more, The *Awen,-* the Welsh *vis poetica,* seems nearly extinguished; and though some few scintillations may still sparkle in two or three of the bards of North Wales, I am much afraid that, like the faint and transient blaze of a nearly-wasted candle, they only forbode its approaching extinction. It is, however, not a little extraordinary, that an author, not versed in the language of this country (as from several passages it is obvious he is not) should take upon himself to pronounce upon the merits of Welsh poetry; a subject, on which to constitute a judge, requiring a long and intimate acquaintance with the language; and on which few, who possess even that advantage, are competent to decide. It is, therefore, scarcely necessary for me to add, that what he has by inference asserted, "that the poetry was not equal to the vehemence with which it was uttered," however it may declare his modesty, cannot, in such circumstances, be admitted to come with any of that weight or authority, which may entitle a man to advance any position to the public.

[...]

The next tourist that claims our attention, is a lady of the name of Morgan. Her publication is called "a Tour to Milford Haven;" though it might more properly be entitled " a description of the town of Haverfordwest, and of the neighbouring country," to which, as far as relates to Wales, it is almost exclusively confined. This journey, it seems, was taken in the year 1791. During the early part, that respect and politeness, ever due to the sex, claim our silent acquiescence; and while she remains on English ground, induce us to take for granted that the facts related are true, and the observations upon them just: no sooner however does the fair traveller cross the Severn, than, from being complaisant hearers, we are called upon to remark and to rectify: no sooner does she set foot on Cambrian ground, than the spirit of embellishment, peculiar, I hope, to the Welsh traveller, instantly seizes her. One would imagine there was some inchantment in this region; or something in the climate, that, in all Tourists, the moment they breathe in it, occasioned a lamentable defect of vision. Some it seems to blind entirely: to some objects appear multiplied: to others reversed or distorted. Soon after her arrival in Brecknockshire, this lady discovers that the men of this country have a terrible way of mending their roads ... Whether the lady and her horse, like the prophet and his ass of old, met with any super-natural obstruction, is not for me to say: it is my part to give the state of the roads, as it appears to vulgar eyes: and the reader will be surprized when he is assured, that eight or nine years ago, a few years before the date of this tour, the commissioners of the turnpikes took immense pains to remove the very inconvenience which the lady and her horse complain of: and that the said commissioners, with that difficulty indeed, which generally exists in removing ancient prejudices, did prevail upon the labourers on this very road, instead of laying huge stones upon or "over it," by which she, the surveyor, had before been frequently deceived, (as they covered it with a layer of earth before they were properly broken) to lay them in heaps upon its *sides*; by which means it has ever since been seen, that they break them sufficiently small, before they are laid over the road. So that, in the lady's account of the matter, there appears at least an odd kind of anachronism: whether introduced for a poetical — or for what other purpose — the Writer herself alone can determine.

After passing these huge heaps, and after a dismal tale of a dismal shower — a dismal dell — and the dismal clinking of chains one mile from Trecastle, not as she tells us a peasant informed her "*tree milst;*" [in Mrs. Morgan's account 'tree milsh'] (a specimen of imitation, by the bye, which can only excite a smile, as coming from a lady, though we could not otherwise avoid observing, that it is much more like the dialect of Duke's Place, than that of the mountains of Wales) this same unfortunate defect of vision, to which I have just alluded, becomes again observable, and discovers itself in a singular manner, when we arc informed, that *all* the cottages in Wales are perfectly white and (hear this, ye unconscious and astonished inhabitants) LUMINOUS! the roof being covered with white slate, resembling — what think you? — a wall ? — a white apron ? — a sheet ? — the inside of an oyster shell? No, no! Guess again. However, not to fatigue the reader with conjectures, or puzzle him to find a simile which it is ten to one he can ever reach, be it known to all men by these presents, that they are like the MOON BURSTING FROM A CLOUD! When the reader is informed of the fact, that forty-nine out of fifty of the Welsh cottages are covered with brown thatch, he may perhaps be apprehensive that the description may be occasioned by something of a moon-blindness: though, after all, it may probably be intended only as a dash of poetical brilliancy; — too brilliant indeed for the owlish prosaic reader to appreciate.

[...]

But her descriptions being confined to the country near Haverfordwest, her observations equally limited, apply only to that place and its vicinity. She does not, indeed, seem to recollect her own observation to her husband in their journey down: — that "these people are not Welsh:" and, consequently, that she cannot, from their practices, deduce the general manners or customs of Wales. In that part of the country, however, where she had leisure and opportunity to make her remarks, I again subscribe with pleasure to their general correctness; though even these I cannot acquit in some cases of exaggeration, and in others of error. To point out a few instances. — The door of a hut of a miner is said to be so low, as to oblige him to creep in on all fours, and he is said to sit in it, as an Indian, upon his hams. From this description one might be led to suppose, that this is the habitual posture of this body of men, as is said to be that of the Indians. The fact warrants no such supposition. It was only the accidental position in which she happened to see a poor fellow under a few turfs, piled up to protect him from a storm or shower of rain, the aperture into which, though low, permits a tall man, on his stooping to enter. — The whole of this, however, hardly deserved notice; there being nothing in these temporary erections peculiar to the principality.

The story of the culm-balls, burnt in Pembrokeshire and Carmarthenshire, having been mistaken for potatoes roasting, (by-the-bye they must have been of a tolerable size) only reminds us of a Hybernicism related there upon this subject: a pleasantry, indeed, which may be amusing to strangers, though worn out among the inhabitants.

The dialect of Haverfordwest does not consist of a mixture of Welsh and English, nor has it any thing of the usual Welsh accent. Little or no Welsh is spoken there, even by the lower classes of people; and their dialect, though of a peculiar nature, and not easily described, has no resemblance whatever to that of Cardiganshire, Carmarthenshire, Breconshire, or Glamorganshire, where the Welsh language is most spoken. On this subject of the variation of languages, there is a very extraordinary circumstance in Pembrokeshire, which has not attracted the notice of cursory travellers. A brook divides the hundreds of Rous and Dangleddy, on one side of which the inhabitants converse entirely in English, on the other as entirely in Welsh; and this has continued so for ages. The same thing may be observed of the inhabitants of Gower in Glamorganshire, though here the line is more ideal, and not so easily ascertained. But when a man of Gower is asked the residence of one in Llangevelach, which is on the Welsh side of the line, it is a common reply, "I donna knaw, a lives somewhere in the welshery;" as if he had spoken of a piggory, or rookery, or any thing of that kind. The Flemings in Gower as well as in Pembrokeshire (for they settled in both) certainly affect to hold the Welsh, and particularly this language, very cheap; no wonder, therefore, that Mrs. M. should be answered in a sharp tone and indignant look, when she presumed to suppose they could gobble our gutterals, or converse in what they esteem a barbarous language.

It is with surprize I find this lady affirming that there are few if any beggars in South Wales. Here again I presume she is only describing Haverfordwest, where I understand they are less numerous. But, to the disgrace of the police of South Wales in general, the towns through which travellers pass, and particularly the doors and windows of inns, are infested with miserable looking objects, as filthy and disgusting, as they are (for of many I can speak from personal knowledge) idle and undeserving.

[…]

When this lady asserts that the lower kind of people in Wales do not live poorly, I fear she only exposes her want of knowledge of their general situation. Great part of the inhabitants, particularly the small farmers among the hills, live in a manner that most people would call wretched. Their fare is infinitely more coarse than that of parish paupers in other parts of the island. What in England are called necessaries of life, are, with them, in many cases, luxuries.

[…]

Mrs. M. still forgetting perhaps that she is at Haverfordwest, observes a peculiarity in the countenance of Welshmen. The same observation, though I own it has never struck me, has been made by several others, and therefore, is probably true. The size and general height of the labouring inhabitants of Cardiganshire seem to have something peculiar. They are mostly thick set, short men, from five feet two to five feet six, muscular, bony, brave, determined, and resolute; (as the French desperadoes who lately landed on their coast can attest (who also found in their neighbours of Pembrokeshire the same energetic qualities) — their dress, which may be almost called their uniform, is a light blue, short coat, with a waistcoat and breeches of the same colour. The women's *whittles* (a kind of short cloak — or piece of flannel — pinned or tied round their shoulders) one of the same make as described by Mrs. M; save that those in Cardiganshire are red, and a long deep fringe: how much the colour and the garment contributed, on the occasion just alluded to, to strike the enemy with consternation, is too well known to be mentioned.

[...]

The next Traveller, whose pea-green skies and yellow ochred mountains cannot fail attracting the eye at least, seems at all events determined to surprize and astonish us; and, in the marvellous, leaves far behind him all his fellow-tourists. Whether, on his approach to the Welsh coast, he may have snuffed in the floating miasmata, that may produce this epidemic disorder, so prevalent among Welsh Tourists, I know not; but he seems deeply infected, even before he has trod in the Welsh soil. It immediately discovers itself on the passage of the Severn; which is, consequently, described, as full of dangers; which never existed, but in his — or some other equally disordered imagination; and as continually liable to accidents, which half a century has scarcely witnessed! Not that it is here intended to deny, or call into question, the story of losing the hat; but it passengers were to be deterred, by this tale, from crossing this water, they might as well be frightened from walking in a street; because, once in fifty years, a tile may have dropped upon the head of some unfortunate person, and occasioned the loss of life.

To review this publication, in order to arrive at the truth, it would be necessary to negative, in some respect or other, almost every account that has been advanced in it. In saying this, however, I wish to premise, that, without any personal knowledge of the writer, I am inclined to ascribe his mistakes more to haste and want of information, than to any wilful misrepresentation. But as merely to deny any given statement may appear abrupt; and, after all, in the present instance, would only intimate what Wales is not, and not what it really is, I shall *take leave* to join the Traveller at Newport in Monmouthshire; and, to rectify a few of his inadvertencies as he proceeds. At Newport, then, I have to acquaint him, that it is *not* celebrated for sewin, but for salmon, which is there equal in flavour to any caught on the coasts of this kingdom; — that the sewin is seldom seen there, but found chiefly in Carmarthenshire, and in some rivers of Glamorganshire; — that the Welsh are *not* proud of it; on the contrary, that it is with them of inferior estimation and price; — that it is not like a trout, but has a greater resemblance to a salmon; — that it very rarely exceeds ten or twelve pounds in weight, and generally not half so much. I have not read Daniel de Foe upon this subject: but if he states it to be the pride of this part of the country, I presume he may have read it in some other traveller, who had read it in some former traveller — marvel or blunder-maker, who had heard it from — the L-d knows whom.

[...]

Advancing to Caerffyli, the tourist indulges himself unboundedly, at the expence of these poor Hottentots (as he calls them) and their huts. That the arrival of a post-chaise in any country town in England, (not a thoroughfare) occasions, at the door of the inn where it stops, a concourse of people, larger or smaller in proportion to the frequency of such carriages, few will deny; and that carriages are seldom seen at Caerffyli, must be admitted: but that, when they do arrive, they occasion consternation, or that the gutturals of the inhabitants are employed to inquire whether the Pope or the French are coming, is a tale—too absurd for serious notice. The acquaintance of the inhabitants of Caerffyli with the Pope, or their care about him, even if he were again in the plenitude of power, is equally slender; and the writer may be assured, that they have as little dread of the French as their countrymen of Pembrokeshire or Cardiganshire; and will probably receive them, if they think proper to pay them a visit, with as little consternation. This place is by no means "an irregular assemblage of huts:" it has several good houses; and at present a well-built inn, probably not erected when this Traveller visited it; though it must then have more than the solitary alehouse he mentions: whether the number be indeed an advantage, may well be doubted.

To prove that a Welshman does not know a coin from dirt, he produces an instance of his guide having one in his possession,—a refusing to part with it. There we have an attempt to imitate the Welsh brogue—with no better success than Mrs. Morgan with her "milst." "What hur think"—"Got bless hur." ... "Got bless hur" is never heard: their manner of expressing the idea would more probably be conveyed to an English ear by "Goat bless *me.*" Another phrase, attributed to the Welsh, though never used by them, is "look vou." ... At Caerffyli, however, where this writer says the English

language is as little known as among the mountains of
Merioneth, and where he asserts he could find only one
person who could speak it, I will venture to aver,
without being acquainted with one third of the
inhabitants, that I know twenty there, who speak it
(most certainly with an accent, not easily described)
more grammatically than in most country places in the
kingdom.

[...]

A Welsh funeral: — "women screaming — children
crying — men swearing — dogs barking" — (the brutes, I
suppose, are trained to join in the chorus, and always
form part of the procession) — odd enough this! — But
this is nothing: the parson and the corpse vanish: and
the author, who attended, could never discover what
became of them! I will, then, beg leave to inform him
from my own knowledge: the corps was decently
interred; and the clergyman walked in and walked out,
in the same manner, and with the same deliberation, as
is usually seen in England — with the exception,
perhaps, of her metropolis, where half the burial service
is frequently omitted, unless the corpse once was — rich
or noble. The funeral, to which this author alludes, being
that of a man of family, and, I believe, respected in the
place, brought together a great crowd; and the noise and
bustle were no more than is usually heard and seen,
where a number of idle people are gathered together
from curiosity.

After a severe and very sarcastic description of the
alehouses at Carmarthen, which may have every thing
to boast of but wit and truth, (for, in fact, the inns here
are not very different from those in England — out of the

great roads:—quædam bona—multa mala—plurima mediveria) and after a pompous display of learning, in which he proposes to detect the *falsehoods* of all his predecessors, from Giraldus Cambrensis, down to himself, (whom I think he has unfairly excluded) he informs us, that he does not believe the Carmarthen people to be the most polite in the world; — that it is (not an uncommon, but) a common market town; — that the reader, if he should visit it, must not be surprised to be gratified with a *picturesque* display (Oh the wit!) of one entire street, formed by mansions of mud; — that dogs are universally used in this part of the world as turnspits; — that sewin weighing 30lb. are found there; that the dress of Welshmen is universally the same; — that the common people despise the use of shoes and stockings; — that the men are distinguished by broad hats and bare feet; and that, if it were not for the criterion of the breeches, the difference of sex would hardly be perceived; and that their ignorance is *amazing*. On these several assertions it would be waste of time to make any animadversions: to those who are acquainted with the country, the bare mention of most of them carries with it, in a great measure, their refutation. What is only of occasional occurrence, this writer calls the custom of the country; and where his facts are true, in part, they are far from being so universal as he would represent them. A Welshman may here and there be seen at a milk-pail: (by-the-bye I am not satisfied—for reasons which I cannot explain here—that the employ is not more appropriate to men than to women) and a man-milliner is now and then met with in London; yet, if a foreigner from thence asserted, that caps and bonnets, in London, were customarily made by men, an Englishman would think pretty contemptuously both of his accuracy and his liberality. The similitude observed between the complexion and appearance of the Welsh and their puppy turnspits is so sagaciously happy, that it would be cruel to hint a doubt of its propriety.

[...]

These are again succeeded by more travellers, of the names of *Skrine, Warner,* and *Aikin;* all published in 1798. The first [to whose private character and real worth all who have the happiness of knowing him will feel proud to bear testimony] certainly does not excel as a tourist, or writer of travels: his style abounds in metaphors, and epithets, singularly and affectedly applied, and frequently extravagantly conceived and oddly expressed: he talks of intervals in a mountainous ridge in Monmouthshire, forming a succession of vallies, *like the cells of a honeycomb;* buildings at Llantrisant, clustered like a swarm of bees, bursts of view, sweeps, stripes of vegetatión, chains of meadows, hills *floating* with water, and feathering woods. The spacious plantations of Buckland in Brecknockshire are sung, though it can only boast of a few shrubs, planted in a lawn, which are said to break upon the sight at the same moment that the *charming* demesne of Paterstone *steals upon the view.* Though every traveller upon that road must know that there is no one point of view between Crickhowell and Brecon, from whence those seats can be seen at the same time. Sometimes his language resembles prose run mad; for instance, we are told that towards the south of Brecknock, the hill of *Canthriff,* cloathed from the summit to its base, with wood, opposes a barrier *finely impending* over the river, and fronting the bold and barren eminence of the Craigie— Unfortunately there is no such impending hill as Canthriff, [or Cantreff, for that is the name of an adjacent parish]. There is a hill or rising ground, which shelves rather abruptly from the river Usk, cloathed with a wood called Clos-y-coed; and which fronts not Craig, or rather Crîg, but a little eminence neither bold or barren, called Slwch, which is so far from being a distinguishing feature in the landscape, that it is degraded by the inhabitants by the dimunitive appellation of *Slwch Tump*. This writer is also seized with the mania, which usually affects Welsh travellers of attempting to explain Welsh words and names, without a sufficient knowledge of the language. *Bwlch* is said properly to signify a rent in a mountain, whereas it may as properly, though it does not as commonly, mean a rent in a garment; and it is in continual use for a gap in a hedge—*Desguilfa,* [a combination of letters peculiarly disgusting to a British eye] meaning Disgwylfa, is said to be a prospect, though it is generally applied to a military station of a centinel, commanding an extensive prospects—Several or similar errors occur in the course of the work; we now and then meet with such a phrase as "too *critic* an eye", which, admitting that it can be justified from good authority, is certainly affected. Johnson's quotation from Pope hardly supports it as an adjective. The mistakes in spelling whole names are almost too numerous to mention—Pont ar dillas, for Pont ar ddulas, (of which the description is not unintelligible, is not correct)—Llanspwddid for Llanspyddid—Calda for Caldy—Russland castle for Dryslwyn castle—Caerphilli for Caerphili, [the difference is very great in Welsh pronunciation] — Wenye for Wenny or Ewenay — Pembray for Pembrey — Glyn hier for Glyn hîr — Caraig Cennin for Carreg Cynan — Cwmtythen for Cwmtoiddwr — Luchyntyaen for Llwyncyntefin, &c. &c.

The next traveller is a clergyman of the name of Warner, who made his tour on foot!!! Here it is impossible to avoid saying two or three words upon this silly and ridiculous whim of converting pleasure into toil. It is, indeed, strange it should be necessary to make an observation upon the subject, to any man who can afford himself a horse, and a pair of saddle bags; but folly, and the inexperience of youth, first introduced this laborious mode of travelling, and fashion and caprice have exerted their influence to keep it alive. The inconveniences that attend it, independent of the fatigues it occasions, which is no inconsiderable objection, are many; the advantages few, and the expences saved by it trifling. The treatment the pedestrian is likely to meet with at most inns [whatever this curate may say to the contrary] is materially different from that which the equestrian receives; and there are few places, indeed, to which the traveller on horseback cannot have access: if such should occur, it is easy to make any occasional deviations on foot; and we shall be ready, after having gratified our curiosity by these slight excursions, to acknowledge, with double satisfaction, the obligations we owe to our useful and submissive companion, who always lightens our fatigue, shortens, apparently, our journey, relieves us often from the necessity of travelling by night, and frequently preserves us from the unwholesome consequences of a sound wetting.

[...]

The last of these three tourists is a scientific traveller, his journey was professedly, and principally, if not wholly, made with a view to improvement, or, at least, amusement in mineralogy — upon this subject, (as far as I am a judge) he writes with considerable abilities, and, it is to be observed, that the Welsh names are more properly spelt than by most other travellers, though he does not affect a profound knowledge of the language, or frequently attempts to explain it. — Little is said as to the customs and manners of the country; but he has said much to the purpose in his preface, in which he very truly acknowledges, that the requisite knowledge of a sufficient number of circumstances from which to deduce national character, is not to be acquired without a long residence, and much intercourse with the inhabitants.

It is not to be *gleaned* in a hasty excursion through a country, where its language, and the general shyness and suspicion which the natives discover towards the English, or, to use their own words, the Saxons, oppose obstacles which only time and perseverance can overcome.

Since the above was written, a publication has appeared, in which the Editor, conceiving several tours into Wales to be scarce and valuable, has hashed and fricaseed them into what he calls a collection, with a garnish of two or three stained prints, or views badly chosen: — a species of book-making very much adopted some years ago, under the title of "Beauties of Sterne" — "Beauties of Joe Miller," — "Beauties of Johnson," &c. &c. and, lately, in two volumes 8vo, the "Beauties of Burke."

This is, doubtless, a very ingenious contrivance; though now, as Trinculo says, "a kind of a — —not of the newest." The work before us, however, chiefly relating to North Wales, a country with which I am little acquainted, I am, therefore, no judge of its merits, or of the merits of those tours, from which it is borrowed or cut down.

'Cymro' (Theophilus Jones), Cursory remarks on Welsh
tours or travels, Cambrian Register for the year 1796,
1799

BIBLIOGRAPHY

Anon. *A Collection of Welch Tours: or, a display of the beauties of Wales, selected principally from celebrated histories and popular tours, with occasional observations and remarks.* London: G. Sael, 1797

Anon. 'An excursion through North Wales', *The Cambro-Briton Volume III. November, 1821 – June, 1822.* London: Simpkin and Marshall, 1822

Barber, J.T. *A tour throughout South Wales and Monmouthshire. Comprehending a general survey of the picturesque scenery, remains of antiquity, historical events, peculiar manners, and commercial situations of that interesting portion of the British Empire.* London: T. Cadell and W. Davies, 1803

Bingley, William. *North Wales; including its scenery, antiquities, customs, and some sketches of its natural history; delineated from two excursions through all the interesting parts of that country, during the Summers of 1798 and 1801.* London: T. N. Longman, 1804.

Black, William. *Reflections on the Relicks of Ancient Grandeur, and the Pleasing Retirements in South Wales.* Cheltenham: J. J. Bradley, 1823

Brome, James. *Travels over England, Scotland and Wales, 1700.* London: Robert Gosling, 2nd Edition, 1707

Camden, William. *Britain, or, a Chorographicall Description of the most flourishing Kingdomes, England, Scotland, and Ireland.* Translated newly into English by Philémon Holland. G. Bishop & I. Norton, 1610. Gibson edition, 1722

Anon., (Allen Cliff(e)). *The Cambrian Directory, or, Cursory sketches of the Welsh Territories*: Salisbury, J. Easton, 1800

'A Countryman'. *A Journey to Llandrindod Wells in Radnorshire, with a particular description of those wells, the places adjacent, the humours of the company there, &c.* London: M. Cooper, 1748, Second Edition, 1756

Cradock, Joseph. *An Account of some of the most romantic Parts in North Wales.* London, Printed for T Davies, Russel-Street, Covent Garden and T. Cadell, in the Strand. 1777

Cradock, Joseph. *Letters from Snowdon: Describing a tour through the Northern Counties of Wales.* London: J. Ridley, 1770

Crouch N (Robert Burton) *The History of the Principality of Wales.* London: A Bettersworth at the Red-Lyon and J Batley at the Dove, in Paternoster Row. 1730

Davies, Walter. *A statistical account of the Parish of Llanymyneich in Montgomeryshire, The Cambrian Register for the year 1795*, London: E. & T. Williams, 1796

'Dyfed Gwinfardd'(Walter Davies). 'Statistical account of the Parish of Fishguard in Pembrokeshire', *The Cambrian Register for the year 1795* (pp. 239-64). London: E. & T. Williams, 1796

Defoe, Daniel. *A tour thro' the whole island of Great Britain, divided into circuits or journies.* London: 1724-27. Reprint London: J. M. Dent and Co, 1927

Dineley, Thomas. *An Account of the Progress of His Grace Henry the First Duke of Beaufort Through Wales,* 1684. Edited from the Original MS in the possession of His Grace the Eighth Duke of Beaufort. London: Charles Baker, Strangeways & Walden, 1864

Donovan, E. *Descriptive excursions through South Wales and Monmouthshire, in the year 1804, and the four preceding summers.* Vol. I & II. London: 1805

Evans, John. *Letters written during a tour through South Wales, in the year 1803, and at other times.* London: C. & R. Baldwin, 1804

Fiennes, Celia. *Through England on a Side Saddle in the Time of William and Mary, Being the Diary of Celia Fiennes.* London: Field and Tuer, 1888

Gilpin, William. *,Observations on the River Wye, and several parts of South Wales, &c. Relative chiefly to picturesque beauty; made in the summer of the year 1770.* London: Blamire, 1782. Second edition, 1789

Heath, Charles. *The excursion down the Wye from Ross to Monmouth.* Monmouth: C. Heath, 1796. Edition 1808

Hucks, J. *A pedestrian tour in North Wales in a series of letters.* London: J. Debret and J. Edwards, 1795

Johnson, Samuel. *A Diary of a Journey into North Wales, in the year 1774*. London: Robert Jennings, 1816

'Cymro' (Theophilus Jones). 'Cursory remarks on Welsh tours or travels', *Cambrian Register for the year 1796*, Vol. II., (pp. 421-454). London: E & T Williams, 1799

Leigh, Samuel. *Leigh's Guide to Wales & Monmouthshire*. London: Leigh & Son, 1831

Lyttelton, Lord George. 'An Account of a Journey into Wales in Two Letters to Mr. Bower', *Dodsley's Annual Register, 1774*, Vol. XVII, (pp.160-64). London: J Dodsley, 1778, Second edition.

Malkin, Benj. Heath. *The Scenery, Antiquities and Biography of South Wales, from materials collected during two excursions in the year 1803*. London: T. N. Longman, 1804

Mervinius ('Mr Harper, a gentleman from London'). 'Walks around Dolgellau. Walk III Dolgellau to Towyn', *The Cambro-Briton*, Vol. II, (pp. 114-121), September, 1820 – June, 1821. London: J. Limburd, Nov., 1821

Morgan, Mary. *A tour to Milford Haven, in the year 1791*. London: John Stockdale, 1795

Newell, R. H. *Letters on the scenery of Wales; including a series of subjects for the pencil*. London: Badwin, Craddock and Joy, 1821

Pennant, Thomas. *A Tour in Wales*. London: H.D. Symonds, 1778

Pennant, Thomas. *The Journey to Snowdon, 1773*. London: Henry Hughes, 1781

Pratt, Samuel Jackson. *Gleanings through Wales, Holland and Westphalia*, Vol. I. London: T. N. Longman, 1795, Fourth edition.

Skinner, John. 'Ten Day's Tour through the Isle of Anglesea, December 1802', *Archaeologia Cambrensis, Supplement*. London: Charles J. Clark, July, 1908

Skrine, Henry. *Two successive tours throughout the whole of Wales, and several adjacent English counties so as to form a comprehensive view of the picturesque beauty, the peculiar manners, and the fine remains of antiquity in that interesting part of the British Island*. London: Elmsley and Bremner, 1798

Taylor, John. *A Short Relation Of A Long Journey Made Round or Ovall by Encompassing the Principalitie of Wales, 1653*. London: James Halliwell, Thomas Richards, 1859

Warner, Richard. *A walk through Wales in August 1797*. Bath: R Crutwell, 1798

Warner, Richard. *A second walk through Wales in August and September 1798*. Bath: R Crutwell, 1799. Second edition, 1800

Wyndham, H. P. *A Gentleman's Tour through Monmouthshire and Wales in the Months of June and July, 1774*. London: T. Evans, 1775

Some recent academic papers and a thesis on travel writing in Wales.

Bishop, Peter. *Vision and Revision: Mountain Scenery in Snowdonia 1750-1880*. Dissertation submitted in candidature for the degree of Doctor of Philosophy. Aberystwyth: School of Art, University of Wales, 2001.

McClain, M. 'The Duke of Beaufort's Tory progress through Wales', *Cylchgrawn Hanes Cymru / Welsh History Review*, 18, 4 (1997), 592-620

Davies, Hywel M. 'Wales in English travel writing, 1791-8: the Welsh critique of Theophilus Jones, *Welsh History Review*, 23 (2007), 65–93

Jones, Kathryn N., Carol Tully, and Heather Williams (Eds.). 'Travel Writing and Wales', *Studies in Travel Writing*, Vol. 18, No 2 (2014)

Particularly:
- Jones, Kathryn N., Carol Tully, and Heather Williams. 'Travel Writing and Wales'.
- Morgan, Mary, Elizabeth Isabella Spence, and Sarah, Prescott. 'Women Travellers in Wales: Hester Lynch Thrale Piozzi'.
- Martin, Alison E. 'Celtic Censure: Representing Wales in Eighteenth-Century Germany'.

INDEX 1 – PEOPLE

INDEX 2 – PLACES